GLOBAL TELECOMMUNICATION NETWORKS: STRATEGIC CONSIDERATIONS

GLOBAL TELECOMMUNICATION NETWORKS:
STRATEGIC CONSIDERATIONS

edited by

George Muskens

and

Jacob Gruppelaar

IVA, Institute for Social Research,
Tilburg University, Tilburg, The Netherlands

KLUWER ACADEMIC PUBLISHERS

DORDRECHT / BOSTON / LONDON

for the Commission of the European Communities

Library of Congress Cataloging in Publication Data

Global telecommunication networks: strategic considerations / edited by George
    Muskens and Jacob Gruppelaar.
        p.   cm.
    ISBN 90–277–2682–5
    1. Telecommunication.   2. Telecommunication—Europe.
3. Telecommunication systems.   4. Telecommunication systems—Europe.
I. Muskens, George.   II. Gruppelaar, Jacob.
HE7631.G58   1988
384—dc 19   87–36759
                                                                      CIP

Publication arrangements by
Commission of the European Communities
Directorate-General Telecommunications, Information Industries and Innovation, Luxembourg

EUR 11389
© 1988 ECSC, EEC, EAEC, Brussels and Luxembourg

LEGAL NOTICE
Neither the Commission of the European Communities nor any person acting on behalf of the
Commission is responsible for the use which might be made of the following information.

Published by Kluwer Academic Publishers,
P.O. Box 17, 3300 AA Dordrecht, Holland.

Kluwer Academic Publishers incorporates the publishing programmes of
D. Reidel, Martinus Nijhoff, Dr W. Junk and MTP Press.

Sold and distributed in the U.S.A. and Canada
by Kluwer Academic Publishers,
101 Philip Drive, Norwell, MA 02061, U.S.A.

In all other countries, sold and distributed
by Kluwer Academic Publishers Group,
P.O. Box 322, 3300 AH Dordrecht, Holland.

CONTENTS

PREFACE

The book collects a number of articles dealing with global networks. They have been prepared as contributions to the second FAST programme of the European Community. This programme intended to contribute to the Forecasting and Assessment of Science and Technology (FAST) by research projects and so-called network-activities. The projects and activities had been grouped under five major headings: work, services, food technology, natural resources, and communication.

One communication project especially struck the attention of IVA. Its serial number was COM8. It entailed the idea of short studies, expert seminars and synthesizing meetings on a broad theme: the tensions between global telecommunication networks, or even one global spider network on the one hand, and the relevance, the autonomy of the national dimension (or dimensions) on the other.

The theme has been outlined initially as broad as a futuristic integrated digital network will be. It has been indicated by terms referring to facilitities for tele-working, flexible labour and capital markets, social, cultural, political and economic consequences of new possibilities for separating the physical environment from the 'relational', by which old patterns of solidarity based on a national economy could be eroded.

The ideas and intentions of COM8 were not only broad but also controversial, aiming at a pluridisciplinary approach of positive solutions for cultural domination, easy protectionism and loss of cultural identity of European nations. They evolved by discussions with the FAST Directorate in the different phases of COM8, by meetings, seminars and a conference held at Tilburg University on 30-31 October 1986. These activities have been organised by IVA. IVA is the Institute of Social Research at Tilburg University. Many outstanding colleagues from sociology, philosophy, communication research, political economy, law, management research, etc. have participated, co-operating with IVA. Seminars were held at The Hague (ISS), Paris (Maison des Sciences de l'homme) and Tilburg (IVA).

So, this book offers a number of their contributions and our general conclusions with regard to the consequences of global telecommunication networks on the autonomy and relevance of the national dimension. They deal with scientific evaluations of developments with regard to information technology. They clarify the options which are, to a certain extent, open to strategic decisions of the parties concerned. For the European nations is of special interest the reversability (up to a certain degree) of the globalization of information networks and their economy by the procurement of local applications of information technology (e.g. by videotex) or by local capital, labour and consumer goods markets which remain important, also in the field of information technology. The other aspects of special interest are for public interests and the support they can get on behalf of the telecommunication policies of European states and the European Community.

The editors of this book hope to find an interested audience under policy-makers within the European communities and the official European Community and those who deal with them at communal, national, international and corporate levels. They might reconsider their objectives and plans on respect of the considerations published. Scientists as we are we also expect to contribute to a technology-oriented philosophy and social science. For this contribution we may find an interested audience of researchers and students.

COM8 and its ultimate product being this book has been additionally funded by the Ministry of Science and Education, and that of Welfare, Health and Culture in the Netherlands. For IVA, George Muskens, head of the Division of Cultural Studies, has been responsible. He has been supported substantially by the co-editor of this book, Jacob Gruppelaar, and, for a long time, by Annet Oosterwijk. Antik double-Dutch has been upgraded by Jake Sudworth.

Secretariat and text production has been done in a traditional way, in house, on non-communicating dedicated text handling machines by Helène van Diemen, Marian de Jong, Bea van Wijk, Rianne van der Velden and Jolanda van Eerdt. Many colleagues have accepted our invitations to deliver their honoured contributions or to organize a special seminar with regard to comparative research (by Cees Hamelink of ISS, The Hague) and with regard of changing concepts of time, space and distance (by Iskender Gökalp of CNRS, Orleans). Contacts and meetings with the interested staff members of the FAST Directorate (Ricardo Petrella, Jean-Luc Iwens and Nicole Dewandre) have been very stimulating, as were both meetings at La Pichelotte with the other researchers involved in COM-projects and with Frits Prakke of TNO, Apeldoorn, who represents the Netherlands on the FAST Advisory Board, being its so-called 10-1 network.

Beside this book contributions to COM8 have been published by IVA, i.e. by way of a report Global networks: a descriptive study and two readers: Global networks and European communities: applied social and comparative approaches and Global networks and European communities: collected papers.

Tilburg, August 1987

Jo Segers
Director of IVA

Global telecommunications developments reconsidered from a strategic and European vantage

George Muskens

As introduction to a collection of papers in which global telecommunications developments are reconsidered from a strategic and European point of view, we are presenting some general themes on the subject. That means that the introduction will not consist primarily of series of summaries of papers elaborating themes successively. It will group the different papers round general themes. These are:

1. The position of the sciences in processes of rapid technological and social change in the fields of telecommunication and information technology. This regards strategic analysis.
2. The second theme is integration of strategic analysis as part of planned Research and Development efforts.
3. The third treats the strategic considerations about policymaking processes providing critical support for the policymakers involved.
4. The fourth general theme is Europe and its role in the changing international economic and political power structure.

This grouping approach of the introduction is undertaken for two reasons. First, it fits the approach of the FAST project from which this book follows. On the basis of these themes new ideas have been gathered and elaborated about the impact of global telecommunication networks on national communities. Among others these ideas should contribute to positive solutions for the problems of feared cultural and economic domination of Europe by foreign powers, of the pursuit of easy protectionism from within and of the threatened loss of cultural identity.

The second is the intention to provide a special interpretation to the papers in this book. They are all important contributions to the growing literature on telecommunication developments from a strategic and European vatage.

The structure of chapters is as follows:

-   Part 1, descriptive studies: two chapters;
-   Part 2, macro-strategic analyses and considerations: four chapters;
-   Part 3, micro-applications and the public and consumer interests: two chapters.

To these parts a methodological and conceptual annex (two chapters) has been added. They are followed by conclusions which arise from a synthesis of all the material in this book. These conclusions are drawn from the four general themes which are elaborated below.

1.   Scientific Responsibility

In democratic societies it is legitimate to challenge policymaking processes by arguments other than those of power and voluntarist choice. In democratic society free choice should be connected to ethical responsibility and reason. So the political institutions of democratic societies include active public opinion and debate. Its constituent parts are the mass media, political parties and movements, and last, but not least, science as far as they are still the living idea of Enlightenment.

Especially when the most recent phenomena of technical and social innovation are the issues to be studied, science should revert to the ideas of Enlightenment. However in philosophy and the social sciences the return to the ideas of Enlightenment, particularly to the critical companionship of science with the modernization of societies, is no longer in vogue. Many colleagues cannot follow their societies which seem to support wasteful innovations (Haug), ecological disasters (Ulrich), nuclear overkill (Aesthetik und Kommunikation) and the cultural and economic domination by countries like the United States of America or transnational corporations (Schiller, Hamelink). Others seem to have reached a post-modern paralogic scenery at which researchers play games without commitment to particular societies and especially not to the most developed industrial and bureaucratic societies (Lyotard). Only in the most 'performative' sectors of applied university programmes such as technology and management has the curiosity for new technical possibilities and human change remained unbroken. So, in the actual so-called post-modern times the societies in which innovation is an important political goal are accompanied mostly by only these sciences. They deliver ideas for such things as Research and Development, the procurement of innovations and their utility.

This development is, of course, much more complex than described. In this respect, European research programmes like FAST or national iniatiatives like SPIN in the Netherlands or Technologie, Culture et Communication in France encourage philosophers and social scientists to study the new possibilities of information and communication technology (e.g. Qvortrup a.o.; Flichy); to develop a new political economy (e.g. Melody) or an 'economy of innovations' (Nelson and Winters); and to answer questions put by national and supranational authorities with regard to societal crises caused by new technologies (Bjørn-Andersen a.o.; Mattelart; Mansell). At the same time, I must acknowledge that invitations to a number of colleagues from philosophy and sociology did not succeed in leading them to publish important reappraisals and challenging hypotheses with regard to actual problems of the global information society.

I think that it is not good, either for science or society, that there is so little serious attention for technological innovation from philosophy and social science. Society, at least the powerful industrial nations in Northern America, Europe and East Asia, have chosen for a policy of technological innovation. Part of it is a massive research effort. If this effort is realized only by technology or management science , the Ring of Technotopia is round: both scientists and policy makers can believe in the technical solutions of problems, in the promises of the things invented, etc.

These sciences fail to approach questions with regard to social and cultural implications or public and consumer interests as central issues. So societies are not challenged or reinforced to take care of them. They do not get what they need. The applied sciences are not as useful as they could be.

Through a programme like FAST societies express their need for a critical reappraisal of the social uses and cultural implications of technological innovation, of the public or consumer interests. Of course, as part of the R+D-expenditures of, for instance, the European Community it concerns only a fraction of it, but the questions are raised and there is no reason why philosophy and social science should not prepare the answers as central issues of their free and academic activities. They should be willing to reassess concepts, theories and methodologies in relation to new (information) technologies, changing patterns of solidarity and residence, new professions, new economic scales and scopes, altering concepts regarding time, distance and spaces, etc., but they do not. After two years of intensive study, a series of expert interviews, seminars and a conference with a great number of outstanding colleagues we can hardly publish provisional attempts at a new conceptualization and methodology of a technologyoriented philosophy or social science. We can formulate the relevant questions as will be done in the methodological and conceptual annexes to this book by Jacob Gruppelaar and Iskender Gökalp. In a rude and provisional way they also indicate critical concepts to be used in a technologyoriented philosophy or social science, as they also can be found in contributions published in the seminar and conference proceedings or in the suggestions for national media and cultural policies by Jean-François Mertens in chapter 5 of this volume.

Of course, it is not encouraging for us who accepted the invitations from the side of our societies, i.e. from the European Communities, to organize a series of scientific activities regarding global telecommunication networks and the relevance, the autonomy of the national dimension. It is, however, no reason to withold ourselves from our duties. In addition to the organization of that series of scientific activities we have to publish the best results of it, being the chapters of this book. We also have to think about other ways to reverse the retreat of Critical Theory from society and the paralogic plays of post-modern philosophy in Western Europe. We must find new positions for our sciences, i.e. for philosophy, history, social science, economics in relation to processes of rapid technological and social change.

These positions can be found, we think, at three levels. They should be explored as parts of new research programmes. We think of:

1. Continued encouragement of those philosophers and social scientists who raise relevant conceptual, theoretical and methodological questions;
2. Scholarships for young researchers in the fields of a technology oriented philosophy and social science;
3. New research programmes for strategic analysis in the fields of information technology, the social uses and cultural implications of it, public and consumer interests, etc.

The first two ways are, to a certain extent, a plea for continued investments in particular aspects of philosophy and social science as, for instance, in parts of the FAST-programme. The third is new in this respect. It flows from the most promising results of our activities. These are the contributions of a number of political economists, innovation economists, comparative researchers, policy researchers and game or negotiation researchers, all members of the social science community. Here they are gathered under a common denominator of strategic analysis.

2. Strategic analysis

Strategic analysis is a field of applied and comparative research to forecast and assess developments such as those regarding global telecommunication networks and their influence on national and international economic, political, technological and cultural power structures. Forecasting and assessment are undertaken from a special perspective, namely that scientific appraisals and reports of trends, expert expectations or public needs serve policymakers and public opinion formation. Policymakers can make better choices when they understand actual trends, evaluate expert expectations or reassess public needs. Choices are unavoidable, e.g. on standardization matters, prerequisites of future networks, tariffs and prices, investments in consumer apparatus or new services, the social and educational consequences of information technology, etc. All these are difficult choices which play at many levels of policymaking and of all those who play a role in public opinion formation. While, it does not forecast and assess an unchangeable future exactly. It enlightens possibilities to change nondesired trends, expectations and needs or to reinforce those which really are desired. It serves a mouldable future.

3. The Strategic Analysis of Global Networks and Services

Choices have to be made with regard to telecommunication networks, equipment, systems software and services as well. At the network level decisions are made on upgrading existing telephone networks, satellite communication systems, or the introduction of complete new connections all over the earth, based on glass-fibre to integrate voice, image, and data communication services in a digital network. Equipment questions regard the tools as such (e.g. personal computers, interfaces, multi-functional PBX-s) as well as the possibilities for production and private offer to the market. Upgraded as well as complete new networks and the equipment used for the (many) communication and information services require a multitude of sophisticated arrangements at the technical, juridical and logistic level to assure an efficient and effective use of networks in general, based on a reasonable and competitive system of costs allocation to different clients and unfettered fast (transborder) information flow. These arrangements have to be developed in the form of systems software, switching and packaging techniques; they may have to be standardized by way of international treaties. For communications and information important questions are; which services can be added to the networks for which market segments and at what conditions, above or besides the general and public tasks of national PTT-s, publishers or broadcasting corporations ?

So, decision makers are continuously faced with development, standardization, marketing and political problems. These problems and the actual state of affairs are described in two chapters of this volume especially chapter 2, in which many relevant data are presented, and chapter 3 in which Peter Vervest gives a thorough overview of European standardization policies.

Although many inventions were unforeseen and many applications differ widely from those conceived by the inventors, decision makers need proposals and critical information about the problems mentioned. They gather it by way of co-ordinated R+D:
- supranational R+D, e.g. as part of EC-programmes (ESPRIT, RACE, APOLLO, FAST) or other programmes like EUREKA;
- corporate R+D, mostly with national and international subsidiaries;
- national R+D in the field of information technology.

Strategic analysis is an important part of these programmes. If it is not it should be, for two reasons. These are:

1. Before technical research into the possibilities of global telecommunication can become of use for service suppliers or customers it has to be translated into political, managerial, consumer and public dimensions. Politically, new information devices do not fit by themselves with the negotiation problems of international standardization bodies. Managerially, it is also not clear directly how they can be added to existing management practices of existing networks. In marketing terms, nobody can forecast how consumers may react or what arrangements and applications will receive public support. No philosopher, social scientist or student in the field of management knows, but it is their expertise to relate new devices, management practices and public preferences with each other, to forecast to a certain degree the relations by extrapolation of trends and historical data and so suggest which might be the best translation of Technotopia into realistic political and industrial action. In this volume they can be found in the contributions of Peter Vervest (chapter 3), William Melody (chapter 4), Jean-François Mertens (chapter 5), Jeremy Beale (chapter 6) and Gerd Junne (chapter 7).

2. Part of the decision making processes are two central issues of the social sciences. These are first the analysis of negotiations, negotiation processes and negotiated arrangements between different relevant parties as there are: engineers and inventors, industrial or PTT or broadcast managers, political decision makers, users and potential users represented for example by trade unions, consumer organizations, professional bodies, etc., or the scientific community. Second, it is a special task of the social sciences to describe populations and explain or even forecast their interest into the matter of concerns, i.e. telecommunication networks, new services etc. They should be commissioned to do so continuously.

The studies in this book, especially those of Gareth Locksley (chapter 8), Lars Qvortrup (chapter 9) en Jean-François Mertens (chapter 5), are analyses of telecommunication developments and explanations of the interests concerned.

4.   Strategic Analysis and Strategic Considerations

If the community of applied social and comparative researchers is ready to take scientific responsibility for development of global telecommunication networks, services and its particular European dimensions, which issues are to be reconsidered ? Which issues are so important that developments and policies regarding them have to be supported by strategic analyses.
I think that we must point at three kinds of issues which deserve ongoing strategic analysis in a European context. These are: 1. International relations; 2. Technical standards; 3. Home affairs. They are strongly interrelated in practice but they deserve special attention because they seem to represent a diminishing European interest.

Only the first issue is relatively non-controversial with regard to European strategic analysis, even though nation states hesitate to give up power to the European Community. The twelve West-European states form a common market, try to survive American and Japanese economic domination or East-European political domination and are intended to settle their international relations in this perspective. A supranational institution like the European Community may constitute an intermediary level of policymaking and negotiation between states and transnational corporations which compete for control of national sub-markets. So these supranational institutions should be supported by supranational programmes for strategic analysis. International relations, global markets and geopolitics are key issues in most contributions to this book.
Is the same true for questions regarding standards and home affairs ? If some policymakers or representatives of the community of applied social and comparative researchers plead for research into such questions as part of supranational programmes for strategic analysis they meet strong counterarguments. Basically it is said that questions of technical standards have to be solved by technical research programmes and that those of home affairs have to be supported by national research programmes. Nevertheless, not for the first time, is it proposed to make technical standards and home affairs issues to be reconsidered within supranational research programmes for strategic analysis. As to technical standards the main argument is that the development of new global telecommunication networks essentially is a matter of international negotiations regarding technical standards for future networks, information carriers, gateways, data-bases and terminals like ISDN, DBS, HDTV and so forth.

States and corporations are negotiating constantly at the level of supranational institutions about standards to be developed and technical problems to be solved while they (still) have many possibilities of choice. So, strategic analysis should support standardization policies substantially. In this volume, Peter Vervest elaborates standardization problems and Jeremy Beale the orientation and organization of European (standardization) R+D.

As to home affairs we feel much more reluctant to plead for substantial strategic analysis. Here, we touch on questions of social and industrial policy or public interests matters, such as education, procurement of new services and cultural identification. It is a rather unquestioned outcome of historical processes of nation formation in Europe that these affairs are to be treated by and within national communities, i.e. by the nation states. If they are not, they are to be treated at a lower level of human organization and policymaking, e.g. the communal or the institutional level, rather than a higher, supranational level. At the former levels complex and institutionalized systems of checks and balances between policymaking, science, democratic institutions, social partnership etc. seem to guarantee that social and public interests receive the attention they deserve compared to private and vested interests. The supranational structures primarily would pay attention to vested industrial, financial, technical and private interests. At the least, their democracies and arrangements for social partnership are weak.
A number of states in Western Europe have transferred part of their social and public responsibilities to the European Community. Its Commission, Council of Ministers and Parliament represent attempts at supranational policymaking which include social and public affairs.

With regard to telecommunications, it is the primary objective of the European Community to create a common and strong market for European companies in the fields of telecommunication networks, equipment and services. As such, this objective can be translated in a rather pure industrial and technical policy, including industrial and technical R+D, a kind of Technotopia which is the image of ESPRIT or RACE. Support of an Integrated Services Digital Network (ISDN) in Western Europe can be quite unquestioned, the commercial approach of satellite television and transborder information flows can be followed.
Yet other policy questions are also posed at the European level. These regard social or educational aspects of industrial policy, substantial choices for R+D, the costs and usefulness of the ISDN telecommunication highways for private households, the substantial choices regarding procurement of services, the value of national cultural identities and of public broadcasting systems within the European countries or even a European broadcasting system (some European parliamentarians strongly support the idea of Europa TV, even after its financial fiasco). At all these points international problems play a (greater or lesser) role. They will do so in

future, to an unavoidably greater extend. Developments are not (only) local or national but parts of, for instance, the planning strategies of transnational corporations to penetrate and control foreign markets. This transnational problem will be elaborated in this volume by William Melody (chapter 4) and Gerd Junne (chapter 7).

Policy choices have their national flavours but are also parts of broad political denominators, preferences and trends. Some of these have to do with the geopolitical problem of what is Europe and what is its position in East-West, North-South or USA-Japan-Europe relations ? This question is going to be treated by Jean-François Mertens (chapter 5) and Jeremy Beale (chapter 6). Others have to do with general policy goals like 'welfare' in the sixties and seventies or 'deregulation' and 'liberalization' in the eighties.

A third home affair with interesting international research dimensions is the need for the mediation of experiences with new information technologies and social innovations in (Western) Europe. There is so much in common that there is a need for a broader horizon than that of the nation state when it is going to invest (or disinvest !) in new information technologies or is going to institutionalize the new possibilities created by information technologies. Results of such internationally oriented research are Gareth Locksley's suggestions with regard to 'social software' (chapter 8) and those of Lars Qvortrup with regard to 'orgware' (chapter 9).

The European Community is an appropriate institution by its traditions, mandate and structures with regard to social and public interests to incorporate international problems in its telecommunication'policy and communication research programmes. Therefore, strategic analysis focused on Europe should provide insight into the following problems of social and public interest and their possible solutions:

1. National and local dependency on the planning strategies of transnational corporations in the field of telecommunication networks, equipment and services.
2. The impact of East-West, North-South and USA-Japan-Europe relations on telecommunication policies in Western Europe.
3. General goals of telecommunication policies.
4. Experiences with new information technologies and social innovation in a broad European context.

These subjects of European research are added to those mentioned , being:

1. The European factor in processes of international negotiations, its power and effects.
2. The standardization of the many systems, networks, tools, machines, etc. which have to be interconnected into reliable networks through which users can communicate effectively and profitably.

These subjects are themes which are treated from the different applied social and comparative contributions to this book, in a number of combinations. Common to them is the readiness of the authors to take scientific responsibility for the development of telecommunication networks and services in Europe. They identify the problems mentioned and possible solutions.

5. European Backgrounds and European Interests

Global telecommunication developments are associated with the changing economic and political power structure of the world. It is feared that the USA and Japan or non-Communist East-Asia are going to dominate the European countries economically and technically. So it is feared that the European nations may loose their cultural identity to generalized, levelled, American middleclass values and habits. The tendency can be reinforced to close national markets and protect national boundaries by high tariff systems, quota imposition on imported electronic devices or telecommunication services and subsidizing of national industries. Even a co-ordinated and integrated European approach as intended by the European institutions is not the primarily favoured perspective of most European states. They hesitate to give up real power to the European Community or other supranational institutions like ESA, EUREKA, NATO, etc., certainly as far as the home affairs mentioned in the previous paragraph are concerned.

But the idea of a European economic, technological, political and cultural community can also be an extension of national interests and cultures to be protected. This community can be a community which is strong enough to withstand the erosion of national political power by electronic trans-nationals or the levelling of culture by American entertainment networks. There are a number of factors which support actions undertaken to strengthen a European economic, technological, political and cultural community. We mention three of them.

First, as indicated a great deal of the R+D-programmes regarding information technology and telecommunication networks are initiated by European institutions and especially those of the European Community: ESPRIT, RACE, APOLLO, FAST, etc. In Europe the electronic transnational corporations fight for national markets for digital telecommunications networks. Most of them began as national telephone and network suppliers but must now operate on a wider economic scale to amortize the huge technical development costs for digital networks. Even the larger national markets within Europe (France, England, FRG, Italy) are too small in that respect. So, here the key issue means applications of digital telecommunications which are more than national, which combine several national markets within Europe. The idea of a European identity, a common market and a community around an integrated services digital network at the European level is reinforced both by the cost of the infrastructure and the co-ordination (full or part) of national, corporate and international R+D by European institutions.

Second, one must realize that Europe is the regional identification of many former global powers. They do not disappear so easily from the global scene. Their languages, especially English, French, Russian and

Spanish, are those of international trade, traffic, diplomacy, science, telecommunications, etc. These are spoken all over the world. In the Americas and Oceania English, French, Spanish and Portuguese are home languages. Intellectuals in Asia and Africa speak these languages while most European intellectuals do not speak the tongues of the milliards living there: Hindi, Chinese, etc. Russian is, at least, the trade language in the COMECON. Many European countries maintain strong ties with former colonies, commonwealths and informal cultural communities outside their actual boundaries or those of the (official) European Community. These can remain an important factor in international communication, e.g. regarding the siting and operation of information services, the exchange of researchers, journalists, travellers and the preservation of different world languages.
Third, there is the European cultural heritage. Three thousand years of cultural history should prove that the European cultural heritage must be strong enough to remain a frame of reference for intellectuals in this and in other parts of the world. The European cultural heritage has as its keystones power, wealth, technological progress, scientific Enlightenment and artistic beauty. It has its roots in ancient Greek and Roman juridical, political and economic systems. It relayed and extended medieval Arab sciences. It survived a great number of European wars during the last centuries. At this moment it is a commonwealth of twelve democratic States. It represents a frame of reference for intellectuals from (the new) Middle Europe and other regions or countries where freedom is oppressed.

Detailed analyses of European history, evaluations of its contemporary problems and discussions about its strategic possibilities to solve them can show policymakers new perspectives and give them new ideas for legitimate actions with regard to problems which cannot be solved at the national level of European countries.
So, the analysis of European traits and factors can shape scenarios for telecommunication policies, the architecture of networks and the development of services or their relations to educational, broadcasting, consumer and cultural policies. By interventions in public debates and corporate planning with books like this the community of applied social and comparative researchers is taking responsibility for the development of global telecommunication network services and its particular European dimensions, based on critical research of society.

LITERATURE

Bjørn-Andersen, N., and others,
    Information society: for richer, for poorer, Amsterdam, 1982.
Europa: Hoffnung und Depression, in: **Aestetik und Kommunikation**, 15, nr. 55, March 1984.

Flichy, P.,
   Les industries de l'imaginaire, Grenoble, 1980.
Global Networks and European CommunitiesCollected papers of the
   conference 'Dealing with Global Networks', Tilburg (IVA), October
   1986.
Hamelink, C.J.,
   Finance and information. A study of converging interests, Norwood
   NJ, 1983.
Haug, W.F.,
   Kritik der Warenaesthetik, Frankfurt Am Main, 1971.
Lyotard, F.,
   La condition postmoderne. Rapport sur le savoir, Paris, 1979.
Mansell, R.E.,
   Contradictions in national communication/information policies: the
   Canadian experience, in: Media, Culture & Society, 7, 1985, pp. 331-
   354.
Mattelard, A.,
   Technology, Culture and Communication: Research and policy
   priorities in France, in: Ferment in the Field, Journal of Com-
   munication, 33, 1983, nr. 3, pp. 59-73.
Melody, W.H.,
   Dealing with global networks: some characteristics of international
   markets, thiis publication, ch. 4.
Muskens, G. and C. Hamelink, eds.,
   Global networks and European communities: applied social and
   comparative approaches, Tilburg (IVA-ISS), August 1986.
Nelson, R.R. and S.G. Winter,
   An evolutionary theory of economic change, Cambridge Ma, 1982.
Qvortrup, L., and others,
   Social experiments with information technology and the challenge
   of innovation, Dordrecht, 1987.
Schiller, H.,
   Communication and cultural domination, White Plains, 1976.
Ullrich, O.,
   Technik und Herrschaft, Frankfurt am Main, 1979.

PART 1

DESCRIPTIONS OF RELEVANT NETWORKS
AND NETWORK POLICIES

GLOBAL NETWORKS: A DESCRIPTIVE STUDY (*)

(*)   This article is based on a report of The Institute of Social Studies at The Hague and additional figures delivered by CSP, London.

1. Introduction

A little over a century ago the first telegraphically transmitted message was the exclamation by Samuel Morse 'What hath God wrought !' To-day an enormous volume of various signals can be transmitted to and received from all corners of the globe almost instantaneously. This achievement hardly causes any exclamations let alone references to the Almighty - although the latter may be invoked when the occasional intercontinental disturbance occurs.
Characteristic of the 100-years of telecommunications development are the gradual upgrading of transmission facilities and the addition of switching. When - late in the history of telecommunications - electronic dataprocessing became available, this enhanced the international scale.
In the course of the 1950s the hitherto distinct technologies of telecommunication and electronic dataprocessing became fully integrated: machine-centered transducers were linked with each other and with human operators. Computer-communication networks were created that consisted of computers with communication channels attached to them that linked the computers to terminals of various sorts. The networks were constructed as centralized systems in which data were transported for processing, storing or forwarding to central computers. They were also constructed as distributed systems with data traffic between decentralized computers and terminals. The widening application of computer-communication networks during the 1960s and 1970s has been made possible by a number of technological developments. These innovative steps have considerably increased the performance, capacity, accessibility and communication capability of computing and telecommunication facilities.

The traditional telephone networks have greatly enlarged their capacity for data traffic through such techniques as modems, multiplexors, optical fibre, packet switching and satellites. Modems are devices that perform modulation and demodulation functions. This means they modulate the digital signal of the computer at the transmission end into the analogue signal that conventional telephone lines transport and at the receiving end they demodulate the analogue signal again into a digital signal. Modems may also have additional functions such as encryption, character code conversion, line testing facilities, etc. Multiplexors are devices that facilitate the transmission of two or more messages simultaneously over a single transmission line. For the expansion of networks they are important since they permit the concentration of data flows for transmission through common higher speed circuits, at lower unit cost.
The development of optical fibres has further increased the data transmission capacity of the telephone network. They make it possible to transport digital signals through light over glass-fibre cables. An 8mm diameter optical fibre cable has about the same capacity as a 20cm diameter copper cable (some 30,000 telephone calls) and is more resistant to conditions that cause disturbances in traffic through the copper cable.

A vital technological development has also been packet switching. This technique makes it possible to dissect information flows into segments ('packets'), to link addresses and other information to these packets and to guide the packets through multiple concatenated links from their source to their destination.

An important development has also been the introduction a non-terrestrial mode of data traffic through communication satellites. Since 1965 six generations of communication satellites have been designed and implemented. The latest satellites have over 30,000 telephone circuits that can alternatively be used for voice and data transmissions. Also groups of telephone circuits can be utilized for wideband data transmissions. With the application of time division multiple access technique the new satellites will become technically better suited for the handling of digital data traffic. Chart 1. shows the satellites in use or proposed in Europe in 1987.

Chart 1.
Satellites in use or proposed in Europe.

SATELLITE	LAUNCH DATE		OPERATOR
EUTELSAT F1	JUNE	1983	EUTELSAT
EUTELSAT F2	AUG	1984	EUTELSAT
TELECOM IA	AUG	1984	DGT, France
TELECOM IB	MAY	1985	DGT, France
TELECOM IC	unknown		DGT, France
ASTRA		1988 ?	SES, Luxembourg
TDF-1		1988 ?	TDF, France
TV-SAT		1988 ?	DBP, W. Germany
TELE-X		unknown	NOTELSAT, Scandinavia
BSB		1989 ?	British Satellite Broadcasting UK
OLYMPUS	LATE	1988	ESA

Some form of European service is also offered by two international satellites, Intelsat VI and VII. There is a proposal for an 'Atlantic' satellite which would be in an orbital slot that has been allocated to the Irish but which would be uplinked from the United States or Europe whilst having a footprint for both Fixed Satellite Services and Direct Broadcast Services over Western Europe.

In addition to these developments the rapid innovation of computer hardware, software and peripheral equipment have contributed largely to the development of computer-communication networks ('telematics' networks).

Such networks became increasingly interesting for:

1) institutions that are involved in inherently international activities (and that consequently rely on telecommunication networks);
2) institutions that are geared towards international cooperation;
3) institutions that can cut the costs of international operations by the sharing of computer-time, computer-processing volume and computer-processing resources.

However, in spite of all these impressive technological advances there is today no global telematics grid. Actually, there is only one genuine international telecommunication network: the POTS (Plain Old Telephone System). The telephone network - which only became really international in the 1960s and 1970s - connects over 485 million terminals in a compatible way and transmits voice, text, and data. The second largest international grid is the telex network. This connects some 2.3 million terminals (principally telex machines) and transmits text and data. Countings of numbers of telephone and telex sets in operation are very inaccurate. The AT&T report on world telephone numbers reported a possible 37% inaccuracy in the numbers. Approximations of these numbers are given in chart 2. below.

Chart 2.
European Community telephone and telex line numbers (1987).

Country	Number of telephone line (x 1.000.000)	Number of telex terminals (x 1.000)
BELGIUM	2.95	23.0
DENMARK	2.46	16.0
FRANCE	22.08	82.0
F.R.G.	24.60	150.0
GREECE	2.92	not available
IRELAND	.61	7.0
ITALY	16.52	74.0
NETHERLANDS	5.60	44.0
SPAIN	8.81	32.0
PORTUGAL	1.32	22.0
UNITED KINGDOM	20.91	92.0

For the transmission of data there are data-networks installed in more and more countries and these are increasingly being linked internationally. There is also a limited number of international dedicated networks for such closed user groups as the banks and the airlines, for intergovernmental co-operation and for commercial computer services. The number

of national data networks is also still fairly modest. The majority of the world's countries do not yet have separate data networks connection, but within the European Community all Member States have been inter-connected for international packet-switched data traffic since 1986.
For the transmission of images a growing number of countries now have cable networks, but they operate typically on the local or city-side level. Cellular radio networks also operate mainly at the national level: the Member States of the EC have adopted four incompatible systems (chart 3.).

Chart 3.
Cellular systems in European countries.

	TYPE OF SYSTEM	No. SUBSCRIBERS (MAY 1986)
BELGIUM	NMT	not available
DENMARK	NMT	54000
FRANCE	RADIOCOM 2000	4000
GERMANY	NETZ C	5000
GREECE	-	-
IRELAND	TACS (EIRECELL)	500
ITALY	-	-
LUXEMBOURG	NMT	-
NETHERLANDS	NMT	9500
UNITED KINGDOM	TACS	64500
PORTUGAL	-	-
SPAIN	NMT	9500

2. International value-added telecommunication networks

The Institute of Social Studies has proposed the following functional typology of international telecommunication networks. A crucial distinc-tion in networks is based on the degree of accessibility: open or closed. Open networks are accessible to every terminal user with the adequate technical and financial means. Closed networks are accessible only to a defined group of users.

Type I.1.: Database access networks
The number of on-line electronic databases has rapidly increased over the past years. In 1986 there were over 3,000 such databases accessible for users. However, not all of them constitute international networks; many are available only within the country of origin. The information is not always unequivocal and as a result only an approximation can be given.

Chart 4.
Global value-added telecommunication network types.

	FUNCTION	OPERATOR	USER GROUP
	TYPE I: OPEN NETWORKS		
I.1.	DATABASE ACCESS	PUBLIC PRIVATE	GENERAL
I.2.	ENHANCED SERVICES	PRIVATE	GENERAL
I.3.	NEWS SERVICES	PRIVATE	GENERAL INTER-CORPORATE INTRA-CORPORATE
	TYPE II: CLOSED NETWORKS		
II.1.	INTERNATIONAL MANAGEMENT	PRIVATE	INTER-CORPORATE INTRA-CORPORATE
II.2.	INTERNATIONAL CO-OPERATION	PRIVATE PUBLIC	PUBLIC SERVICES GOVERNMENTAL ACADEMIC

Our search suggests there are about 30 major database access international networks operated by private companies.

Type I.2.: Enhanced services networks
These are the value added networks (VANs). Most of these are only national in their operations. International VANs are few in number. The largest is Tymnet. Other smaller networks include Telenet, GEISCO's Mark III, Infonet, Cybernet, and Comshare.

Type I.3.: News services
The large international news services (such as Reuters, United Press International, Associated Press, Agence France Presse, and Inter Press Service) and some of the largest national news agencies (such as in the Federal Republic of Germany and in Spain) operate international networks for the collection, processing and distribution of news. These services are in principle open to any terminal user who is ready to pay for the information supply. Provided the terminal is type-approved by the national authority any user can subscribe to the services of the Reuter's network, for example.

At the same time, however, the news services may also offer their communications facilities to specified groups of journalistic users. The networks are thus commercially made available to other media organizations. Thus the Financial Times uses Reuters transmission facilities, and the Daily Telegraph uses AP. In the USA, for example, various syndicate services use the AP or UPI high-speed networks to reach their customer-newspapers. The third-world agency, Inter Press Service (IPS) carries material for the news pool of the non-aligned countries. These activities do in fact violate some PTT's regulations about the subleasing of circuits to third parties. For this reason all the information carried on the networks of the news services is considered to belong to these services.

This indicates the third layer of the network operations of the news services. They also use their international telecommunications facilities for intracorporate applications. As such the networks are defined as accessible only to the closed intra-firm group of users.

Type II.1.: International management

Networks that perform international management functions for a closed group of private corporate users are basically two: the banking network S.W.I.F.T. and the airlines network S.I.T.A. Then there are the intra-firm networks that international business users install for the co-ordination of transactions among geographically dispersed units of the same corporation.

Such networks are operated by the world's largest industrial and financial companies. From the avaible information it would seem that out of the Fortune 1000 largest international firms some 250 operate, one way or another an international network for internal use.

Type II.2.: International cooperation

There is a multitude of intergovernmental networks within the United Nations system, the NATO, the European Communities, and among national goverments, inter alia for criminal investigation (e.g. the INTERPOL network). There are also various networks serving international co-operation between different public bodies such as the telecommunications system of the World Meteorological Organisation. Networks may also be installed for international co-operation between such public bodies as port authorities. International networks are also operated as service to academic co-operation among unversities and research institutes in various countries. Again, a very tentative estimate puts the number of networks of this type at 20.

This - tentative - estimate suggests a total of some 300 international telecommunication networks that are accessible to individual, corporate, and public user groups in the EC Member States. An equally tentative estimate suggests that out of these international networks some 150 are operated by European entities or have strong European participation.

3.   Prominent networks

The following networks are described in more detail:

Type I.1.   (Database access networks): DIANE
Type I.2.   (Value added networks): TYMNET
Type II.1. (International management networks): SWIFT, SITA, Intra-
firm-networks.
Type II.2. (International co-operation networks): GTS, WMO, EPDPA,
EARN

DIANE

In March 1975 the EC Council of Ministers agreed to set up a Common
Market telecommunications network. It was decided that the PTT administrations of the nine member states would constitute the Euronet Consor-
tium for the operation of the network. The network would enable terminals in EC countries to access databases in these countries. The network
was called Euronet and the databases were called DIANE (Direct Information Access Network for Europe). The basic principles for the Euronet
decision were:
1)   the network would follow agreed international standards;
2)   the tariffs should not discriminate against any EC Member State;
3)   the network could carry non-Euronet traffic and non-EC Member
States could join the network;
4)   the network should be developed into a full European public datanetwork.
In March 1980 Euronet started commercially by providing access to over
100 databases. For the 1980-1984 period the Euronet objectives were:
a)   to develop Euronet into an operational public on-line information
network;
b)   to promote technology for the enhancement of information services;
c)   to develop a common market for scientific and technical information.
On 1 January 1985 the Euronet equipment was switched off and replaced
by the linkage of national packet switched networks. DIANE now provides
through these networks access to more than 600 databases in fields such as
agriculture, medicine, biology, engineering, physics, chemistry, energy,
environment, law, economics and social sciences. In the 1981-1984 period
the use of DIANE increased from 40,000 hours (duration of access) to over
96,000 hours.
Euronet-DIANE has stimulated the creation of a unified command language that enables conversation between widely differing computers and
adapts to most of the bibliographic and textual databases currently linked
with the network. Euronet-DIANE has promoted co-ordination among
database hosts thus enhancing their services to users. Presently more
research is being undertaken on the European Commission's initiative to
improve direct access to the databases and explore new storage and
retrieval technologies, such as compact discs.

TYMNET
The largest and most successful international value added network is
TYMNET which began operations in 1971 as a wholly-owned subsidiary of
the computer service company Tymshare. The access to remote data
centres formed the basis for the development of the network. In 1977 the
US Federal Communications Commission granted the licence for the
operation of public data service. In 1986 Tymnet - meanwhile acquired by
the McDonnell Douglas company - is the world's largest public packet
datanetwork with 2,000 switching nodes, 500,000 miles of leased lines and
connections with some 68 countries. The network transmits some 100 billion characters monthly. The network has very comprehensive security
measures and built-in error detection mechanisms.
The enhanced services the network offers include:
- protocol conversion capabilities,
- electronic messaging and electronic data interchange,
- flight planning,
- credit card validation,
- time sharing,
- numerical control applications,
- access to technical, medical and economic information.
With the packet technology Tymnet employs multiple users can share the
same packet. This multiplexing of data within packets means considerable
cost reductions for users. In order to avoid traffic congestion and circum-
vent outages the network has an automatic alternate routing selection
feature. The list of Tymnet customers reads like the Fortune 500 list of
the world's largest companies.

SWIFT
An important illustration of an international telecommunications network
established for co-operation among a closed group of specific users is
provided by SWIFT (Society for Worldwide Interbank Financial Telecommunications). The idea for this network was born in the late 1960s when a
group of large European banks studied the possibility of improved international transaction procedures and concluded that international banking
needed an accurate, rapid, safe and standardized funds transfer system.
As a result of the study and the positive responses from the banks
involved, the major European, Canadian and US banks established SWIFT
in May 1973. Four years later in May 1979 the network became operational. By then almost US $ 1 billion had been spent on the network and the
equipment that was procured from Burroughs, ICL and General Automation.
The SWIFT network consists of computer centres at various locations
across the world connected data transmission lines leased from public or
private telecommunications carriers. The computer centres are linked to
regional processing centres to which member banks connect by means of
computer-based terminals on their premises. Banks are free to choose any
compatible interface to link with the network. The present SWIFT I

network is basically a message store and forward system providing the following range of services: customer transfers, bank transfers, credit/debit advices, foreign exchange and money market confirmations, account statements, documentary credits, interbank securities trading, balance reporting, and payment systems.

The peculiar nature of the network lies in two characteristics:

I)   all messages are formatted in accordance with a standard specification; this improves efficiency of transactions and reduces misunderstandings;

II)   a combination of physical, technical and procedural security measures renders the network safe from unauthorised access or fraudulent transactions.

Network traffic has increased between 1980 and 1984 from an annual 47.2 million messages to 129.9 million messages. In 1986 the network handled approximately 750,000 messages daily for some 1,500 banks in 50 countries. As from 1986 a new system, SWIFT II, has been introduced capable of processing over a million messages a day and allowing for interactive dialogue and file transfer between users.

SITA

In 1949 eleven airlines established a reservation system with low-speed teleprinters: the Societe Internationale des Telecommunications Aeronautiques (SITA). By 1974, 184 airlines from 90 countries were part of the network. In 1986 SITA was the largest closed user group network serving some 300 airlines worldwide throughout some 170 countries.

In 1981 the SITA network transmitted 4.400 billion interactive messages and 450 million conventional messages. The types of messages the network transmits are: various reservation messages, transmission of teletype tickets, requests for endorsements of tickets, on-hand baggage information, forwarding of mishandled baggage and found and unclaimed checked baggage, tracing procedures for missing checked baggage, requests for incapacitated passengers for special handling arrangements, forwarding advice special handling arrangements, forwarding advice messages on security matters, and procedures for passengers travelling on space-available basis.

By way of illustration: the flight of a Boeing 747 between New York and Amsterdam involves some 30,000 messages. Most of them, some 27,000 relate to the passengers (names, requests, hotel reservations, etc), some 2,000 relate to freight and the remainder to various flight execution details. The SITA network encompasses almost 29,000 terminals in 16,600 airline agencies. In addition to the telecommunications network SITA operates two large dataprocessing centres in London and Atlanta.

The telecommunications network consists of automatic switching centres, concentrators, and satellite processors. Message traffic is routed through circuits leased from public or private entities. The numerous access terminals around the world are linked to some 200 switching centres operated and maintained by SITA. Interactive message traffic on the SITA network includes information exchanges between operators and computers in conversational formats. Through Common Use Terminal Equipment installed at airports (e.g. check-in counters) short transactions (of some 80 characters) can be conducted with average response times of three seconds enabling airlines staff to communicate with their own central computers. SITA also provides an air/ground interactive message service for real-time exchanges between aircraft in flight and the ground facilities of an airline.

Conventional message traffic contains mainly the transmission of telegraphic messages of some 200 characters in length. The network operates for these transmissions SITATEX (transmission of text documents between office systems) and SITAFAX (transmission of facsimile text).

Presently SITA is upgrading its network architecture following open network interconnection standards designed by the International Standards Organisation. Indications are very strong that the airline community is prepared to invest heavily in advanced telecommunications and information technology.

Intra-firm networks

Large international business corporations are for their effective and efficient management dependent upon mechanisms that assist in the co-ordination of widely dispersed activities. This makes telecommunications an essential tool for the international firm. It has been estimated that on average a company may spend US $ 14 million on telecommunications for every US $ 1 billion in revenues, but for organisations in certain sectors which are highly international and/or information oriented the proportion is often much higher.

International corporations install private networks for the following applications:
-    decision support to management,
-    monitoring of inventories and production volumes,
-    monitoring of market, price and currency developments,
-    transfer of funds,
-    intra-company accounting,
-    access to databases,
-    transport and processing of R&D information,
-    transport and storing of personnel records.

Some illustrations of intra-firm networks are: IBM's private network RETAIN with databases in the USA and the UK. The network is accessible to IBM engineers through terminals all over the world. It provides updated technical details on disfunctions of computer systems.

The electronics manufacturer Motorola has a private network that gives access from the company's locations around the world to the programmes and databases in computer centres in Illinois and Arizona. The network uses 26 dedicated circuits throughout the world, 102 high-speed printers and 4,000 interactive terminals. Each day over a billion characters are transmitted through the network. It is used for engineering, design, inventory control, production-schedules, sales data, product test parameters, invoices and a large variety of time-sharing computer applications.

Several of the large international banks have their private leased-line telecommunication networks, such as Chase Manhatten Bank, the Bank of America and Citibank. Citibank's GLOBECOM network interconnects the overseas branches of the bank in some 100 countries. Computer switches are located in New York, London, Hong Kong and Bahrein. Store and forward message facilities handle over 300,000 transmissions monthly.

Diversified-financial company American Express operates an international network with nine large dataprocessing centres and some 70 big and 226 small computers. The network handles daily over 250,000 transactions involving the authorization of credit cards. The average response time of these transactions is five seconds. American Express spends in excess of 500 million dollars annually for the maintenance of its network.

Meteorological Services: GTS and WMO

The world's meteorological services - gathered in the World Meteorological Organization - have created an international network for the exchange of weather information. This Global Telecommunication System (GTS) is accessible only to meteorological services, and by exception to two European non-WMO member organizations, ESOC in Darmstadt and ECMF in Reading. The GTS - established in the 1970s - connects through a variety of transmission techniques (from 50 baud HF links to 9,600 baud satellite channels) the three layers of the network.

On the national level the National Meteorological Telecommunication Networks operate utilizing telephone, telex and radio linkages. These NMTNs connect into the Regional Networks that operate in the six regions defined by the WMO: North America, Africa, Australia & New Zealand, Europe & Middle East, Asia, Latin America). The RMTNs are branches of the Main Trunk Circuit connecting with high-speed linkages the world's main meteorological centres such as Washington, Moscow, Melbourne, Offenbach and Bracknell. The MTC transmits some 50 million characters daily plus some 50 to 100 weather maps in facsimile.

EPDPA

In the late 1970s several European port authorities got together to explore the possibilities of co-operation and co-ordination in data processing. Developing a standardized European format for information exchange between ports was seen as essential given the many information-related functions in ports. Ports collect, process and distribute volumes of information about ship movements, their cargoes and ship characteristics, such as dangerous substances properties or dangerous substances handling procedures.

In 1979 the European Port Data Processing Association (EPDPA) was established as a voluntary association for European ports to co-operate in installing an interport telecommunication network. Since 1979 a number of studies and pilot projects have been conducted leading towards the

implementation of the final network. As conceived now the network will
be used by port authorities and port users for the transmission of messages
on ship movements and dangerous substances. The network will use computers, intelligent terminals and telex terminals. Telephone access will
also be facilitated. Messages will be exchanged in standardized formats.
The EPDPA network will have message-storage and forward facilities and
be capable of functioning 24-hours a day.

Academic institutions: EARN

In 1986 IBM-Europe took an initiative to establish the European Academic
and Research Network (EARN). This provides an international computer
network to academic, educational and research institutions. Extensions
from the European academic community to the Middle East, North
America and Africa are foreseen. The network will operate on leased
transmission lines with speeds up to 9,600 baud and will use store and
forward message techniques.
EARN users can access the network for: message exchange, data interchange, computer conferencing, remote database enquiries and remote
library searches. IBM intends to support the development of the network
technically and financially and wants to promote its international usage.
CEPT has authorized IBM to operate EARN on a leased-line configuration
with the following conditions:
-    there should be a development towards the use of international
     standardized procedures;
-    the authorization is for a limited period only;
-    the leased lines are tariffed according to the volume of messages
     transmitted.

4.   The European telecommunications equipment market

The development of the international telecommunications equipment
market (chart 5.) raises the question whether all the major European
manufacturers can survive.

The crucial factor in this is the capacity to recoup investments in research
and development. Particularly the demands now made on digital telecommunications switching equipment can only be met with excessive development expenditures on the part of the provider. Such expenditure for design
and development of systems will only increase over the years ahead. If, for
example, the UK companies Plessey and GEC spent in the late 1970s/early
1980s some US $ 80 million a year for the development of their System X,
the next generation of this system would cost them over US $ 100 million
annually. In 1986 the recouping of R&D expenditure on digital switching
systems is only possible if the supplier can expect to sell to a significant
segment of the international market. In 1984 the world market for equipment such as telephone sets, PABXs and transmission and switching
equipment amounted to some US $ 34 billion. The distribution of this
market among the twelve leading companies is shown in chart 6.

Chart 5.
  Balance of Trade in Telecommunications: Leading Industrial Nations (1986).

	$M Imports	Exports
United States	3218	1718
Japan	123	1839
United Kingdom	398	300
West Germany	161	757
France	92	472
Italy	191	167
Sweden	150	959
Canada	205	597
Taiwan	107	260
Hong Kong	256	370

Source: National Telecommunications and Information Administration.

Chart 6.
  World and European market for telecommunication equipment, 1985.

COMPANY	World revenues (($M)	European market share
AT&T	11,918	
Alcatel (inc. ITT)	7,510	42.9%
Northern Telecom	3,936	
Siemens	2,972	11.6%
NEC	2,773	
GTE	2,612	
Ericsson (inc. CGCT)	1,738	13.0%
Plessey		10.5%
GEC		9.7%
Italtel		6.4%
Others		5.9%

Source: Observatoire des Strategies Industrielles (OSI) of the Direction Générale de l'industrie, France, cited in Telecom Magazine, nr. 3, April 1987..

With the growing R&D investments it is expected that by 1995 a market segment of 16% needs to be controlled in order to survive. This would mean that the world market could sustain only six companies. Presently the eight European telecommunication manufacturers develop different strategies in order to secure their survival in the years ahead. Some firms focus on joint ventures with large non-European companies, like Philips with AT&T (since 1983) and the French CGE with ITT (since 1986). Others concentrate on their expansion into overseas markets and engage only in limited co-operative arrangements, like Siemens and Ericsson penetrating the US market. A third group of companies supports primarily European co-operation, like Plessey and Italtel: they favour an Airbus-consortium type of arrangement.

Distinct from the USA and Japan, the European countries have not liberalized the provision of basic transmission and switching services. Only the British government has allowed two main basic services suppliers (British Telecom and Mercury). In the other EC Member States the basic service networks remain State monopolies.

In the area of enhanced services the situation is diverse. In general, such services as videotex and electronic mail are liberalized in the UK and France. Liberalization has been proposed in the Netherlands and in Belgium, but is resisted in Denmark, Greece, Italy, and the Federal Republic of Germany.

In the UK, for example, since the liberalization the number of value-added network services for which government licenses had been issued had risen to 615 services operated by 149 companies by mid-1985. See chart 7. for VANS in the UK and chart 8 for those in the major European countries.

In France the government strongly encourages the development of new electronic services. This is part of the effort to place France in a leading position in the electronic industry (according to the plan La Filiere Electronique, launched in 1982). France applies a flexible regulatory policy and does not aspire to a PTT monopoly over enhanced services. Today's market for VAN services is estimated at FFr 4 billion per annum and could grow to some FFr 15 billion per annum by 1991.

Openings towards liberalization of VAN services are evident in the Netherlands and somewhat less clear in Italy. Most resistant to the liberalization of telecommunication is present regulatory policy in the Federal Republic of Germany. The controlling force in basic and enhanced services is the Deutsche Bundespost that favours the protection of the telecommunication infrastructure and its social obligations over the demands of business users for competitive services.

Almost all EC Member States have installed packet switched service networks which are basic to many VAN services. These PSSs create international network accessibility in so far as the interfaces to them conform to X.25 interface standards and the networks are themselves interconnected by standardised international links. As the demand for

Chart 7.
Registrations under VANS general licence in the U.K. at 2 February
1987.

COMPANIES OFFERING VANS SERVICES:	221

SERVICES REGISTERED

Automatic ticket reservation and issuing	16
Conference calls	16
Customer data bases	66
Deferred transmission	63
Banking services	5
Long term Archiving	30
Mailbox	90
Multi address routing	56
Protocol Conversions between incompatible computers and terminals	84
Secure delivery services	29
Speed and code conversion between incompatible terminals	49
Store and retrieve message systems and telephone answering	112
Tele software storage and retrieval	26
Text editing	33
User management packages	58
Viewdata	62
Word Processor/Facsimile	46
Total Services	841

Source: Department of Trade and Industry, U.K.

VAN services grows also the PSSs are expected to expand. It is not yet
clear how packet switched services will fit in with the later development
of integrated digital services networks. For PSSs in EC Member States see
chart 9.

Subscriber Equipment

In this area practically all EC Member States have shifted from monopoly
control to competitive supply of subscriber's equipment; including tele-
phonesets, private branch exchanges (PBXs), facsimile machines, etc.

Chart 8.
Major European VANS.

COUNTRY	PROVIDER	SERVICES
Austria	PTT	PDNS, Videotex, CUGS
	LINC	Email
	Geisco	Email, FMDS, MDNS, CUGS
	IP Sharp	FMDS, MDNS, CUGS
Denmark	PTT	Email, Videotex, CUGS, PDNS
	Geisco	Email, FMDS, MDNS, CUGS
	IP Sharp	FMDS, MDNS, CUGS
	IBCS	Email, TF
Finland	PTT	Email, Videotex, CUGS, PDNS
	Regional Telcos	Some other Videotex
	Geisco (via distributor)	Email, FMDS, MDNS, CUGS
	IP Sharp	FMDS, MDNS, CUGS
France	DGT	Email, Videotex, MDNS, PDNS
	DGT/IBM	MDNS (joint venture)
	Geisco	Email, FMDS, MDNS, CUGS
	IP Sharp	FMDS, MDNS, CUGS
Holland	PTT	Email, Videotex, PDNS
	Geisco	Email, FMDS, MDNS, CUGS
	IP Sharp	FMDS, MDNS, CUGS
Ireland	Telecom Eirean	PDNS, Email, Videotex, CUGS
	Geisco	Email, FMDS, MDNS, CUGS
	IP Sharp	FMDS, MDNS, CUGS
Italy	Geisco	Email, FMDS, MDNS, CUGS
	IP Sharp	FMDS, MDNS, CUGS
Norway	PTT	Email, Videotex, PDNS
	Geisco	Email, FMDS, MDNS, CUGS
	IP Sharp	FMDS, MDNS, CUGS
Spain	Geisco	Email, FMDS, MDNS, CUGS
	IP Sharp	FMDS, MDNS, CUGS
Sweden	Televerkert (PTT)	Email, Videotex, PDNS
	Geisco	Email, FMDS, MDNS, CUGS
	IP Sharp	FMDS, MDNS, CUGS
Switzerland	PTT	PDNS
	Radio Suisse	Email, Videotex, CUGS
	Geisco	Email, FMDS, MDNS, CUGS
	IP Sharp	FMDS, MDNS, CUGS
UK	ADP Network Services	Email, Videotex
	Aquiz Holdings	Videotex
	Atlantic Telecom	Teleconferencing
	Audiotext	Recorded Information Services
	AVS (Context)	Videotex
	Basic Computing Services (Holiday Master)	CUGS
	BT	Email, Videotex, CUGS, TF, PDNS
	Broadsystem	Recorded Information Services
	Cable and Wireless/Mercury	Email, TF, PDNS
	Celicom	Protocol Conversion
	Compower Ltd.	POS
	Connex Communications	Videotex, etc.
	Contact Telecommunications Services	Telephone Answering, Sales & Marketing Services

COUNTRY	PROVIDER	SERVICES
	Thomas Cook	Videotex, Ticket Reservation, Related Services
	Darome International (The Darome Connection)	CUGS
	Datavision Telesystems	Videotex
	Datec	Email, Videotex
	Debenhams Applied Technology	Videotex, Credit Authorization, Protocol Conversion
	Digital Paging Systems	CUGS
	Fastrak/Midnet	Videotex, CUGS, MDNS, PDNS
	Funds Transfer Sharing	EFT
	Geisco	Email, FMDS, MDNS, CUGS
	Hull City Council Telephone Department	Recorded Information Services, Call Diversion
	IBCS	Email, TF
	IBM	Videotex, CUGS, MDNS, PDNS
	ICL	Email, Videotex, CUGS, MDNS, PDNS
	ICS Computing	Videotex
	Internet Technology	CUGS
	IP Sharp	FMDS, MDNS, CUGS
	Istel	Email, Videotex, CUGS
	Kensington Data	Email
	LINC	Email
	Lloyds Bank	EFT
	Lydiastar	Telex Services
	MDS Computer Systems (WINC)	Email
	Mercury/ICL	MDNS (joint venture)
	Mimac Unit	Videotex
	NVA Consultans	Videotex
	Ocean Transport and Trading	Videotex
	Oceanics Communications	Videoconferencing
	Reuters	Videotex, FMDS
	Standard Life Assurance	Videotex
	Teltour	Protocol Conversion
	Ticketmaster	CUGS
	Transnet	MDNS
	Travicom	CUGS
	Value Added Networks	Videotex
	Vitel Group	Videotex
	Wang	Videotex
	Western Union Priority Mail	PDNS
	Williams Lea Communications	Messaging
	Wiltek	Messaging, Protocol Conversion
West Germany	Deutsche Bundespost	Email, Videotex, PDNS
	IBCS	Email, TF (international only)
	Geisco	Email, FMDS, MDNS, CUGS (international only)
	IP Sharp	FMDS, MDNS, CUGS (international only)

Key:
Email	Electronic mail
Videotex	Videotex/viewdata
CUGS	Closed user group services
TF	Telex forwarding
PDNS	Public data network service
MDNS	Managed data network service
FMDS	Financial market dealing systems
POS	Point of Sale
EFT	Electronic funds transfer

Source: Telecomeuropa/DTI, cited in: Datapro Research Corporation, Value Added Networks (VANS), July 1987.

Chart 9.
Packet Switched Services in EC Member States.

COUNTRY	PSS NETWORK	INTRODUCTION DATE
BELGIUM	DATA COMMS SERVICES	1982
DENMARK	DATAPAK	1983
FRANCE	TRANSPAC	1978
GERMANY	DATEX-P	1981
GREECE	HELPAK (HELLASPAC)	1983 (1987)
IRELAND	EIRPAC	1984
ITALY	ITAPAC	1984
LUXEMBOURG	LUXPAC	1983
NETHERLANDS	DATANET 1	1982
UNITED KINGDOM	PACKET SWITCH STREAM	1981
PORTUGAL	TELEPAC	1984
SPAIN	IBERPAC	1971

Source: Eurodata Yearbook 1987.

Only for data modems do some States continue to hold a monopoly control (chart 10.).

Chart 10.
Provision of modems in EC Member States.

	PTT MONOPOLY	PRIVATE SUPPLIERS
BELGIUM		*
DENMARK		*
FRANCE		*
GERMANY		*
GREECE		*
IRELAND		*
ITALY	*	
LUXEMBOURG		*
NETHERLANDS		*
UNITED KINGDOM		*
PORTUGAL	*	
SPAIN	*	

Source: Eurodata Yearbook 1987.

5.   ISDN in EC Member States

On March 29, 1984 the European Parliament adopted a resolution that
proposed to the Commission: to co-ordinate work on ISDN, to move
towards a common European network and common broadband services.
According to the Commission a pan-European ISDN is the critical opportunity for the integration of telecommunication services in Europe. It is
also seen as vital to the creation of an integrated European telecommunication equipment market.
This European effort to harmonize technical standards, network configu-
rations, tariffs, and subscriber equipment type-approvals coincides with
considerable interest in the EC Member States in the development of
national integrated services networks. Most national telecommunication
authorities expect that an ISDN would provide the kind of services large
corporate users demand. Thus ISDN could make them competitive vis-à-
vis private networks and undercut a possible skimming off of the services
market by private interests.

The EC Member States have in varying degrees embarked on steps that
will eventually lead to the integration of their national networks.

BELGIUM = the introduction of digital transmission and digital switching
during the 1980s will lead to a commercial ISDN after 1990; from 1984
fiber optics was introduced as the principal future trunk transmission
means. The main private supplier (Bell Telephone Manufacturing Company) has played a vital role in the development of the digital switching
system: ITT - System 12 - that is operational worldwide.
DENMARK = the Danish telecommunication entities are developing digital networks although they have expressed some doubt about the possibility of fully installing an ISDN; a broadband network is in development; this
network - based on fiber optics - is intended primarily for cable television, but could possibly be used for other communication services. The
main private suplier NKT Telecommunications formed an affiliate NKT
Electronics in 1981 that specializes in optical fibre development.
FRANCE = compared to other EC Member States France has the highest
proportion of installed digital transmission and switching; various pilot
ISDN projects have been initiated and experiments with optical fibre
based broadband networks are taking place; further developments will
depend on the outcome of these tests. There is a commitment to spend
some FFr 60 billion to link up the country by 2000 with an optical fibre
trunk network.
French telecommunications industry - primarily the merger of Thomson-
CSF with CIT-Alcatel with CGE and recently with ITT - provides a wide
range of expertise in digital switching systems (e.g. the Alcatel E-10, one
of the first successful digital telephone switching systems in the world,
and ITT System 12) and fibre optics.
GERMANY (FR) = the Deutsche Bundespost plans to install only ISDN
switches after 1988; a nationwide narrowband ISDN is expected by 1993

and from 1992 the first phase of an integrated broadband network should start; in 1979 the first fibre optic links were established in Frankfurt and Berlin and in 1982 a broadband integrated optical fibre local telecommunications network (BIGFON) was introduced with pilot projects in several cities. The company Siemens sees for its Communications Group an important growth area in the development of optical fibre based digital communication systems. Standard Elektrik Lorenz -a subsidiary of ITT - offers the System 12, has directed its R&D towards ISDN and plays a leading role in the development and installation of optical fibre cables.

GREECE = the Greek telephone network will not be digitized before mid-1992 and only very tentative plans have yet been made for ISDN.

IRELAND = the Irish P&T started to installate digital exchanges in 1981 and expects to have achieved extensive coverage by 1988; also for 1988 the first ISDN experiment is planned; experiments with optical fibre have started.

ITALY = the Italian telecommunication authorities have been committed to ISDN since 1972; by 1985 digital transmission techniques accounted for 70% of the network; ISDN pilot projects are planned in 1988 and the integrated network is expected to reach a million subscribers by 1994; in Rome and Turin some fibre optic links have been installed. The largest Italian telecommunications manufacturer, Italtel, supplies digital transmission and switching systems as well as optical fibre links.

LUXEMBOURG = digitization of the telephone network is on the way but no detailed plans have been published for ISDN. Siemens has supplied the digital exchanges.

THE NETHERLANDS = since 1981 digital transmission has been introduced on a large scale; the PTT plans the connection of some 38% of the subscribers to digital exchanges by 1995; trials with optical fibre links have started and installation of a broadband fibre optics network for business users in Amsterdam, the Hague and Rotterdam (Digital Backbone) is under way. Since 1983 the Philips/AT&T combine has supplied digital exchanges. The NKF group, which Philips acquired in 1970, designs several types of optical cables for telecommunication systems and since 1983 NKF Telecommunication Cable Systems has specialized in the large scale manufacturing of optical fibres with very high bandwieths.

PORTUGAL = a digital system is planned to be introduced during this year. Around 30% digital technology is already in place in the regional networks. No ISDN plans have yet been detailed.

SPAIN = a start toward digitalization was made in 1980. The plan is to gradually build this network in to a full ISDN via an IDN network some of which is already in place. The first ISDN lines to CCITT specifications will be operational by 1988.

UNITED KINGDOM = British Telecom is seriously committed to digital subscriber services and started pilot services in 1984; research on fibre optics started as early as 1966 and the first trials were conducted by 1975; it is expected that by 1990 half of the trunk network will be optical fibre. Mercury, the second licensed Public Telecommunications Operator (PTO) started to build its alternative national network in 1983. This network is all digital, and employs optical fibre and digital microwave radio for both long distance and local links.

GEC Telecommunications - part of the General Electric Company - is one of the main suppliers to British Telecom. It manufactures optical fibre and produces the digital switching system, System X. The Plessey Company also manufactures digital transmission and switching systems (the System X developed jointly with GEC) as well as optical fibres.

Chart 11.
Current market shares in EC Member States for digital exchange supply.

COUNTRY	SUPPLIER	MARKET SHARE
BELGIUM	ALCATEL	80%
	GTE	20%
DENMARK	ERICSSON	80%
	ALCATEL	20%
F.G.R.	SIEMENS	60%
	SEL	40%
FRANCE	ALCATEL	84%
IRELAND	ALCATEL	40%
	ERICSSON	40%
ITALY	ITALTEL	50% (est)
LUXEMBOURG	SIEMENS	100%
NETHERLANDS	PHILIPS/AT&T	75%
PORTUGAL	SIEMENS	55%
	ALCATEL	c. 30%
SPAIN	L.M. ERICSSON	20%
	ALCATEL	80%
UNITED KINGDOM	GEC	40%
	PLESSEY	40%
	ERICSSON, STC,	
	AT&T	20%

Although experimental work on digital telecommunications has developed since the mid-1950s, integrated digital networks become only in the 1980s a realistic commercial proposition. The first phase is the upgrading of the analogue switched telephone network into a digital PSTN. This phase has started in most EC countries. The second phase entails the transition of the digital PSTN into a narrowband integrated network with a transmission speed of 64,000 baud. Several EC countries expect this to happen by the early 1990s. The third phase is the development of an optical fibre based broadband ISDN. No EC countries have yet developed detailed plans for this last stage.

SOURCES:

PTT Datanet Study: draft final report, prepared by Information Dynamics Ltd for the Commission of the European Communities, 1986.

European Telecommunications Review, Financial Times Business Information, 1986.

European Communication Services: towards integration, Logica, 1986.

Interviews with representatives of telecommunication authorities in the Netherlands, Belgium, Luxembourg, France, Federal Republic of Germany, Italy, Denmark, and the UK during 1986.

CSP International research on European Telecommunications Development.

Eurodata Yearbook, 1987.

Monopoly and Mergers Commision Study, 1985.

Dataquest of the European Market Shares of Lines delivered in Europe, 1985.

Daterpro Research Corporation, Value Added Networks (VANS), Detran, N.J., July 1987.

Telecom Magazine, 4º 3, April 1987.

STANDARDIZATION AS A GOVERNMENT POLICY TOOL

- West European harmonization of
tele-information services -

P.H.M. Vervest

1. Introduction

Modern computer and communication technologies make it possible to construct a global telecommunication network as a new infrastructure for the exchange of information. A large number of new facilities become possible which will have a profound impact on traditional services (1). The monopolies of the PTT's are under severe scrutiny; and the globalization of information exchange is gradually affecting the national sovereignty of telecommunications.

The development of a global network, however, requires the interconnection of separate networks as well as the harmonization of network services. This paper addresses the issues of industrial and R & D policies as a means for such harmonization. In particular, the question of investigation is as follows: 'Which are the possibilities and limitations of industrial and R & D policy as a means to co-ordinate the developments in international European telecommunication networks'.

The paper takes in particular the point of view of innovation policy research and tries to establish the main opportunities and bottlenecks. The intention was not to provide a complete overview of the many, differentiated national policies but to focus on the initiatives of the European Community. Moreover, the developments of tele-information services are studies rather than the underlying transmission and switching facilities.

The next section explores the developments in networks and the possibilities for new services. There is an increasing variety of networks and services: the conclusion is that there is a need for a new conceptual framework for international harmonization, which is described in sections 3 and 4. The organization of the standardization work is given in sections 5 and 6. It is argued that standardization will become a deliberate tool of innovation policy.

2. Developments in telecommunication services

Innovations in transmission and switching facilities determine to a large extent which network services are technically feasible; however, a broader perspective should be taken in order to understand the changes in telecommunication services. Kitahara (1983) (2) points two important directions in the long-term development of telecommunication services (see Figure 1): 1. future telecommunications will increasingly merge with mass media; and 2. telecommunications will increasingly expand to information processing.

The merger of personal-type media and mass media will be made possible via a common communications infrastructure for transmission with adequate bandwidth to accommodate different types of information, such as voice, text, facsimile, video, audio, etc. In particular, developments lead from interpersonal to machine-to-machine communications. It will result

Figure 1
Enlargement of the range of telecommunications.

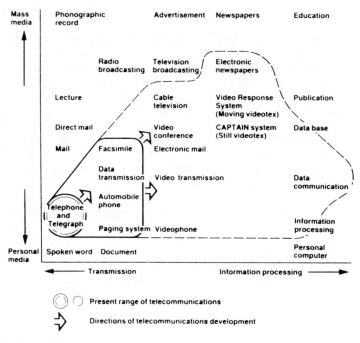

| Mass media | Phonographic record | | Advertisement | Newspapers | | Education |

Radio broadcasting · Television broadcasting · Electronic newspapers

Lecture · Cable television · Video Response System (Moving videotex) · Publication

Direct mail · Video conference · CAPTAIN system (Still videotex) · Data base

Mail · Facsimile · Electronic mail

Data transmission · Video transmission · Data communication

Automobile phone

Telephone and Telegraph · Information processing

Paging system · Videophone

Personal media · Spoken word · Document · Personal computer

◄────── Transmission ────── Information processing ──────►

◎ ◯ Present range of telecommunications

↪ Directions of telecommunications development

Source: Kitahara (1983)

in a situation where the exchange of information is performed by a
machine, a computer-based terminal, which can act 'intelligently' on
behalf of its end-user, the human being. Whether the pattern of communication is one-directional such as conventional radio and television (broadcast information delivery) or two- (bi-) directional (like in traditional
telephony), will in future no longer determine the way in which the
communications infrastructure will be constructed, operated and
managed.
The second important direction is from transmission to information processing. In future it will not only be a matter to transfer data from one
location to the other, but far more than before, means are needed both to
facilitate the transfer ('communications processing') and to process the
information itself. Communications processing offers convenience to the
users, such as speed, protocol and media conversions, without altering the
content of the information being transferred. Information processing,
however, changes the content of the information itself.

A new distinction becomes necessary, i.e. between bearer services - i.e. services that enable information transfer without further assumption on the structure of that information - and telecommunication services. Telecommunication services make assumptions on the structure of the information, such as telephony for voice communications and telex for text communication.

Tele-information services: Because of the capturing and storage of information inside the communication system, all kinds of manipulations become possible. This has stimulated the interest in global services: computer (message handling) systems interconnected on a worldwide basis can provide all kinds of transfer and processing services, while maintaining a high freedom for both sender and receiver. The rapid development in terminal equipment, in particular communicating personal computers, and the ongoing storage of vast amounts of data in computer systems (on-line data bases), are some of the key activators of this development. As a result, all kinds of new tele-information services can be offered - defined as information services via telecommunications, such as data base services, electronic funds transfer, electronic publishing, electronic shopping, goods movement, and information management services.

The role of Value Added Network services: The development of new tele-information services is ultimately determining the applications of the telecommunication infrastructure. There are two different routes to develop these tele-information services. The first one is via office automation in large organizations. Office automation gradually extends its scope from the department level toward intra-site communications via local area networks. At the same time there is a development of inter-site and corporate systems that integrate different organizational processes (purchasing, manufacturing, logistics, marketing and administration in particular) via a company wide area network.

Such corporate - often international - wide area networks (WAN) become a company resource for access by non-members of the organization, i.e. for the organization to communicate with its environment such as suppliers and customers. The large organization can then provide services such as information on products, organizational procedures or more general information; it can also share resources with its environment, like electronic mailbox, data bases or data processing/computer power. Even more important, transactions between the organization and the environment can be handled electronically and procedures could be imposed upon less powerful suppliers and customers. In fact the corporate network can be used as a strategic means to increase the competitive strength of the large organization.

The other route to develop tele-information services is via Value-Added Network (VAN) service providers, defined as (Butler & Cox, 1984): 'A value added network service is a service based on a telecommunications network by which messages are processed or stored so that some value is added to the message as it is transferred from the message sender to the message receiver. In addition to the network operator, value added network services involve two other categories of participants: the service provider, and the service users (or subscribers)'.

Thus, the kernel of VAN services are electronic mail and message handling facilities; this usually narrows down to (3):

- connection of incompatible computer terminals of different manufacturers or of different models, by converting protocols, speeds, codes, formats and media;
- access to and from a variety of networks and the interlinking of different nets ('internetting');
- concentration of traffic and optimal path selection; error detection/correction, improving of reliability and security;
- message routing, storage and processing;
- access to data bases and computer application programs, including remote job entry and remote execution of jobs over distributed computer systems.

Potential suppliers of VAN services are the traditional telecommunication service providers (PTT's and carriers) and computer timesharing bureaux. Moreover, cooperative leagues and associations of professionals, small and medium size companies seek a new opportunity to enforce the cooperative structure among their members via a similar concept as WAN.

The need to interconnect: Throughout history governments have controlled the provision of telecommunication service more or less directly (4). It is because of the increasing variety in services, as discussed above, that current political regimes for telecommunications are under scrutiny and revised in many parts of the world. One of the most critical objectives is to allow the variety in services, but at the same time to make sure that interconnection is possible and that infrastructures can be shared.

What is needed, is a framework to analyse the problems with the objective to ensure 'open systems interconnection'. Since 1976, the International organization for Standardization (ISO) has been working on such a model (5). In conjunction with the work of the International Telegraph and Telephone Consultative Committee (CCITT) on Message Handling Systems (6), a conceptual model has been constructed, called Open Systems Interconnection/Message Handling Systems (OSI/MHS). If defines a 'message handling' boundary in between communication oriented functions (data transfer functions) and application functions (meaningful information). The following sections discuss the model and the protocol architecture.

3.   OSI/MHS as conceptual model

ISO defines the term Open Systems Interconnection as standards for the exchange of information among systems that are 'open' to one another for this purpose by virtue of their mutual use of the applicable standards (7). System is defined as: 'a set of one or more computers, the associated software, peripherals, terminals, human operators, physical processes, information transfer means, etc., that form an autonomous whole capable of performing information processing and/or information transfer'.

An 'open system' should obey OSI standards in its communication with other systems: this will allow not only the transfer of information between systems but also the capability to interwork, that is to achieve a common (distributed) task. The OSI architecture is an abstract model for systems interconnection. Each system is viewed as a hierarchical division of a number of subsystems. Subsystems of the same order, but belonging to different overall systems constitute a layer. Thus, the (n)-subsystem of system A is on the same level as the (n)-subsystem of system B: in this way, the (n)-subsystems of A and B collectively constitute a peer layer. Except for the highest layer, which represents the systems' application, each layer provides services for the next higher layer. The OSI architecture distinguishes seven layers as given in Figure 2.

Figure 2
The ISO seven-layer reference model.

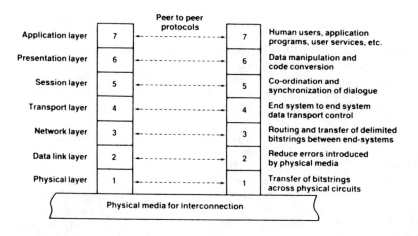

The OSI principles for layering are the following: 1. Layers are defined so as to group similar functional entities together. 2. Each layer adds to the services provided by the layer below, except for the lowest layer. 3. Each layer has one or more peer protocols for the interaction among its functional entities. 4. Different protocols may be used within the same layer without affecting the layer service definition. 5. Interactions across layer boundaries are minimized. 6. The number of layers is kept to the minimum consistent with the above principles.

CCITT message-handling functional model: CCITT has defined message handling as a function of the application layer (layer 7 of the OSI model). It forms one of the first specifications of a user system that is part of the application layer in accordance with the OSI model. A Message Handling System (MHS) is defined by CCITT as the collectivity of user processing equipment, referred to as User Agent (UA), and Message Transfer Agents (MTA).

The UA and MTA can be compared to the postbox and postoffice as in traditional postal service. The UA is an electronic postbox, where messages are delivered or posted. The MTA is the postoffice, responsable for relaying messages between different postboxes.

A number of related MTA's constitute a Message Transfer System (MTS), like postoffices are organised as a 'system'. The MTS is the interconnection of distributed systems on the level of message transfer, called the Message Transfer Layer (MTL) as shown in Figure 3. The MTL is the conceptual boundary between the application layer and the lower-level communication layers. Its position is on the lowest part of the application layer and other application functions are positioned on top of this MTL. As of October 1984 CCITT has defined the Interpersonal Messaging service (IPM) - or User Agent Layer (UAL) - for the relaying of messages for human end-users. The MTS functionality, however, extends beyond that of interpersonal messaging.

Directory services: An important extension of the MHS model are the directory services. First, the directory services enable one to identify the other party. The variety in message handling systems and the different conventions for naming and addressing, will make the compiling and maintenance of a public directory a formidable task. The updating of such a directory will be a continuous effort of processing the mutations of various directory systems. This may lead to a distributed directory system in such a way that every private MTA has an associated Directory Service Agent (DSA), to which all relevant information from the other directory systems must be copied, under the management of the overall public directory.

A second function of the directory is to include information on the type of messages (at presentation layer and/or application layer) and the method to obtain access to private or specific public systems. Moreover, the directory can be seen as a means to control access and to provide specific facilities for security. It may also provide domain management services and conformance testing services.

4. Protocol architecture for standardization of tele-information services

The work of CCITT, ISO and other organizations (IFIP, NBS, ECMA, IEEE, ANSI, etc.) has resulted in an overall protocol architecture for the development of standards aimed at the interconnection of information

Figure 3

Message handling protocol structure following OSI/MHS.

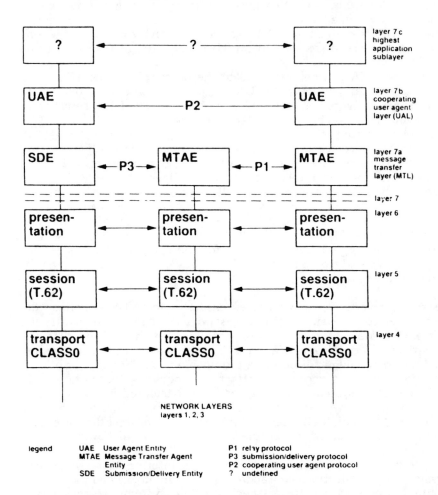

legend   UAE   User Agent Entity   P1   relay protocol
              MTAE   Message Transfer Agent   P3   submission/delivery protocol
                       Entity   P2   cooperating user agent protocol
              SDE   Submission/Delivery Entity   ?   undefined

systems. It is also the basis for the standardization of tele-information services. The protocol structure has been laid down in Figure 4. It is composed of the following sets of standards (Recommendations):

- IS 7498 (ISO, 1983) on Information Processing Systems - Open Systems Interconnection - Basic Reference Model and specific layer standards (including DIS 8473, 8348, DP 8602 for connectionless transmission).
- CCITT Recommendations X.200, X.300 and X.400 Series.
- CCITT Recommendations on telematic services as well as on bearer services.

47

Figure 4

Protocol architecture for standardization of tele-information services.

OPEN SYSTEMS INTERCONNECTION – BASIC REFERENCE MODEL

X.200, X.210, X.250, IS 7498, DP 8509	Standardized applications			Private applications
	Telematics[2]	Office services	Data processing	

Layer 7 application layer

Office services: DOCUMENT STRUCTURE AND INTERCHANGE T.73 DP8613
Data processing: REMOTE DATA HANDLING
Private applications: [3]

Telematics column items: TELETEX F.200, F.201, T.60, T.63, T.90, T.91, X.430, DP 9063/2, DP 9064 2; FACSIMILE T.0, T.2, T.3, T.4, T.5 DP 9063/1, DP 9063/2; Mixed-mode teletex /facsimile T.62 T.72, T.73; VIDEOTEX F.300, T.100, T.101; OTHER

Office services column items: DIRECTORY, X.DS1, X.DS2 X.DS3, X.DS4, X.DS6, X.DS7; MAILING F.40, F.350, X.400, X.401, X.408, X.420; FILING DP 8571; PRINTING; OTHER DIS 8879

Data processing column items: FILE TRANSFER ACCESS AND MANAGEMENT DP 8571; JOB TRANSFER DP 8831, DP 8832; PROGRAMMING AND INTERPROGRAM COMMUNICATIONS; OTHER DP 8632, DP 8651, DP 9007, DP 9040, DP 9041

Layer 7a application sublayer	X.410, X.411 DP 8505 (MOTIS), DP 8649, DP 8650	
Layer 6 presentation layer	T.50, T.51, T.61, T.73, T.100, X.409 IS 6937, DP 8822, DP 8823, DP 8824, DP 8825	
Layer 5 session layer	X.215, X.225, T.62 DIS 8326, DIS 8327	
Layer 4 transport layer	X.214, X.224. T.70 DIS 8072, DIS 8073, DIS 8602	

Network oriented layers	X.213, X.244, X.300, X.310, V.100, V.110, I.120, I.210, I.211, I.212, DIS 8348, DIS 8473, DP 8648, DIS 8802/1					Private Local Area Network (LAN) and/or Wide Area Network (WAN)
	PSTN	CSPDN	PSPDN	ISDN	LAN[4]	
Layer 3 Network layer	telephone + X.25	X.21	X.25, X.3, X.28/ X 29, X.32 DIS 8208,DP 8878	I.450, I 451, X.30, X.31	DIS 8802/3, DIS 8802/4, DIS 8802/5, DIS 8802/6	
Layer 2 Data link layer	T.71 or X.25		LAPB X.25 DIS 7776	I.440, I.441	DIS 8802/2	
Layer 1 Physical layer	e g. V 24, V 25	X 21, X 21 bis, X 22	X 21, X 21 bis DIS 2110	I 430, I 431		

notes: 1. ISO standards are either International Standard (IS); Draft International Standard (DIS); or Draft Proposal (DP). CCITT Recommendations start with capital F., T., V., X., or I.
2. interworking with Telex (TWX) is foreseen, cf. F.201
3. examples are proprietary architectures such as SNA-DIA/DCA by International Business Machines (IBM) or specific application protocols such as MAP by General Motors
4. The following LAN technologies are standardized:
   DP 8802/3 Carrier Sense Multiple Access/Collision Detection
   DP 8802/4 token bus
   DP 8802/5 token ring
   DP 8802/6 slotted ring

-      Local area network standards developed by the Institute for Electrical and Electronic Engineers (IEEE) and ISO.

A distinction is made between standardized application and private applications. Private applications are based on proprietary architectures, developed independently of standardization institutes by manufacturers or user organizations. System Network Architecture (SNA) and Document Interchange Architecture (DIA)/Document Content Architecture (DCA) is an important proprietary architecture developed by IBM. In general a proprietary architecture is not built for open systems interconnection and tends to exclude unlike systems from the environment. Communications across the boundaries necessitate gateway processors, which will restrict inter-system communications to the lowest common denominator.

The more sophisticated inter-system applications are, the higher the level of standardization must be. In particular three types of standards become increasingly important: (1) office document architectures, (2) industry-generic transaction formats, and (3) interprocess control standards.

(1)   Document interchange formats define the data structures of the information for transmission in such a way that both sender and receiver can interpret this structure. Each document will be composed of different portions of document content, with a specified relationship between these portions. This is called the document structure. ISO has been working on an office Document Architecture (ODA) with a complementary Office Document Interchange Format (ODIF). CCITT defines a Simple Formattable Document (SFD) in X.420 and a telematic documents interchange format in T.23 (the character set is defined in T.62).

(2)   Another set of important standards are forms standards for business transactions. Much work for transaction standards has been performed by the Transportation Data Co-ordinating Committee (TDCC) in the USA. They have developed the Electronic Data Interchange (EDI) standard, with a generic software structure so that industries with similar data structures can adjust the standard to their specific requirements. EDI is composed of tables with respect to transaction set names, segments in each transaction set, segment names, data elements in each segment, and data element specifications. Another important development has been by the American National Standars Institute (ANSI) which addressed the issue of multi-industry transaction standards.

(3)   Increasingly information which is distributed over different systems must cooperate for a common task, such as for computer integrated manufacturing, data base enquiry, logistic and purchasing. Standards are needed that allow the use of distributed information as an integrated resource for certain tasks. For this reason General Motor's has developed its Manufacturing Automation Protocol (MAP), based on the seven layer model, but including an eighth layer, the Manufacturing Message Format and Syntax (see also Boeing's TOP).

5.   The promotion of standards in West Europe

Over the past years European governments have increasingly become
aware of the necessity to develop and enforce standards which comply
with the OSI framework. Two programs by the European Community are
specifically important:
1.   European Strategic Program for R & D on Information Technology
(ESPRIT), covering (8):
-    advanced micro-electronics (submicron technology, computer-
    aided design, materials and opto-electronics);
-    software technology (development methodology, production and
    maintenance, tools and management);
-    advanced information processing (knowledge engineering, in-
    formation and knowledge storage, external interface, computer
    architectures);
-    office systems (office systems science and human factors, advanced
    workstations, communication systems, filling and retrieval,
    integrated office systems design);
-    computer integrated manufacture (CAD/CAE/CAM, machine
    control system, integrated system architectures and system
    applications).
2.   R & D on Advanced Communications Technology in Europe (RACE),
which is specifically aimed at R & D for integrated broadband com-
munications.
Related EC programs are (the following list is not complete);
-    EIES (Esprit Information Exchange System).
-    INSIS (Interinstitutional Information System).
-    BRITE (Basic Research in Industrial Technology in Europe).
-    CREST (Comité de la Recherche Scientific et Technique).
-    COST (Coopération européenne dans la domaine de la recherche
    Scientifique et Technique).
-    FAST (Forecasting and Assessment on Science and Technology).
-    APPOLLO (Article Procurement with Online Local Ordering).
Another influential organization is the Conference of European Post and
Telecommunications Administrations (CEPT) which formulates joint ad-
ministrative and technical programs among the European PTT's. CEPT is
not an officially recognized intergovernmental body, but it harmonizes
implementation programs of its member PTT's; in this way CEPT influences equipment procurement by its members. An important agreement was made by CEPT in November 1985 in the Memorandum of
Understanding on European telecommunication Standards. It is open for
adherence by CEPT members and lays down two important objectives:
1. CEPT technical recommendations will be used to establish European
Telecommunication Standards (NET's); CEPT will initiate the means to
give these standards sufficient mandatory force, in particular to seek the
establishment of a new Directive of the European Community on such
standards. 2. The standards will be used in the purchasing specifications of
PTT's and for connection of terminal equipment to their networks.

Besides the EC and CEPT significant initiatives are undertaken by SPAG and CEN/CENELEC. The Standards Promotion and Application Group (SPAG) is an interim organization of the Roundtable of European Industrialists to coordinate their interests toward the EC initiatives (9). SPAG is active in three areas: technical coordination with standards-making bodies; validation and certification of standards; demonstration projects, of which MHS is the first to be realized.

CEN (Comité Européen de Normalisation) is the European association of national standardization institutes; CENELEC is the equivalent for electrotechnical standardization with government representatives of 17 national electrotechnical committees. CEN and CENELEC have intensified their activities to harmonize information technology in Europe; in collaboration with CEPT they have established the Steering Committee for Information Technology (ITSTC) with an official mandate from the BC (10).

Figure 5 gives a schematic diagram of the European structure for implementing standards. The proposed procedures are as follows:

1. Basic documents by CCITT, ISO, ECMA, and others are first converted into 'reference standards'.
2. These form the basis for functional standards (European Norms) as rules for the applications of specific functions, including rules for the use of the functional standards themselves.
3. Specific European Norms are developed for certain aspects (safety, ergonomics, quality) and for certain hardware and software elements.
4. European Norms are also to be developed for test methods and conformity verification.
5. These norms lead to commanding (EC) standards for specific equipment, including - inter alia - compatibility requirements.

The recent European initiatives by the EC and the Roundtable of European Industrialists show the need for standardization at a global scale in the area of communication and information technologies. West Europe opts for R & D cooperation and standardization in order to create a technological as well as an economic unity. The dominance of manufacturers and governments on the one hand, and the absence of user representation on the other hand, is remarkable.

6. Standardization as a government policy tool

A conceptual model as well as adequate standards seem necessary for the long-term development of tele-information services. Government can therefore stimulate and lead the innovation process by way of standardization policy. In particular the availability of expertise and the industrial interests associated with standards determine the way in which standards policy can be constructed (11):

Figure 5

Organizational structure for standardization of information technology in Western Europe.

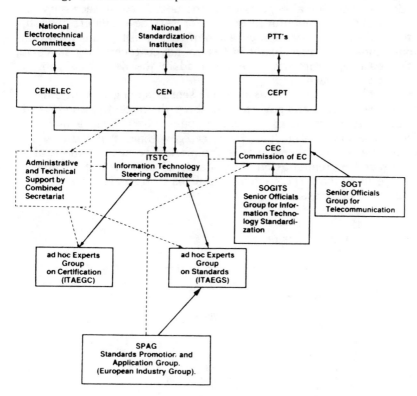

1.   The availability of expertise is necessary to obtain consensus on
standards; if expertise is available throughout a variety of categories
- manufacturers and service providers as well as government and users -
this will have a positive influence on the acceptance of innovations; in
other words, standards that are accepted before diffusion of the innovation, will highly promote the innovation and diffusion processes themselves.

2.   Industrial interests are another factor for the process of innovation;
if manufactorers and service providers are the prime beneficiary of
standards, they will promote the development of standards on their own
account, for instance in order to create new markets; if these interests
are not that obvious, or if manufacturers and service providers will not
take the lead in standards development, the user interests in forcing
standardization are essentially left to government and/or a limited group
of powerful users.

As shown in Figure 6 the above factors lead to four different scenarios for which government innovation policy should be constructed. In the liberal-technology scenario there is no agreement among technical experts, nor is there widespread technical expertise for the definition of necessary and acceptable standards; manufacturers and/or service providers take the lead in the definition and implementation of appropriate standards. Consensus on standards is also absent in the contrived-technology scenario, but in this case governments take the lead in the definition and the enforcement of standards.

There are two scenarios that assume consensus among manufacturers, service providers, users and government about the necessity and criteria for acceptability of standards. These assume that adequate technical expertise is available throughout industry, government and users. The market-led standards scenario leaves the market to initiate the factual development and implementation of standards; alternatively governments can take the initiative. The various scenarios lead to different government innovation policies.

Figure 6
Standardization scenarios.

standardization initiator consensus among manufacturers, service providers, users, and government	manufacturers and/or service providers	government
no consensus	liberal-technology scenario	contrived-technology scenario
consensus	market-led standards-promotion scenario	government-led standards-promotion scenario

Liberal-technology scenario: The basis of this scenario is the autonomy of technological developments and the 'logic' of the market to determine what it needs and to assimilate innovations as and when it is feasible. Government policy is aimed at the generation of new technology and at the liberalization of the maket, i.e. the creation of an equal playing field for the application and dissemination of technology into the market. Regulatory provisions are kept to a minimum and are intended to promote competition as an instrument for market innovation. An explicit standardization policy is not followed; moreover, standards are seen as the result of market forces (de-facto standards), not as a negotiated contract among stakeholders in the market.

As 'equal' market player, government will procure innovative products and services, but will not specifically favour new products. Subsidies to individual firms are granted for the generation of new technology, not so much for the application of new products in the organization or for marketing. There is a definite policy to stimulate the scientific and technological infrastructure, necessary for the generation of new technology; it is specifically directed toward a competitive knowledge infrastructure, leading to a many new product ideas. Science and technology policy also aims at lowering user barriers and creating a favourable attitude toward newness. The liberal-technology scenario is completed with a policy to encourage young starter companies, a flexible production infrastructure and a favourable financial climate.

Contrived-technology scenario: The 'Leitmotiv' of this scenario is that innovation can be contrived, technology and market needs can be assessed, and governments can strategically manage the innovation process. Industrial and trade regulations are especially important. Monopoly positions of state-controlled firms can offer a technological base for innovation; monopolies of service providers make a controlled assessment of the innovation possible.

Technological development is stimulated as well as controlled via government procurement policies. This is also effected via subsidies to individual firms. Moreover, a specific science and technology policy supports the government strategic objectives. Small and medium size companies cater for the necessary flexibility of large companies, but are not a significant innovation factor.

Consensus-standardization scenarios: Under assumption that there is common understanding of what the market needs and what technology can do, government policy aims at the standardization of new products prior to the factual market introduction. All involved parties - manufacturers, service operators, users, etc. - are engaged in defining primarily functional standards. There are two alternative situations: either manufacturers and service providers agree upon the necessity of (voluntary) standards, or not. In the latter case government should take the lead in ensuring consensus standards. In both cases government interference is mainly the result of consulting the market players. Regulation is seen as a necessary instrument to enforce standards and to retaliate the market, if non-standard products gain acceptance in the market. While dominant market positions are not promoted, this need not harm innovation as long as the approval of standardized products is independent of the dominant player.

Government procurement policies follow standards rather than innovation and are applied to effect the generation of standardized new technology. Subsidies to develop standards by individual firms are given. The scientific and technological infrastructure is very important in a consensus-standardization scenario, not so much as a means to create new ideas, but as a way to define overall and comprehensive architectures of technological

Figure 7

Government policies.

	liberal-technology	contrived-technology	consensus-standardization
• regulation	minimal	all-important	follows the process
• procurement	neutral	industrial policy	standard equipment
• subsidies to individual firms	generation of new (basic) technology	generation of new (applied) technology	standards development
• science and technology infrastructure	competitive knowledge	trade-able knowledge	consensual architecture
• small and medium size companies	starter policy	flexibility for large organizations	lowering user barriers

pathways. Government policy aims at a rather uniform knowledge structure and interchangeability of ideas. The study of user functionality is promoted and user barriers are seen as a necessary evil to prevent non-standardized innovation. Policies for small and medium size companies are specifically to lower user barriers.

7. Summary and conclusion

This paper discusses the possibilities and limitations of industrial and R & D policy as a means to co-ordinate the development in international European telecommunication networks. Rather than examining the technical developments in transmission and switching facilities, the fundamental changes in telecommunications industry are analyzed; in particular, the development of the infrastructure for new tele-information services. In order to develop this infrastructure as well as the associated basic services, a conceptual framework is needed. The first efforts for this framework started in the mid 1970s and have resulted in the OSI/MHS model. This model is described in sections 3 and 4. While competing architectures exist. OSI/MHS is increasingly accepted as the basis for standards development. Moreover, the model can serve as the organizational framework for European harmonization.

At the basis of industrial and R & D policy in European telecommunications lies this need for harmonization. The essence of 'global' networks may be that national policies become highly dependent of international developments. Over the past years West Europe has been establishing a new framework for harmonization (see section 5). This is not only a matter of the technical definition of standards. Increasingly standardization gains a political and economic dimension. Technical experts, who fully understand the delicate balance between technical feasibility and fore-seeable market demand, are scarce. At the other hand, European indus-trial interests necessitate that consensus on 'right' standards exists before the market can be developed. Section 6 outlines the various scenario's and puts standardization policy into the overall perspective of innovation, industrial and R & D policy.

The European Community faces an enormous challenge for technological harmonization in telecommunications. The development of the promising market for tele-information services requires the interconnection of the various European networks and the harmonization of network services. This will not be possible on a nationalistic and scattered European scale: will the Community act in time ?

Finally, from a research point of view, the case of innovation in telecom-munications sheds a new light on the traditional concepts of industrial and R & D policy (12): standards are a new way for governments to develop, direct, and precipitate the market acceptance of new technologies.

Notes

(1)   Cf. Nora, S. Minc, A., **The Computerization of Society,** The MIT Press, MA, 1980; an interesting overview of developments is also given in: Cantraine, G., Destine, J. (ed.), **New Systems and Services in telecommunications, Proceedings of the International Confe-rence on New Systems and Services in Telecommunications,** held November 24-26, 1980, North-Holland Publishing Company, Am-sterdam, 1981; Compaine, B.M. (ed.), **Understanding New Media - Trends and Issues in Electronic Distribution of Information,** Ballinger Publishing Company, Cambridge, MA, 1984.
(2)   Kitahara, Y., **Information Network System - Telecommunications in the Twenty-First Century,** Heinemann Educational Books, Lon-don, 1983, p. 9.
(3)   Vervest, P.H.M., Wissema, J.G., **Eelectronic Mail and Message Handling in the USA - Results of the May 1984 Study Tour,** Erasmus University Rotterdam, October 1984; see also Vervest, P.H.M., Wissema, J.G., **Electronic Mail and Message Handling in Japan - Results of the February, March 1985 Study Tour,** Erasmus Univer-sity Rotterdam, April 1985.
(4)   Cf. Stamps, G., **The Future for Electronic Document Distribution,** Institute for Geraphic Communications', MA, 1982, p. 161-175; Beesley, M.E., **Liberalisation of the Use of British Telecommu-nications network,** Department of Industry, London, January 1981; Evans, D.S. (ed.), **Breaking up Bell - Essays on Industrial Organiza-tion and Regulation,** Elsevier Science Publishing Co., New York, 1983; Trebing, H.M., **Issues in Public Utility Regulation, Proceeding of the Institute of Public Utilities Tenth Annual Conference,** Michigan State University, 1979.

(5)   Information Processing Systems - Open Systems Interconnection - Basic Reference Model, International organization for Standardization, ISO/IS 7498, ISO/TC97/Sc16 (rev.), Geneva, 1983.

(6)   CCITT, Recommendation X.400, Message Handling Systems: System Model - Service Elements, Study Group VII, International Telecommunications Union, Geneva, 1984. See also X.401, X.408, X.409, X.4.10, X.411, X.420, and X.430.

(7)   ISO (1983) p. 2; cf. Day, J.D., Zimmerman, H., The OSI Reference Model, Proceedings of the IEEE, p. 1334-1345, Vol. 7, No. 12, December 1983.

(8)   Cf. The Midterm Review of ESPRIT - Commission of the European Communities, Brussels, October 15th 1985, submitted by the ESPRIT Review Board, under chairmanship of A.E. Pannenborg.

(9)   Current participants in SPAG are AEG, Bull (CII-Honeywell Bull), CGE (SIT/Alcatel/SESA), GEC, ICL, Nixdorf, Olivetti, Philips, Plessey, Siemens, STET (SGS/Italtel/CERCI/CSELT, Thompson/EFCIS.

(10)   Note also the Senior Officials Group for Information Technology Standardization (SDGITS) and the Senior Officials Group for Telecommunications (SOGT), which are advisory boards to the Commission of the EC, composed of senior officials of member countries. Reference is also made to 'EUREKA', an initiative by the French government in 1985.

(11)   A standardization-scenario analysis has been made in Innovation in Electronic Mail, North-Holland Publishing Company, Amsterdam, forthcoming.

(12)   Rothwell, R., Zegveld, W., Reindustrialization and Technology, Longman Group Ltd., Harlow, 1985; Rothwell, R., Zegveld, W., Industrial Innovation and Public Policy - Preparing for the 1980s and 1990s, Frances Pinter (Publishers) Ltd., London, 1981.

PART 2

GLOBAL STRATEGIES

DEALING WITH GLOBAL NETWORKS: SOME CHARACTERISTICS OF INTERNATIONAL MARKETS

William H. Melody

1. Introduction

The theme that technologically advanced economies are in the process of moving beyond industrial capitalism to information-based economies that will bring profound changes in the form and structure of the economic system is becoming ever more popular in the social sciences (1). Rapid advances in computer and telecommunication technologies are making it possible to generate information that was herefore unattainable, transmit it instantaneously around the globe, and - in a rapidly growing number of instances - sell it in information markets. Some authors claim that the most developed countries already devote the majority of their economic resources to information-related activities (2). The computer, telecommunication, and information content industries are among the most rapidly growing global industries, and are expected to remain so for the next decade or longer. Many national governments are counting on these industries to provide the primary stimulus to their future economic growth.

It is generally recognised that the most important resource determining the economic efficiency of any economy, industry, productive process, or household is information and its effective communication. The characteristics of information define the state of knowledge that underlies all economic processes and decision-making structures. Fundamental changes in the characteristics of information, and in its role in the economy, should be central to the study of economics. The state of information in the economy has pervasive effects on the workings of the economy generally. It has intensified impacts on those sectors that provide information products or services, including, for example, press, television, radio, film, mail, libraries, banks, credit bureaus, databanks, and other 'information providers', as they are now called (3). And the establishment of information markets brings about changing conceptions of public and private information, as well as the property rights associated with marketable information (4).

The extension of telecommunication systems has expanded the geographic bounds of markets, thereby increasing competition in global markets among the largest transnational corporations (TNCs), and extending the scope of potential monopoly control. At the same time, survival by local and regional and even national firms that must compete with TNCs is often made more difficult and sometimes impossible. To the extent that expanded markets encompass different political jurisdictions, they influence - and often constrain and direct - the political agenda of affected governments. And to the extent they promote unbalanced exchanges of goods, services, people, and particularly of the content of mass media, they provide the basis for cultural domination as well.

We are now in the process of a great expansion of the world's telecommunication system, not only in terms of geographical coverage, but also in types of communication services (including high-speed data and video) and substantially increased capacity. Virtually instantaneous communication can be obtained in enormous volumes at substantially reduced unit cost on global networks. The increasingly global scope of this change raises a variety of issues of political policy that transcend national governments. Indeed, it forces together economic and political dimensions of trade and government in a way that precludes separate treatment, effective analysis is to be achieved. The economic issues that are raised constrain the scope of independent action by national governments and require that international economic issues become an increasing preoccupation of national governments. It also tends to shift power from national governments to TNCs and to thrust international agencies into a new role as negotiating fora where national governments and TNCs jockey for political and economic power in both international as well as domestic national markets.

These developments also have important cultural implications. In technologically advanced societies the mass media represent the major set of communication institutions for spreading information, ideas, values and beliefs throughout society. The economic and political power of the mass media have long been recognized and analyzed within a national context. The mass media, and particularly television, is seen by the TNCs as an enormously profitable vehicle for international marketing through commercial cable television and direct broadcast satellite networks. Thus the implications for national cultures have become tied closely te developments in the international economy in general, and in international telecommunication in particular.

2.   The Information and Communication Sector (5)

Issues relating to information and communication have become central to public policy in all nations and in an increasing number of international agencies. The major reason is the rapid economic growth in the industries that constitute this sector - micro-electronics; computer hardware, software and services; telecommunication equipment and services; the mass media and a plethora of new data bank and information services - growth that has been stimulated by rapid and continuing technological change. The direct economic effects are compounded by the fact that this sector provides important infrastructure services for most other industries, as well as government agencies and other institutions. Information gathering, processing, storage and transmission over efficient telecommunication networks is the foundation on which developed economies will close the twentieth century as 'information economies'.

This sector likely will become even more significant to the development of national economies than any of the major transport expansion eras of the past (canal, rail or highway). As a result the information and communication sector already has become a central concern of domestic industrial policy for most developed countries. In the UK, for example, the privatisation of British Telecom (BT), the Alvey, Hunt and Peacock Commissions, the adoption of preliminary policies relating to cable television and direct broadcast satellites, government approval of the monopolisation of the only UK legal data base in the US, and its disapproval of an alliance between BT and IBM on telecommuncation technical standards are but a few recent illustrations. Similar issues of public policy have been raised in many countries.

Yet the economic implications go much beyond the domestic economy. Expansion and increased efficiency in the information and communication sector serves to integrate the domestic economy more easily into the international economy by means of efficient international communication and information networks. As international economic integration is expanded, control over the domestic economy by the national government is weakened, and the impact of domestic public policies is reduced. These developments are forcing national governments to recognise the need for a full range of international trade policies addressed not only to direct trade in information and communication equipment and services, but also to be the implications of world wide networks for other industries. For example, they are central to current policy discussions in a number of areas at the EEC, as well the preparations by all countries for the next round of GATT meetings.

The international banking industry already has restructured its organisation and methods of operation in light of the enhanced opportunities for transferring money and data instantaneously around the world. Many TNCs have been able to improve economic efficiency and control by centralising more decisions at their world headquarters. This has removed significant decision-making power, as well as research and development, from 'national' subsidiaries that have been reduced to the status of branch plants. Medical, tax, credit and professional information relating to one country is being stored with increasing frequency in another. This raises important policy questions in a number of areas, including national and regional sovereignty, the terms and conditions of access to information, privacy of personal information and the vulnerability of a country's economic and political decision-making systems to losses of essential information because of breakdowns in crucial information and communication networks that occur outside the country.

Significant changes in information and communication networks require a reinterpretation of traditional notions of public and private information and the terms and conditions for access to it. Information itself is becoming a marketable commodity in many new instances, and proposed changes in copyright laws now under discussion would permit a further expansion. Continuing growth in the information and communication sector is permitting an expanded role for a wide variety of private markets, but these markets are very imperfect, raising questions of government regulation of domestic and TNC monopoly power in national and international markets.

Clearly many people and organizations will benefit substantially from the expansion of the information and communication sector, but many also will lose, in both relative and absolute terms as traditional public services are displaced, downgraded or made more expensive. For example much of the information now in public libraries may be privatised and only accessible through telecommunication information services. The telephone system is being upgraded to the standards of an integrated services digital network (ISDN) that is more efficient for the plethora of new information services, but significantly more expensive if only basic telephone service is required. A major challenge for social policy will be to find methods to ensure that developments in the information and communication sector do not exacerbate class division in society and the benefits are spread across all sectors of society. This will require new conceptions of the 'public interest', new interpretations of the requirements of social policy, and the design of new systems for its efficient and effective implementation.

Some nations undoubtedly will find it in their interest to promote the implementation of the information and communication technologies at a faster pace than others. Depending upon the structure of, and implications for, the domestic economy, other national priorities and the particular values of each nation, the optimal pace and structure of implementation will differ, in some cases substantially. The US and Japan see enormous benefits from international trade in information and communication equipment and services for their domestic economies. Most developing countries, with extremely low rates of telephone penetration, many urgent domestic priorities and large trade deficits, are much less enthusiastic. For most countries, including those in Western Europe, the implications are very mixed. Domestic structural implications are likely to be very significant and policy development more complex.

3.   The extension of market boundaries: theory and practice (6)

According to conventional market theory, an expansion of available information, together with enhanced and improved telecommunication, should permit more efficient decision making and the extension of markets across geographical and industry boundaries. It should increase competition. It should allow resources to be allocated more rapidly and efficiently. The conditions of real markets should approximate more closely the assumptions of theory, where markets are frictionless and operate under conditions of perfect information. Indeed much of the literature on the information economy considers these developments to provide unmitigated benefits to society (7).

But close examination indicates that the benefits of these technologies will not be distributed uniformly across markets, that certain segments of society will be made poorer both in absolute as well as relative terms, and that the structure of markets in many industries will be affected in fundamental ways (8). These new technologies permit many markets to be extended to the international and global level. But only the largest national and transnational corporations and government agencies have the need for, and the ability to take full advantage of these new opportunities. For them the geographic boundaries of markets are extended globally, and their ability to administer and control global markets efficiently and effectively from a central point is enhanced. These changes have been a significant factor in stimulating the wave of mergers and takeovers involving giant TNCs in recent years. The diseconomies of size and scope provided by the increasing administrative costs and reduced effectiveness of information processing and communications in very large organisations can be reduced substantially, if not overcome by the application of information and communication technologies.

The manner in which these technological developments are being implemented creates a significant barrier to entry for all but the largest firms, thereby accelerating tendencies toward concentration (9). In fact smaller firms are likely to find themselves disadvantaged because of the new technological developments. For example, the telecommunication systems in the United States and other technologically advanced countries are being redesigned to meet the technically sophisticated digital data requirements of high volume, multiple purpose, global users. For traditional, simpler communication requirements, such as basic telephone services, the new upgraded system will serve quite well, but at substantially increased cost to smaller users (10). The telecommunication options available to small, localised, and even regionalised businesses do not reflect their unique needs. Rather, their range of choice is dictated by the national and global needs of the largest firms and government agencies. The most efficient telecommunication system for their needs has been cannibalised in the creation of the technologically advanced system.

In most industries the new competition is simply intensified oligopolistic rivalry among TNCs on a world wide basis. The firms that can now leap across market boundaries are already dominant firms in their respective product/service and geographic markets. Their entry has a major impact on the structure of the supply side of the market and requires a strategic response from the established dominant firm(s). This is not atomistic competition responding to market forces that reflect individual consumer demand, but rather a type of medieval jousting for territorial control.

The focal point of this oligopolistic rivalry is on differentiated adaptation of particular technologies and product lines of sale to nation states. Major decisions involving multi-million-dollar commitments over many years are made relatively infrequently, for example, selecting a satellite system or a line of computer or telecommunication equipment. The rivalry is directed to obtaining a long-run position of market entrenchment and dominance in particular foreign national submarkets.

The rivalry among TNCs for entrenchment in new national markets differs fundamentally from traditional market theory in several respects. First, short-run market clearing prices are not the focal point of the rivalry. Rather, short-run pricing policy is simply one of many strategic tools for achieving the long-run objective of market entrenchement. This rivalry stands far outside the short-run pricing behaviour examined by traditional oligopoly theory.

Second, competitive advantage is obtained not primarily from the superiority of a product or service in the eyes of individual consumers exercising choice, but rather from effective persuasion of government leaders in foreign countries. The objective is to secure a position of special privilege in entering national markets. The privileged market position then is ensured by the national policy of the purchasing countries with respect to such matters as licensing, tax, tariff, currency exchange, capital repatriation, entry barriers imposed on rivals, etc.

In attempting to achieve these long-term dominant market positions, the TNCs are assisted by governments of their respective home-base countries. The home governments adopt policies and positions that will assist their respective TNCs, and sometimes they even participate in institutional marketing. Thus, the oligopolistic rivalry among TNCs involves a strong element of nationalism and direct government involvement on both the demand and supply sides of the market exchange.

Adoption of the new technologies tends to increase the significance of overhead costs, not only for the information and telecommunication activities, but also with respect to greater centralisation of functions and capital/labour substitution, for example, robots. Thus, the inherent instability in oligopoly markets is magnified by the instability created by an increased and very significant proportion of overhead costs.

Taken collectively, these changes introduce new elements of risk and uncertainty. But they also provide new opportunities to shift these risks and uncertainties away form TNC investors and managers to the particular localities where production occurs, and to the institutions that reside there, that is, local government, labour, and consumers. TNCs also can diversify their risks by expanding their absolute size and geographical coverage. The larger the TNC, the more resources at its command for allocation within the firm rather than through capital markets. The greater the geographical coverage, the more risks can be diversified by the TNC, although these risks could be disastrous for any particular production location dependent on the TNC. In addition, the enchanced market power strengthens the TNCs ability to exploit both resource and consumer markets.

Because the new technologies permit rapid transfer of new types of information, they permit more frequent short-run decision making by TNC managers. In global markets, the terms of trade, currency exchange rates, interest rates, and money movements are often as important to real profitability as the actual production of goods and services. With new opportunities for frequent, short-run decisions there is likely to be an increased emphasis on day-to-day financial transfers, if not ongoing speculative manipulation. This will create additional instability for any particular resource supplier or production location that might fall out of favour as a result of short-term shifts in financial and currency markets.

Historically, the current revolution in telecommunication technology can be compared in certain respects with the effect of the introduction of the telegraph upon the structure of markets in the United States over the period 1845 to 1890. In his study of these developments, Richard DuBoff concluded: 'The telegraph improved the functioning of markets and enhanced competition, but it simultaneously strengthened forces making for monopolisation. Larger scale business operations, secrecy and control, and spatial concentration were all increased as a result of telegraphic communications' (11). In fact, he says, 'increasing market size helped 'empire builders' widen initial advantages which at first may have been modest' (12). DuBoff's assessment provides a useful benchmark for examining the current global developments that illustrate similar economic trends, but effects that are substantially magnified and modified as described here.

4.   The role of national governments

For the TNCs, the domestic markets in their home countries provide a springboard to their activity in global markets. The home governments identify more directly with the international success of particular TNCs because they play an important role in the home country's domestic economy.

Home governments tend to exhibit greater tolerance for increased domestic monopoly power because it enhances the power of their resident TNCs in international markets. This can range from a reduced emphasis on the application of laws promoting competition to the actual encouragement of domestic cartels. Many countries have promoted domestic monopoly power in some industries for the purpose of creating a larger corporate presence that they hope will have the power to compete with the largest TNCs.

As oligopolistic rivalry in global markets becomes more intense, national governments are more actively attempting to manipulate the terms of international rivalry to the advantage of 'their' TNCs. Thus, the TNCs are becoming more direct instruments of macro-economic policy through R & D subsidies, tax concessions, tariff conditions, trade agreements, and other policies. This includes the assumption of market risk by home governments in the form of R & D funding, investment guarantees, government-industry joint ventures, and government assistance of home-based TNCs in international market negotiations through applying political pressure to foreign governments. Today this kind of government involvement is labelled 'industrial policy'.

This new approach reflects a change in the role of government from adopting policies designed to stimulate the marketplace environment generally, toward adopting more focused policies designed to assist specific companies. As such, it reflects direct interference in the market. It identifies the economic prosperity of the nation with the financial success of the largest home-based TNCs. The role of government then becomes one of using its political power to manipulate the rules by which the market works to the advantage of the TNCs that it has chosen to support. These policies provide significant barriers to entry to those firms not selected, which includes all domestic firms not large enough to exploit international markets.

Under these conditions competition in the domestic market can be seen as potentially damaging to the ability of home-based TNCs to compete successfully in global markets. Anti-monopoly domestic policies becomes less important, if not antiquated. Monopoly and cartel behavior are accepted as tolerable, if not promoted. Even monopolistic exploitation of domestic consumers becomes tolerable as providing the necessary strength, power, and resources to compete successfully in the global markets (13). Politically it is much easier to provide subsidies by simply allowing a home-based TNC to exploit monopoly power in the domestic market rather than going through the cumbersome political process of first taxing and then granting subsidies.

In this new political economic environment, the conception of the public interest within a nation also changes. Traditional concerns about the prices and quality of public utility services and the universality of coverage of public service declines. For example, in the United States, basic telephone service as a priority of social policy is being questioned, if not yet abandoned, by the Federal Communications Commission (FCC). The international success of home-based TNCs, as measured by sales, profits, and a favourable balance of payments, becomes a primary objective of government public policy. This success is viewed as fueling domestic employment, productivity, and national wealth. Domestic consumers and social policies are seen to benefit from the trickling-down of benefits from successful TNCs.

The real change is a much closer identification of the national and public interests with the corporate interest of the dominant home-based TNCs. It is truly ironic that these industrial policies typically are justified by invoking the ghost of Adam Smith and free market competition. In fact, they represent a fundamental mistrust of the free market. We need not be reminded that, in fact, Smith argued that the wealth of nations would be enhanced if domestic competition were encouraged rather than sacrificed to the myopic criterion of mercantilistic success (14).

In addition, national government policy designed to promote the power of TNCs in global markets may well be an exercise in gradual self-strangulation. The nature and direction of government policy intentions are always heavily constrained to some degree by market conditions and the power of corporations and other large economic units to prevent their effective implementation. Canada has been attempting to implement independent economic and cultural policies for generations. But it has neither the economic nor the political power to implement them effectively in the face of domination by US-based TNCs. As national governments tie themselves more closely to the promotion of corporate power of their TNCs, they are at the same time reducing their own degree of freedom to adopt domestic or international policies contrary to TNC interest.

5. The role of market theory

Traditional market theory provides a perfect rationale for this expansion of TNC market power. By assuming that technology is authonomous and beneficial, that oligopolistic rivalry for long-term dominant positions in foreign national markets is competition, and that market-clearing prices maximizing short-run profit will yield optimal long-run resource allocation, the theory simply reflects the short-run market power positions of the dominant firms. Such concepts as static equilibrium, marginal cost, and consumer surplus are perfectly pliable in their subjective application. Indeed, within this theoretical framework, nothing can be rejected that travels under the appropriate theoretical labels.

The most relevant market model for examining the consequences of competition in the information age is one of indeterminate, unstable oligopoly wherein the TNCs deliberately employ short-run pricing strategy to achieve long-run entrenchment and monopoly power in national markets, foreign and domestic. For detailed analytical development of this type of market model, one must look to the historic work of people like Joseph Schumpeter (15) and other institutionalists following in the same tradition such as Christopher Freeman (16). Within this oligopoly model, the market provides ample room for negotiation to affect outcomes in both the short-run and long-run, with a wide range of possibilities. Therefore attention must be paid to negotiating structures, criteria and alternatives, an area of analysis that has been well developed.

The new oligopoly markets cannot be explained without reference to dependency theory. Incorporation of the possibility of dependent market relations simply recognises that buyers and sellers are not part of a unified homogeneous market. The locational separation of economic functions may be total. Each of the following activities may take place in a different country: supply of primary resources; the production activity; markets; location of profit recognition; and central control over the continuing reallocations of resources. Many localities are dependent on a specialised production plant of a TNC used to serve markets on another continent. In fact, different economic, political, social, and cultural systems generally provide a basic for significant specialised advantage to a TNC, or a significant barrier to production and marketing. In the 'information age', dependency relations within global markets take on a new significance.

6.   Research needs and policy options

Although Western societies have so institutionalised computer and communication technologies that they are becoming ever more dependent on these technologies, there are wide areas for policy choice that will significantly influence: the direction and speed of technological changes; the institutional arrangements for managing and controlling them; the type of product and service applications; and the characteristics of the information content that is generated and transmitted using these technologies. This always has been the case. But for the future the stakes for society are much higher than they have been in the past. Therefore, research directed to revealing the full range of policy options and their long term implications for society is essential (17).

The direction and pace of developments will be influenced primarily by government policies in the telecommunication sector, not by technological developments in the computing industries. The telecommunication sector historically has been subject to monopolisation and direct control by national governments. Telecommunication has been one of the most protected, insulated and monopolised industries in the economies of virtually all nations. International agencies in the field have tended to operate as a cartel of national monopolies, establishing policies to prevent or limit encroachment into the domain of the telecommunication monopolies.

The traditional policies and practices of telecommunication monopolies have been called into question in most Western countries. It began in the US in the late 1960s, and gradually spread north to Canada and across the oceans to Japan and Western Europe. But the speed of policy changes has been extremely slow. The US is still wrestling with most fundamental policy issues that were raised initially almost two decades ago. Canada, the UK and Japan have just begun lengthy processes for reevaluating a wide range of regulatory and tariff restrictions that now limit the application of information technologies and services. Some countries have yet to begin this reassessment. With the exception of OECD, which has no direct power to effect policy changes, international agencies have been slow to recognise the evolving policy issues, and often seemingly inescapable of addressing them on any terms other than eleventh hour ad hoc incremental adjustments.

It is perhaps ironic that in the name of 'deregulation', more regulatory activity has been generated than ever existed in the so-called 'regulation' era. Under monopoly conditions (especially public monopolies) there needn't be a lot of regulatory activity. Most decisions taken by the monopoly supplier are not challenged or challengeable. Controversial issues are negotiated quietly among a few dominant interests, or resolved by the direction of government authority. But under deregulation, there is a mixture of monopoly, oligopoly and competitive markets, many sensitive issues to resolve at the margin between competition and monopoly markets, and more affected parties with interests to be considered and the financial backing to warrant vigorous advocacy.

In the US and Canada, the telecommunication regulatory agencies are busier than ever attempting to adress telecommunication policy issues. When the UK privatised - some say 'deregulated' - telecommincation, it became necessary to create a regulatory commission, OFTEL, when none was previously necessary (18). International regulatory agencies, such as the International Telecommunications Union (ITU) and the International Radio Consultative Committee (CCIR) are virtually overwhelmed with policy and regulatory problems. Under 'deregulation', regulation is more important than it ever has been.

7.   Conclusion

The developments outlined in this paper will bring to the foreground and accentuate, perhaps as never before, the oligopolistic character of most national and global markets. The globalisation of information and tele-communication networks provides a major step toward the globalisation of markets in most other industries. In making the reality more visible, the problems may be addressed more directly. It will provide a stimulans to reorient market theory form abstract notions of atomistic competition to the challenging reality of indeterminate, unstable oligopolistic rivalry, and the formulation of public policy to address the many serious problems raised by this type of market structure.

It should also force a recognition of the growing political dimension of economic markets, the increasing economic dimension of governmental political policies and the dominant influence of international economic developments on national economies and on domestic policies. Even technical issues that heretofore were left to the engineers to sort out have risen to a level of key economic and political importance. The international technical standards for such new developments as the integrated systems digital network (ISDN) and high definition television will have an enormous impact on the economies of many countries, including the UK, providing either a significant competitive advantage, or disadvantage, depending upon the technical standards adopted.

It is apparent that, despite a definite shift toward an increased role for market forces in the telecommunication field, the primary influence upon future developments will not be the invisible hand of the competitive market, but rather the more visible hands of those crafting administrative policy decision in global oligopolistic markets. By providing the infra-structure for a plethora of electronic information services, telecommuni-cation policies will have a major influence on the characteristics of information content services that are developed. The move in many countries to privatise and deregulate the telecommunication sector in recent years has served to expose to public view and debate the super-structure of administrative policies and regulations that lie beneath the limited market competition that exists on the surface. Competition is not a substitute for policy and regulation. It is a tool of policy that, under some circumstances, can facilitate the achievement of the objectives both of economic efficiency and universal telephone service; under other circumstances it can promote efficiency at the expense of social policy; under still other circumstances it can promote neither. It is the task of policy research and analysis to examine the circumstances and determine the appropriate role of competition, whether the telecommunications industry is publicly or privately owned.

In the past the role of market forces generally hasnot been an integral part of policy analysis. Too often the market was viewed simply as a direct substitute for public ownership, regulation, or both, and perhaps a compe-titor to bureaucrats or policy makers. This grossly overstates the power of both. There always will be a major role for both administrative policy guidance and market forces. The historic policies and practices of natio-nal telecommunication monopolies clearly have been superseded by events. An increased role for market forces is inevitable, and an increased role for active competition in some markets and services may be desirable.

But this is not the end of policy direction and regulation. It is a shift in the balance between administrative regulation and market forces. Hopefully, it is the end of passive and secret policy making consisting of little more than a superficial acceptance of the status quo and simplistic self-serving justifications for the continuation of special privileges. It is the beginning of a more thorough and explicit analysis of policy alternatives and their implications, and of active policy implementation in a dynamic market and technological environment.

The restructuring of private and public enterprise will require reassess-ments of the implications for services to the public, and new definitions of appropriate roles for government and public policy in the new environ-ment. In particular, the increasing role of private information markets will require a reassessment of public information needs and the best way to statisfy them.

Developments in the information and communication field are also breaking down the traditional separation of cultural issues from political and economic issues. Whereas in the past it may have been possible to consider cultural policies and mass media regulation as separable from political economic issues and industrial policy, now it clearly is not. Cultural policies and industrial policies are two edges of the same sword. Policy analysis must recognise that whatever the policies, their implica-tions will cut in both directions.

But perhaps the most significant implication of the globalisation of tele-communication services, information networks and ultimately the markets of most major industries is that effective policy responses will have to be developed at the international and global levels. This will require that the nation states yield power and authority to regional and international government bodies and regulatory agencies. To date, inter-national agencies ranging from the EEC to the United Nations have been extremely weak because the member countries have been extremely reluctant to yield any significant powwer. With very strong global TNCs and weak international policy-making agencies, nation states will be faced with a fundamental choice. Either they will be forced to abdicate a significant amount of power over their domestic economies to the TNCs, or they must voluntarily surrender it to international policy-making agencies. This is the major policy dilemma that global networks are imposing on nation states, and which will be played out over the next generation.

References

(1)   Two of the earlier expositions of this theme are: Daniel Bell, **The Coming of Post-Industrial Society: A venture in Social Forecasting** (New York: Basic Books, 1973): M. Porat, 'Global Implications of the Information Society', Journal of Communication 28 (Winter 1978), pp. 70-80.

(2)   Fritz Machlup, **Knowledge: Its Creation, Distribution, and Economic Significance**, 3 vols. (Princeton, N.J.: Princeton University Press, 1980-1984); Porat, 'Global Implications'.

(3)   See for example, Dallas W. Smythe, **Dependency Road: Communications, Capitalism, Consciousness, and Canada** (Norwood, N.J.: Ablex, 1981); and William H. Melody, 'Direct broadcast Satellites: The Canadian Experience' (1982), published in German in **Satelliten-Kommunikation: Nationale Mediensysteme und Internationale Kommunikations-politik** (Hamburg: Hans Bredow Institute, 1983).

(4)   Herbert I. Schiller, **Who Knows: Information in the Age of the Fortune 500** (Norwood, N.J.: Ablex, 1981); and Rohan Samarajiwa, 'Information and Property Rights: The Case of the News Agency Industry' (Prague: International Association for Mass Communication Research, August 1985).

(5)   William H. Melody 'Implications of the Information and Communication Technologies: The Role of Policy Research' **Policy Studies Journal** (Ocotober 1985), pp. 46-58.

(6)   For a more detailed analysis, see William H. Melody 'The Information Society: Implications for Economic Institutions and Market Theory' **Journal of Economic Issues**, (June 1985), pp. 523-539.

(7)   See, for example, Ithiel de Sola Pool, **Technologies of Freedom** (Cambridge, Mass.: Harvard University Press, 1983).

(8)   William H. Melody, 'Development of the Communication and Information Industries: Impact on Social Structures' **Symposium on the Cultural, Social, and Economic Impact of Communication Technology,** (Rome: Unesco and Instituto della Enciclopedia Italiana, 1984).

(9)   Edward S. Herman, **Corporate Control, Corporate Power: A Twentieth Century Study** (New York: Cambridge University Press, 1981).

(10)   William H. Melody, 'Cost Standards for Judging Local Exchange Rates', in **Diversification, Deregulation, and Increased Uncertainty in the Public Utility Industries**, ed. H.M. Trebing (East Lansing, Mich.: Michigan State University, MSU Public Utilities Papers, 1983), pp. 474-495.

(11)   Richard DuBoff, 'The Telegraph and the Structure of Markets in the United States, 1845-1890, **'Research in Economic History 8** (1983), pp. 253-277.

(12)   Op. cit., p. 270 footnote omitted.

(13)   For a detailed illustration with respect to the Canadian experience, see Robin E. Mansell, 'Industrial Strategies and the Communication/Information Sector: An analysis of Contradictions in Canadian

Policy and Performance' (Ph.D. diss., Simon Fraser University, 1984); and 'Contradictions in National Communication/Information Policies: The Canadian Experience, **'Media Culture and Society** (Spring 1985), pp. 33-53.

(14) Adam Smith, **An Inquiry into the Nature and Causes of the Wealth of Nations,** 5th ed. (New York: Modern Library, 1977 (1776)).

(15) Joseph A. Schumpeter, **A History of Economic Analysis,** ed. E.B. Schumpeter (New York: Oxford University Press, 1954).

(16) Christopher Freeman, **Economics of Industrial Innovation,** 2nd Edition (London: frances Pinter, 1982).

(17) William H. Melody and Robin E. Mansell, **Information and Communication Technologies: Social Science Research and Training: Volume I An Overview of Research** (London: ESRC, 1986).

(18) Wigglesworth, W.R.B., 'Deregulation of Telecommunications in the UK', **le Bulletin de l'Idate,** No. 21, November 1985, pp. 30-40.

THE DEVELOPMENT OF TELECOMMUNICATIONS:
A STRATEGIC ANALYSIS

J.F. Mertens

1. Introduction

A study of strategic behaviour around a network could a priori proceed along very different lines, depending on the purpose. The purpose of this study has two very specific aspects, which determine to a large extent its organization. The first is to serve as an aid to public policy-making, and the other that this is for long term policy making, at an exploratory stage-which implies that the analysis will remain at a very qualitative level.
The study would clearly be quite different if it had to serve e.g. as an aid to a given firm's corporate planning, or as an expertise in judicial proceedings (say antitrust), or if it was an academic study in industrial organization or the economics of regulation.
As a consequence of this aim, it seems better to distinguish two different levels in the analysis:

a)   first analysing the likely strategic behaviour of the other players for given public policy environment (section 2);
b)   next to analyse as a consequence what public policy mixes seem most appropriate for different public objectives (section 3).

Such an approach has the inherent danger of biasing the point of view towards viewing the situation as a two-stage game, with public authorities as the first movers and the rest of the market following. It is quite obvious, even from casual observation, that this would be wishful (or dreaded) thinking, a caricature of reality. In fact, technological developments (e.g., next breakthrough in switching technology, or in bypass technology ?) company policies, and both the sociological and the international environment severely limit public policy options and their effectiveness. Many countries may have wished to have a strong and competitive telecommunications equipment industry, and still it seems that to some extent those that succeeded best were those that tried the least.
A more accurate view is probably to consider more symmetrically a great number of independent and interdependent decision centers - not only all kinds of public authorities across the world, corporations etc., but also less formal ones like the media, various pressure groups, maybe in our context the scientific establishment or rather the engineering community etc. -, all of them constrained to work within the framework of a global market economy. Furthermore, this overall constraint, as well as e.g. the internal dynamics of scientific discovery, confront those decision centers with a number of major sources of uncertainty, on which they have very little leverage. Some people may like such an informal system of mutual checks and balances, as being finally a guarantee of individual liberties against Big Brother, others may regret it as a limitation to the sovereign power of the nation-states. The overall constraint imposes among others severe limitations to any interferences of public authorities with market forces: except when motivations are very serious, and no other mechanisms are available that would better respect market forces and still satisfy the same objectives, the hoped-for benefits may be outweighted by the incentive distortions and efficiency losses inherent in any such inter-

ference. Nevertheless, as we will see, even a very limited domain as the one under consideration already confronts public authorities with numerous tasks but it appears that very often, the same objectives can be achieved with several different mechanisms, some of which require much less intervention by the authorities than others. So constant attention will have to be paid to this risk of bias in the analysis.

In section 2, we examine first the major actors:network managements, suppliers and customers. Here already we need for analytical purposes a clear distinction between network and customers premises equipment, and between network and services provided over it, to distinguish the corresponding suppliers, which appear to form three very different industries. Next we consider the major players' strategic options, and finally we examine the aspects which are most specific to networks: externalities, public good aspects, 'storage' possibilities for the demand and lack of them for the supply, and finally the high sunk cost and high-tech features, and their implications.

In section 3, we consider the policy options for public authorities. First we consider the different aspects of regulation of the switched network, and next the functionality to be demanded from this network. Then we deal with the same questions for broadcasting. We consider - because of lack of space very shortly - issues which are less directly of a regulatory character, and that concern much more fundamental values: The desirability and the feasibility of public control over telecommunications' content; it appears that such control, even if desirable, is likely to become less and less feasible, certainly in all interesting cases - those where it would really be desirable. Those limitations suggest a more positive attitude, more in line with basic human rights, might be to renounce any such aim. And we consider the more general cultural implications telecommunications may have. The fundamental motivation of a public project like the one under consideration lies in this realm, and it is bound to have far reaching implications of this nature, so those questions relating to more fundamental values definitely have to be considerd here, both became of their paramount importance per se and to assure the adequation of means to ends. Finally those questions also bear a close relationship to the industrial policy matters, which are considered in the last part.

2.   Competition around a network: the setting

Here we examine briefly who are the major players, what are their main strategy options, and which aspects most specifically distinguish competition around a network from competition in any other market.

A.   The major actors

The major actors are: 1. network-management; 2. suppliers; and 3. customers.

1.   It is crucial in this analysis to treat network management as a separate actor, as distinguished from the authorities which represent the public interest - even with PTT's. Failure to do so would almost evacuate the problem: since network management embodies the public interest, just give them the widest powers, and everything will be optimised in the public interest (neglecting the efficiency losses in managing unnecessarily large organizations).

This would negate everything we have learned both from the economics of regulation and from agency theory: if we assume continuation of the monopoly in the provision of network services, economics of regulation tells us how difficult it is to align the interest of the monopolist with the public interest. Indeed, direct subordination of the firm to public authorities - as is more usual in Europe - tends to subject management policy to the short-run political interests of the politicians currently in power - which can be extremely disruptive in an industry requiring such long-term planning. 'Public interest' per se is too vague and subject to too many different interpretations to be of any use as a management guideline.

And economics of regulation shows that the most frequently used principles of regulation fail to align the interest of the monopolist with public interest - e.g., rate of return regulation leads to overinvestment (Averch-Johnson effect). But even if it was possible to align the interest of the organization with public interest, agency theory still shows the difficulty of aligning the interests of management with those of the organization. It is therefore essential to consider network management as an actor per se, whose 'utility function' incorporates probably some more or less vague and personal idea about public interest, but also, as in any organization, a strong interest for making the organization bigger, extending its domain; and finally, a fair degree of risk aversion.

2.   Among suppliers to the industry, it seems useful to distinguish: a) the network equipment suppliers, b) the CPE (customers premises equipment) suppliers, c) and the service suppliers.

2.a. The boundary line between service suppliers and general business that uses the network to offer its services to clients is quite arbitrary - it depends on the subjective appreciation of the importance of the communications part in the service.

E.g., we would rank among service suppliers providers of electronic mail, of alarm and wake-up services, of videotex, of other database access services (e.g. financial database (Quotron, Reuters, the Source, etc.)), of protocol conversion services, etc. Would not be ranked among them telemarketing firms and 'home-shopping' TV-channels, banks - even if they offer ATM-networks, credit-card verification networks and 'home-banking' services.

On the other hand, the boundary line between the functions of the network and the service suppliers is quite clear: the network's role is to transports bits, irrespective of their meaning or protocol. Whatever service has to know the content or protocol of a message is not a network service. Just likt the road network administration does not need to know what you transport in your car, or to organize bus services or trucking services. Similarly, the postal services does not need to open letters, or to manage newspapers or banks, or to offer translation services. The language or the script used in the letter is the people's own business, and usually they manage pretty well to coordinate.

This is not to deny the importance of protocol standardization for instance, but, with a digital network, this is no longer at all the business of the network (cleary, on an analog network, the way to encode voice was intimately related with network design). Protocol standardization is of crucial importance, but this is the proper role of standards organizations, etc. - possibly with some additional prodding by public authorities. Meanwhile, the postal service has no business neither in translation services (language translation) nor in the french academy (language standardization).

2.b. Similarly, the definition of CPE is very clear: it is any equipment standing on the customers premises and connected (directly or indirectly) to the network, from line termination (point U in ISDN jargon) on to all telephones, terminals, PBX's, LAN's, computers, ATM's, and whatever he may have on his premises and connect to the network.

Even in a residential set-up, one may envision that, within the next few years, households with ISDN service will wish to connect in one single LAN all the audio and video equipment, all homecomputers, telephone sets, intercom, telephone answering machines, maybe also fax equipment, and all alarms, meters, sensors and controls-connecting this LAN both to the CATV line and the telephone line.

This LAN and everything attached to it is the homeowner's responsibility (even applications like remote meter reading do not require the network to go farther than U; usual encryption techniques easily guarantee its security), and no business of the CATV company or the telephone network. Note that this argument essentially says that the network's business stops at point T in ISDN jargon, to preserve the customers flexibility, (and hence to foster an important and highly competitive CPE-industry). Network managers typically argue that similarly, to preserve flexibility on the network side (i.e. to allow the network to change its technology without affecting the customer), the network has to extend up to point T - i.e. include a small black box called NTI in ISDN jargon that provides a standard interface between user and network.

Schematically, one has the following diagram:

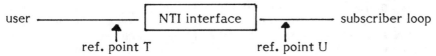

There is some truth in this claim; it is also true that ref.point T provides the 'cleanest' boundary point between network and user, and the most consistent with our previous finding of the role of the network as a 'bit-hauler' - like the postal network or the road network. However, technological change and upgrading is typically much faster on the CPE side than on the network side - and this is expected to remain so, despite a likely increase in the pace on the network side with the advent of ISDN and furhter developments. So the networks' argument applies a fortiori on the customer side, implying that the network should definitely not meddle further than T - as soms PTT's have attempted, through their influence on ISDN standardization (this is like having around 1900 the railroad managements set the standards of the road network); this confirms our observation in the last paragraph about their likely utility function.

Nevertheless, the FCC's position, that the network should stop at the 'physical' demarcation point U, has definite merits too, and for our present purposes - to make the conceptual distinction between CPE and network equipment - the exact difference between T and U is not crucial; we will return later to this point (III.A., II.B., end III.F.).

2.c. It is important to distinguish between CPE suppliers and network equipment suppliers because the market structures, and very often the suppliers themselves, are very different. Network equipment supply - e.g. in switching - is an industry dominated by a couple of very big firms, with high sunk costs (development costs for today's switches are often quoted to be of the order of half a billion $ and more). On the other hand, CPE supply is a highly diverse and extremely competitive industry, where these same major firms coexist with a host of smaller firms which play such diverse strategies as competing in a specialized niche, subcontracting or being second source for majors, or being at the technological forefront for one specific product (as e.g. in the markets for personal computers, or for LAN's, or for PBX's). Still other firms play the lowest cost producer, very high volume strategy.

Entry costs are typically much lower - e.g., the development costs for Intecom's switch (a high-capacity, state of the art PBX) were below 20 million $; with an experienced management team and a good business project, such an amount is easily raised from venture capital.

Finally, the marketing is completely different, since in the first case the firms address themselves to only a few, very knowledgeable, major buyers - the telcos -, while CPE is a mass marketing business, typically using established distribution channels, except for big ticket items where some firms (e.g. Intecom, cfr. supra) have established an own salesforce.

A healthy telecommunications industry crucially needs the two types of firm: The major firms' typical role consists of teh more fundamental or big ticket R&D developments, (sometimes) a systems integrator and normsetting role, and to bring products to mass production and get way down the learning curve - playing if necessary a survival-game strategy.

The other firms' typical contribution is to fill a series of niches too small or too specialized to fit into the strategy of the big firms, to bring new ideas to the market-often, but not necessarily, they are at the technological forefront and play only the very early stages of the product lifecycle -, and to provide the most plausible avenue for entry into the big league (e.g. DEC's entry into computers; or in switching equipment starting with PBX market before entering network switching), maintaining in this way some competitive pressure on the big firms.

Interaction between the two categories is multiform, and very healthy for each one: it takes e.g. the form of second sourcing and subcontracting agreements, of exchange of expertise through industry contacts and through personnel movements, and of buyouts.

Finally, the importance of this sector of small firms - and hence of the CPE market - stems also from the fact that they form essentially a continuous, connecting tissue between all major 'high-tech' markets - telecommunications, computers, office automation, factory automaton and CAD-CAM, electronic financial services and payments, consumer electronics - and backwards into semiconductors. And in almost all of these markets they play a similar dynamic role w.r.t. the majors.

3.   Customers are best separated in three different categories: big business, small business, and residential. They differ to some extent in the nature of their demand: Business in general really needs a series of services (hardly offered in Europe) like 800 and 900 numbers, and foreign exchange service, at highly competitive proces. Big business has a high demand, given present service offerings and tariff structure, for private lines and private networks - including dynamic network reconfiguration. It is to be hoped that the networks will offer sufficiently flexible services and at sufficiently competitive prices such as to shift most of this demand to virtual private networks (with dynamic reconfiguration), and even to network services themselves: since there would apparently be a gain in overall efficiency (e.g. because business peak demand occurs at different hours than residential peak demand), such competitive offerings should be possible. They must also include good datagram-type services, not only for the electronic transaction networks, but also for a multitude of other transaction or non-transaction applications (including at the residential level).

But anyway, the above mentioned services are a basic need for business, and we should certainly avoid putting European business at a competitive disadvantage by refusing them these services or by pricing them uncompetitively. They should be offered on a non discriminatory basis - in the limit down to the scale of households - as basic network offerings.

-     Small business may have a high use of a great number of specialized services from independent suppliers over the network (accounting, data base inquiry, monitoring of alarms on premises, whatever).

-     Residential customers share to some extent those characteristics of small business; in addition, however, they provide a demand peak at different times than business peak demand, and they will require that the use of such a fancy network for just basic voice be not substantially more expensive than a basic voice network would be. Since typically total peak demand is due to business, a tariff which is sensitive to load conditions (or even just to time of day) should have this effect.

82

B.   Strategic options of players around a network

Let me make clear to start with that I do not intend to discuss here competition between networks. This is doubtless a very important question, so much that it deserves a study per se; but in my mind, the issues addressed here - the fast implementation of an ISDN-type, bit hauling network - are much more urgent, probably crucial to the overall competitiveness of Europe. It seems therefore better to concentrate efforts on this issue, and even to try to take advantage of the strength of the PTT-monopolies to get the implementation fast, rather than having them feel defensive and expend all their efforts to defend their fiefdoms instead of working on the network.
Other issues, like the above, or like the possibility of going to even more ambitious technologies (broadband e.g.) are in the meantime probably better kept on the back-burner - 'under study' - at least until ISDN is solidly on track. Of course, whatever experiments can be done in the meantime locally, or in some countries, are very welcome, but I speak here of EC-wide policy.
We will quickly survey the main strategy options of equipment providers (1), of business in general w.r.t. the network (2), of service providers (3) and of countries (4).
1)   For equipment manufacturers 5 options can be distinguished:
a.   These firms can choose to go for worldwide competition, getting on the forefront of technology, introducing continuously new and better products, while maybe abandoning to others the more mature and the declining products.
b.   Another choice is to compete under the protection of national (European) tariff and non-tariff barriers, using mainly mature and/or second-hand technology.
c.   Smaller firms can use the same strategies as the previous two, but in specialized niche markets.
d.   A different possibility is to compete not in technology, but in mass manufacturing - like any other strategy, such a strategy needs a specific competitive advantage - like cheap labour, or very skilled labour, or government subsidies.
e.   A last type of strategy is portfolio management like, e.g. to close, to sell out and to diversify, reinvesting cash flow in other countries or activities; or to engage in buyouts of smaller firms, or in the creation of smaller firms in a venture-capital type activity; or to engage in mergers, swaps and/or restructuring activity.

Any well-established firm has to have some strategy of type (e). Besides that, any of the above strategies - both separately and in conjunction - can make sense for individual firms, depending on their circumstances and on the intensity with which they feel the current rate of return constraint. It is however necessary to stress here - in a somewhat similar vein as in Sections A.2.C and A.2.D - that a healthy industry sector crucially needs both firms pursuing strategy (a) (and its niche variant) and firms pursuing strategy (d) - and some overlap between the two sets of firms. Strategy (d) is the way to play the learning curve; without such firms we would lose alle manufacturing know how. Even if such a strategy sometimes entails to have to locate plants abroad - e.g. when temporarily there is no efficient manufacturing process available that efficiently uses highly skilled labour -, those moves have to be done, for the sake of keeping the manufacturing know how - and the market. This also explains why consumer electronics is such a strategically important sector.

Recall finally that, while the above strategies were discussed mainly in manufacturing terms, a similar array of choices is available for marketing, and the choices are to a large extent independent.

2) With regard to other business one should distinguish the use of telecommunications in a business strategy when it is an integral part of the main business line from a use just for purpose of internal organization. The first type of application includes for instance all forms of mass-merchandising ('mail order') through the network - whether switched or broadcast (cfr. e.g. the current 'home-shopping' TV-channels in the U.S.).

A variant includes all means for firms to bypass intermediaries completely, and to get direct contact with customers. Currently one sees only some warning signs of this (e.g. G.M. setting up computer programs that would allow customers to select themselves a car, through the whole maze of different lines and options - also airline reservation systems may be moving in this direction-) but the trend could soon become quite important. Both the above trends are already very strong in the financial services sector ('no load' mutual funds selling direct (WATS lines) instead of through brokers; discount brokerages having all their operations by telephone; ATM networks and home-banking; mortgages sold by telephone, etc.).

All these applications depend heavily on a number of network services we mentioned, before, like 800-numbers e.g. When they will develop in Europe, they promis a drastic increase in competitivity of the European distribution sector (with major structural changes), and unification of the European market.

The other type of application is to improve internal organization, coordination. It may also enable more subcontracting of tasks to small outside firms or to consultants working at home, or allowing employees to work at home; better inventory policies and better coordination of multinational plant systems fall also under this heading.

All these possibilities (home-shopping, home-banking, home-movies (video), home-computing, maybe home-work, home-education and video conferencing) clearly announce a decrease in the growth trend of transportation - they also mean a smaller competitive advantage for Europe from a high population density.

But, much more importantly, they may help in getting in part around the high inflexibility costs (moving costs, termination and social security costs, etc.) of european economies (e.g. by subcontracting, by replacing employees by independents working at home, etc.). But all these positive effects depend crucially on a wide variety of value added services that get easily tailored to individual needs - hence on a transparent network with free competition in services - and on the willingness of the networks to provide business with whatever types of bearer services and competitive tariff schemes that are needed.

To conclude, a headstart with a good ISDN-like network could mean a substantial competitive advantage for business in general in Europe.

3)   Service providers face the choice between broadcast mass services and individually tailored services by 2-way communications. In the first case they still have to choose between subscriber-paid channels and free channels whose expenses are covered by other proceeds of the business (e.g. home-shopping), or by advertising, or by sponsoring firms, etc. In the second case, there exists similary an alternative between an offering to the public at large, like database enquiry systems might be, or a reserved, high prices offering to specialized public.

This raises major policy issues. Indeed, while sometime such choices may be essentially determined by the type of product offered, and may serve the whole interested public at a roughly competitive price, other times the choice may result from monopolistic market discrimination.

It may be useful to illustrate this by an example; there is no claim whatsoever here that the monopolistic behaviour on the part of these firms actually occurs; it is quite likely on the contrary that the choices were in fact determined by the currently available media and their costs; the example should just be taken as a hypothetical case.

Firms like Quotron or Reuters might offer more or less high cost financial information to brokers and other financial institutions who will be ready to pay any price to preserve their competitive advantage, and once such a market is captured, entry by competition becomes much more difficult (very low marginal cost for incumbent). But, given an appropriate CATV network, they might also (at same or even lower total cost) broadcast publicly all over Europe on a single digital TV channel all current quotes on all world financial markets (stock-, bond-, currency-, futures-, options-, commodities-, etc.), together with some ancillary statistics like P/E ratios, dividend yields or volume data. This would still leave room for a more specialized interactive service, that would e.g. allow to retrieve historic data, or balance sheets, earnings statements and 10-K forms. But is is conceivable that the availability of the public service would so much undercut revenue from professionals - who could for instance also use the broadcast service to do a lot of filing in their private databases, in order to have to rely much less on the interactive service if this one is expensive -, that is might be more profitable for such firms not to offer the broadcast service at all. To preserve the incentives for innovation, innovators have to be able to capture such rents. However, both as a matter of competitive policy, and (this being essentially a public good) as a matter of social welfare, public policy may want to push for the second solution.

Remedies like antitrust litigation are difficult to use, especially in a sector like this (service provision) where every firm would be a potential target to watch, because of the natural monopoly aspects. Also it seems difficult and maybe inappropriate to have public authorities offer all those services as public goods. An alternative is outlined in the paragraph on Broadcasting Media Policy which would among others make europe-wide broadcast channels essentially free, and hence allow to rely much more on market forces and on competition to police these markets.

4)   The U.S. and Japan have a (in the U.S. case very) liberalised telecom market as:
-     a competitiveness tool for their economy,
-     a competitiveness tool for their government (internal organization, security and intelligence, military, etc.);
-     a privileged market for their telecom industrie to remain at the forefront of technology, leaving only licensing and/or more established technologies to foreign companies. (I mean 'foreign' in the usual sense; whatever sophisticated 'local content' rules are completeley irrelevant in such a strategy: the only thing that matters is where the R&D, the know-how, the headquarters of the company are located).

It is perfectly compatible with such a strategy, on the one hand to encourage a centralized, non competitive system in Europe, to constrain the technology of major european firms to older, well established technologies, and to prevent small-firm, high-tech competition from springing up in Europe, and on the other hand, to push for commercial liberalisation in Europe (trade negotiations, etc.) for those products where they have been able to use their own competitive market for testing, development, getting way ahead on the experience curve and acquiring huge economies of scale.

What may be lacking in this strategy (in the U.S. case at least) are: A central push through federal or nation-wide administrations to accelerate and further progress, among others in the field of standardization, and lack of public awareness of the economic concept of a 'public good' and of its consequences, and hence to take advantage of externalities (cfr. infra for such possibilities).

Underdevelop countries can buy well established products, when prices are already way down, sometimes even on the second-hand market. They can displace countries like Singapore etc. in the manufacturing of such products (whenever intensive in not-too-skilled labour). They can educate the work force and subsidize local high-tech and R&D.

These options leave them in a relatively favourable position (in this area I mean): sacrificing only a couple of years of technological advance, they get both technology and products essentially for free. In this framework, 'local content' does make some sense.

C.   Network specific aspects

-     **Externalities:** A typical instance of externality is the fact that connecting one more person to the network increases all other subscribers' utility: they can now call - or be called - by some additional person.

Thus, of several networks coexist, they have to interconnect smoothly, to maximize consumers' suplus. This externality factor lies also at the root of the major importance of standards (not network standards, but user standards: the french academy's business, not the postal office's).

-        Another typical network is its **public good** aspect. The broadcasting function (CATV network) is an almost pure instance: except for the fixed and sunk cost of connecting one more person, one subscriber's viewing or not has no cost consequences and no impact on the other customers' enjoyment. But similarly in the switched network, at all but peak hours one call has essentially no cost effect and no impact on other persons' utility.

-        **Non-storability of the supply.** During peak hours, this is no longer true, because this call increases the probability that other persons' calls will be blocked, which suggests a rationing at peak hours by price (demand is to some extent storable), essentially proportional to the duration of the call and the number of different (saturated) switches through which it has to pass - a price per bit. Even much more refined tariff structures are easily conceivable - up to having the network's routing algorithm continuously readjusting shadow prices (per bit transmitted, i.e., bandwidth times duration) in each switch and in each switch line, and computing from those total consumption of the call.

If the routing algorithm's objective function was to minimize total cost to consumers due to blocked calls - measuring the cost of a blocked call to the consumer, e.g. as a constant plus a fixed markup above the amount he would have paid for the call, and assuming blocked calls have on the average the same duration characteristics as the unblocked calls - then the above shadow-proces would (together with some completely minor factors like additional power consumption) describe the true 'marginal opportunity cost' of a call. (The minimization algorithm will obviously assume that the statistical distribution of new calls and terminating calls in the next few minutes will be similar to the one in the last few minutes).

-        A last telecom characteristic is obviously the **high fixed cost** - even high sunk cost - and **high-tech environment,** both in manufacturing and in the provision of network services. One consequence is to make competition between incumbents more 'prisoners' dilemma'-like, where for each player, moving to a more capital-intensive technology, with higher sunk costs but lower variabel costs is often cost-saving, hence a dominant (i.e. best, whatever other players do) strategy, but those strategies taken together lead overall to a much less profitable equilibrium, since competition will drive proces down to the much lower variable costs. (Some people would even speak of destructive competition in such a context). The other effect of the high sunk costs is obviously to create high barriers to entry. Taken together, those two effects predict a strong tendency towards cartellisation. We will nevertheless argue (III.E) that anti-trust authorities should not take too harsh a view at every attempt to stabilise the market, lest they drive European industry to bankruptcy in this sector. Bu we will argue all along that everything has to be done to help and stimulate the smaller and newer firms, the potential entrants, and certainly to avoid discriminating against them.

3. Major policy options for public authorities

A. Regulation of switched network

Definition of Network Boundaries: Both the functional boundary of the network (to provide a highly flexible array of transparent bit-hauling services) and its physical boundary (the entrance to the customers premises) at which we arrived earlier, also coincide in first approximation with the maximal (cfr. 2 below) extent of natural monopoly.

This is confirmed by the evolution of technology: first, modern switches go more and more towards a fully distributed architecture, of which the logical conclusion is to put all enhanced services in CPE and VAN's (and probably most in CPE). For example, modern PBX's put already the voice digitization codecs in the individual handsets, not in central switching equipment. Second, even for households we see more and more intelligence coming into the customers premises - not only homecomputers, but microprocessors of all type - and, as mentioned before, the same trend as in business will push towards integrating all this equipment in a single LAN. In such a perspective, the incremental cost of some more intelligence on premises, for this huge mass market, will quickly become extremely low, while the incremental utility of having it there rather than centrally located will be much greater due to synergetic effects. For example, a tape- or cassette-recorder connected to such a LAN would provide not only the function of an electronic mail and voice-mail receiver and storage device, but also, through its connection with the home computer, a sophisticated telephone answering service, allowing e.g. to tailor messages to individual callers, and furthermore all usual functions it has today, both in audio and video and as a computer storage device. Connection on the LAN of intercom and telephone service also allows the tape-recorder to play the role of a portable dictaphone; and any new developments would still much more increase the utility of the equipment in place - e.g. digital voice to text conversion algorithms would also enable to replace the secretary, besides the ability to give voice instructions from anywhere to any regulator or computer in the home. Similarly, for digital image to text algorithms; the tape-recorder would in such cases also serve as buffer memory, say between incoming digital images and the translator. And so on.

Such a scheme makes much more sense and is much more useful than having centrally located, standalone electronic mail, voice mail, voice store and forward services and so on. Even a feature like call forwarding could be easily implemented e.g. by an appropriate 'agenda' program on the home computer, using the datagram capability of the network.

In this argument on natural monopoly extent one should not quibble about small detail; for almost any business there exist some other things that it could also do with some additional economies of scope or other integration; that is not what is meant by a natural monopoly; for reasons of efficient management, it is anyway usually better even for the company to forsake these possibilities, in order to focus better on its main role. The same applies a fortiori in such a complex business as network management.

In addition, there is finally the argument that allowing the network to expand its boundaries further would create huge, technologically integrated, monolithic structures, where the slightest change in one service offering may have consequences throughout the system, and require every time again careful network planning. Every change, even for a very small set of customers, becomes a major network decision, and has to be implemented throughout the network. With then the equipment standing there for years. In addition to this inflexibility cost, there is the economic cost that such a situation favours ordering of equipment by huge quantities at once, hence stimulating an uncompetitive degree of concentration on the supply side, and a chance only for well established, mature technologies.

One or More Networks ? It is difficult in econometric studies to disentangle the three different scale effects due to: changes in calling frequency, in population density and in geographical size of area served. The first comparison would be the relevant one if it was contemplated to have many competing networks, each one connected to every subscriber. The second one would be relevant, when each subscriber would be connected only to one network, which would transfer his calls to the network of the called party as close to destination as possible. While the last one would become relevant if a U.S. style reform was contemplated - having distinct monopolies each serve smaller geographical areas.

Rough data suggest however that, while such economies of scale definitely exist, their effects are not necessarily major within the relevant range, i.e. excluding extreme cases. E.g., Canada's size is of the same order as Western Europe, with population maybe twenty times lower. Still, telephone costs in Canada appear not to be substantially higher - in many cases in fact lower. Does this mean that we could do in Europe with up to twenty competing networks, without substantial loss in effeciency ? One would not even have to go that far for having a healthy dose of competition. Anyway the possibility is intriguing.

But quite likely a U.S. -type solution is even far superior from the point of view of competition; customers are not locked in by one company (i.e., for long distance). Form that point of view, it is interesting to obeserve that telephone costs of small countries in the E.E.C. (even Luxemburg) do not appear to be very substantially higher than in the major countries... One could in the limit think of local telcos serving very small areas - say of the order of a with maybe the municipalities, something like the electricity network in Belgium - with maybe the municipalities auctioning of the franchise every x years to operating companies...

These questions are very important and deserve careful study. However, provided other regulatory measures suggested in this section are taken, they are probably less urgent than the main object of concern - the fast upgrading of the network and stimulation of CPE and related industry. Also, they are probably less a matter of community concern: to some extent, nothing prevents different countries to implement somewhat different schemes in this respect.

But the economic feasibility of such schemes implies maybe that the community might credibly threaten to move towards the application of antitrust legislation to the networks, if this was useful to persuade them to go along in other respects.

Capital Markets Discipline ? It would probably be useful to subject network management to capital markets discipline. (This would not prevent some goverments to retain a substantial or controlling part of the shares if they wish so). This would have the double advantage of insulating to some extent network management from troublesome and excessive desiderata of day to day politics, and of keeping their investment decisions in line with the true cost of capital in the economy.

Tariff Constraints: Allocative efficiency demands that callers be charged the (short-run) marginal cost (as defined before in II.C.3) of their calls. (For the customers information, phone books would list typical average prices, and the consumer would for instance have the option to set up a call in such a way, that as soon as his call is routed, a datagram causes the price per minute to be displayed: he would then still have the option of hanging up, paying only for the datagram and the first few seconds of the call. Or customers would just be charged the typical average prices). Calls would then in effect be auctioned off.

Efficiency of the monopolist's investment decisions requires it to equate the marginal cost of investment (at the efficient scale) to the discounted value (at market cost of capital) of expected future revenue from the marginal investment at the above marginal cost prices (taking also expected evolution of equipment prices into account).

Therefore the revenue to be expected, under a correct investment policy of the network, from charging the callers at marginal cost should roughly cover all variable costs in the telephone plant - remains to be allocated the cost of the local loop plant, plus the long-term fixed costs and overhead.

The annual financing and maintenance cost of local loops (including the dedicated fraction of the local switch) can be fairly well allocated to individual terminations - e.g. by spanning tree-like methods. However, in view of the previously cited externalities, one should probably charge each user (as a fixed charge) for only part of the cost of his termination. Also, to preserve universal service, there should probably be a ceiling on that part which is charged to him, at least for basic service. The remaining part of his loop's cost could then be charged on some prorata basis to his callees - reflecting in this way the externalities mentioned. Similarly the remaining overhead and fixed costs could be apportioned to individual calls, and charged also to the receiving party (except say for calls under $\frac{1}{4}$ minute, then the callee could ask that the callig party be fully charged, to prevent harassment calls): callees stand to some extent as a proxy to the callers, preserving in this way the allocative efficiency of charging the caller only for short-run marginal cost. (With as byproduct an elimination of incentives to bypass: bypass would not avoid a firm having to pay its part of all its callers loops; and for intensively used loops, like those of the several locations of the firm, the additional charge per call will be negligible, so nothing can be gained from bypassing them - further, when the firm calls outside, the charge for its local loop to its correspondents will also be very small.

The schemes used to prorate local loop costs and to apportion overhead to individual calls could involve a mixture of factors - like number of calls, number of bits hauled, and marginal cost of the calls (A whole literature, both game-theoretical and non game-theoretical, is relevant in this respect, laying down various pricing principles - Shapley value pricing, core-pricing, various froms of nucleolus pricing, Ramsey pricing, etc -). They should however be designed such as to provide a total price schedule exempt from cross-subsidization (more technically, in the core of the cost-allocation game) (Their they might also involve e.g. some moderate floor on connexion charges): no subset of total demand should be charged more than the cost of providing this on a standalone basis (e.g., to prevent putting some industries or companies at a competitive disadvantage); or, to speak more in equity terms, the efficiency gains from the monopoly provision should benefit everybody.

Given the importance of the natural monopoly efficiency gains, as argued by network spokesmen, it seems very likely that such a pricing scheme is in fact feasible, along lines such as suggested above (assuming the network's investment policy is correct).

To recapitulate, the network's pricing scheme should be constrained to be competitive, in the sense that:

a.   the callers should be charged roughly at very short-term marginal cost;

b.   there should be essentially no cross-subsidization.

Monopoly: Exclusiveness or not ? Monopoly provision can be understood in two different ways: either as a waiver form general anti-trust legislation, allowing to operate even on a monopoly basis, or as an exclusive right granted for provision of such and such services.

With a pricing scheme as described above, no rival firm could ever enter profitably, so even in the first hypothesis, the full benefits of monopoly provision would be preserved. However, to help police the fact that indeed such a pricing scheme is used, it may be helpful to take the first meaning; in particular allowing unlimited resale and bypass, by whatever technologies (including e.g. microwave and satellite): the pricing scheme itself should make such ventures uneconomical. Not doing so would not only be unfair and put some industries or other groups at a competitive disadvantage; it would als provoke a generalized and economically wasteful search for bypass: rooftop satellite dishes, in some future maybe direct rooftop to rooftop or rooftop to satellite light signals (who could ever prevent this...), maybe cordless telephone in a whole neighbourhood connected to a single concentrator - technological possibilities are boundless, and it would be a futile waste to try enforcement of such prohibitions. And the possibilities arise not only in the technological area: e.g. all types of value added services would concentrate themselves in the most liberal countries, with the most competitive tariff structures, at a great damage to the others.

To give more teeth to such a proposal to let the competitiveness of the tariff structure be in part policed by the allowance of entry (including resale and bypass), one could in addition have some rules - as in any good anti-trust legislation - to prevent predatory retaliation by the monopolist.

Investment Policy Regulation: As we have said sub (A.4), an efficient investment policy requires equating the cost of marginal investment to the discounted value of revenue from the marginal investment at the short-run marginal cost prices. This follows from the rule to maximize the discounted value of a hypothetical cash flow, whose outflows in each year are the actual outlays of the network (including overhead, maintenance, debt repayment (net of fresh debt issued) etc.), and whose income is the total consumer surplus provided by the network that year (i.e., the sum over all calls and other services of the maximal amount customers would have been ready to pay for such services).

Clearly monopolist's profit motive would lead him to invest less than optimally to drive prices up. On the other hand, the classical forms of regulation, like rate of return regulation, have in principle the defect of leading to overinvestment, to broaden the rate base (Averch-Johnson effect). And we have seen in the beginning that to rely on the judgement of network management has the two inconvenients that: 1. management has its own preferences and other motives, not necessarily aligned with the above; 2. the 'public interest' objective is too vague to serve as a management guideline, and too much subject to various government pressures motivated both by different views and often also by short-term political interests.

But other alternatives are possible. For example, the following suggestion is inspired by modern agency theory: set up a separate, private, profit maximizing company, with partly paid shares, whose cash flow would be e.g. 2% of the above described hypothetical cash flow of the network. This cash flow would actually be paid by the network to the company, but since it would be the network that would have sold the shares of the company on the market, the network would have received the discounted value of these future payments.

The profit motive itself would drive such a management to set the right investment and other policy for the network, and it appears it would face no major incentive to depart from a competitive tariff structure as previously described.

One could ask an independent small group of econometricians (say nominated by the European Economic Association, or by a court under advice from the E.E.A.) to devise (including the use of cross-section and polling methods) a set of formulas to estimate the consumer surplus form the detailed accounting and billing data of the network, and those formulas would be subject to periodic revision under a similar procedure.

Such a regulation method would ensure efficiency. One could rely on competition of some sort for the investment decisions: anybody could at any time ask the network to install any given additional capacity - network management would just pool these requests, say over 1 year periods, for cost effectiveness. He would pay the cost of the investment, and thereafter receive the 'shadow price' proceeds of all traffic sent of that capacity unit by the routing algorith. Such a scheme does not need the econometricians (relying on competition), and it would lead to efficient investment (or excessive, but then at the cost of the investors if they prove too aggressive). And it would be somewhat closer in spirit to the U.S. system of competition on the long distance market.

To summarize our conclusions on the regulatory aspects:

1.   The issues of network boundaries and of transparant network operation, as well as the issue of competitive pricing, are urgent and crucially important.

2.   To implement these quickly and efficiently, we need the full strength and cooperation of the PTT's, and to be able to build on their great dedication and expertise. It is not worthwile to sidetrack this by provoking a confrontation on other less urgent issues.

3.   The other issues (privatization and/or competition, proper regulatory mechanism for investment policy, etc.) are highly important. But they are probably because of (2) best kept in the meantime under study - which is anyway much needed in this domain - if possible with the cooperation of the PTT's; and for the rest left to the initiative of national governments for the time being - there is no objection against somewhat different mechanis, in different parts of the EEC in this respect.

B.   Network functionality

We stressed all along that the network should be more like the public road network than the railroad network: supporting in a transparant way all kinds of services (bus services, trucking services, parcel delivery services, taxi services, private automobiles, bikes, whatever, car or trunk rental services, and public services traffic, highway police, roadside help, etc.) and a whole industry around them, without the network's management being involved at all in these services.

This means offering services corresponding to the first three levels of the

ISO standardization. But we insisted also on the importance of a very flexible offering within this framework - both in the nature of the services and in the pricing scheme. Because of back of space we have to leave out the technical conditions for this flexibility.

We only remark that it is most important to have a clear functional architecture, independent of specific services or hardware implementation. This means (a) realizing there will be many ISDN's rather than one - the country networks, one or more international networks maybe, some countries with several public networks, the private networks of major companies, the LAN's on customers' premises. Hence (b) a customers' termination should be functionally equivalent to an ISDN-ISDN gateway. (c) Also the basic services would be to establish a virtual ISDN within a real (or other virtual) ISDN, and concatening several ISDN's (virtual or real) into one ISDN through one or more gateways. Setting up a virtual ISDN clearly includes as very particular cases the set up of a call, or of a private line, etc.; while the concatenation is the basic operation the customer has to do with his CPE.

Such a 'functional' definition would preserve a maximal flexibility, commercial and technological, both for customer and network - and even allow for locally quite different hardware implementations. Indeed, any change of technology on either side, provided the functional aspects remain fixed, can then be easily accommodated by just changing an interface card in CPE - and for such high volume items, prices should be extremely low.

C.   Media Policy

We first outline a CATV option, as said sub II.B., to promote competition in the provision of all kinds of mass-oriented services, by making high bandwith at low cost available. Again, because of lack of space, we have to leave out the details of the regulatory aspects of these services. With regard to censorship or control of broadcast messages we conclused that it is not clear where it should start or stop. We therefore think that it seems much more appropriate to refrain from any such censorship altogether, and for Europe to stand again in the lead on the issue of basic human freedoms.

Outline of a CATV option: While PTT's set up a bit-hauling, ISDN-type network, with flexible services as outlined above and with a competitive tariff structure, they will have their hands full and it is best to let them concentrate on that objective, which is certainly by far the most urgent. That objective concerns mainly the functionality of the switched network, and requires little or no investment in the local loop plant (except for termination equipment). During that period the LAN's on customers' premises will also take shape and be standardized, and the whole thing will provide a sustained demand for electronic equipment manufacturers (both network and CPE).

In the meantime, one could work through broadcasting authorities and

CATV companies to prepare the next generation local loop plant, such as to provide also a nice level of demand for the opto-electronic industry.

Capacity of fibers is for practical purposes potentially infinite: with coherent transmission, the capacity of a single fiber may go up to 10000 digital TV channels (or 10 million conversations). In order not to commit to a very heavy local loop plant investment before this technology (and the corresponding switching technology - Texas Instruments for example has just constructed a first 'optical switchboard' on a chip) starts to stabilize, one could first build a Europe-wide CATV network in very high capacity fiber, with e.g. one LAN-type loop per bloc or per neighbourhood, passing close to the corresponding local telephone switch (in prevision of the second stage).

All major European radio and television chains would output directly on this network, as would all service providers. Simultaneously, a process of digitization of all radio and television emissions could be started. Finally, one should also implement a reasonably cheap system of pay-television - which is essential for the development of a sufficient variety of services. Many different ways are conceivable to do this.

In a next stage, once ISDN is well established, one could start using the huge spare capacity in local CATV loops installed in the first stage, and increasing it by: 1. sending in each local loop only those channels that are actually in demand and 2. using the excess capacity in the loop as a local area network connecting with the local ISDN switch, thus dramatically increasing - at least statistically - the ISDN bandwidth available to customers.

In this way, many options will still be open at this stage, even at the regulatory level: all the way from installing autonomous switching equipment on this CATV network, together with some crosslinks with the other networks, and going to a telecommunications industry which is competitive down to the local loop level, to fully integrating both networks and going to one single huge monopoly.

At that stage, customers will have very substantial bandwidth available on an ISDN-type network, the opto-electronic technology will have matured, and the size and nature of potential demand will be much clearer, while still no substantial investments will have been committed to the telephone local loop plant. So, the more urgent needs being satisfied, and depending on what seems more appropriate at that time, one will still have the options of:

-       either decide to increase the depreciation schedules on the copper local loop, and doing all replacement and new installation with fiber, such as to move progressively to an all-optical ISDN network with individual loops for each subscriber, which would also provide all broadcast functions;

-       or decide to move to a similar solution, but where subscribers are connected in a LAN-type technique to the network, and progressively scrap the local copper plant;

-       or various mixtures of those solutions.

D.   Cultural policies

A cultural policy with regard to the development of telecommunications should distinguish 1. negative effects and 2. positive policies.
1)   Technological developments as sketched above have a number of quite worrysome potential effects, like disappearance of small village, local community-life, of local cultural events like concerts etc. and of proper use of language, emergence of a degraded English as a new lingua franca, encouragement of a more passive attitude, at a substantially lower level of intellectual activity, increased exposure to all kinds of foreign cultural influencess and finally a degradation of work-conditions. Details were censored out by the editor, for lack of space. Taken together, such effects mean a decrease in the quality of life and the quality of work for many people, and a strongly diminished national and cultural identification through a decreased sense of local and national solidarity and an international levelling of culture, reducing it to its most elementary forms.
Such things would be disastrous for Europe, meaning the complete loss of its unique strength, viz. the amazing richness and diversity of its many cultures. The greatest attention of authorities to these questions is required.
Most worrying is the fact that several of these aspects seem related to classical symptoms - or causes - of a decaying civilisation, like absence of any collective project or vision, generalised scepticism, proliferation of sects and marginalised people.
However, upon closer examination, these effects appear to be only very unspecifically related to a project of advanced telecommunications network, which at most reinforces current trends, and may finally only bring their day somewhat closer. One might nevertheless justifiable consider that, just to buy some additional delay for some of these effects, it would be worthwhile to delay or even to derail the whole project. Indeed, the differences between possible modalities of such a project, which we discussed somewhat before, seem to have little or no bearing of these effects.
Two points should however be considered in this respect: one is that the major sources of worry among the previously cited and the ones most directly linked to an advanced telecommunications network, are rather easily identified, and have pretty obvious, direct remedies in hands of public authorities, through their education and cultural policies, through their labour market policies, etc. (cfr. infra for some examples).
The other is that while delaying or stopping such a project may buy us some additional delay for some of those effects, any delay in the project may cause Europe to lose altogether one of its major benefits, which is also to some extent cultural in nature. Indeed, now (i.e. May 1986) the possibility still exist for Europe to implement such a project before the U.S. of Japan. But if one of those countries gets a headstart, they will be standard-setters, and their industry will be much further on the experien-

ce curve, so that they will dominate the market. And any chance for Europe to regain a serious foothold in a major part of high-tech will probably be gone for long. Now this would represent an enormous cultural setback too. Indeed, the only way for Europe to retain a cultural leadership, is to retain it in science and technology too. Also, an almost complete dependence on foreign powers and companies in most of high tech would mean a major loss of economic and even political independence - which are a necessary condition for any cultural leadership. Finally, it would mean quite an impoverishment too, Europe becoming a second order zone of low-tech industry, unable to use a big pool of high skilled individuals, and having therefore to compete on wage levels. Indeed, we cannot dispense with huge imports - if only of raw materials; to pay for them we have to compete somehow on export markets. The qualification of our labour pool would have to be lowered or be unemployed. Those would be dramatic social and cultural consequences too.

This might suggest that the most appropriate course of action would be to apply specific ad hoc remedies to the negative effects, while letting the network project proceed at full speed.

Another factor to be considered that the effects are not necessarily all black:

- To the previously mentioned symptoms of a decaying civilisation, one could justly oppose that a remapping of the world, a major change in Weltanschauung has always been extremely stimulative for culture and civilisation. Today's pace of scientific discovery, and the telecommunications' role in pushing frontiers further, turning the world into one big village, are certainly very promising in this respect.

- Something can be learned too from a parallelism with the advent of the printing press. It certainly spelled the doom of the compyist's art, which was definitely a mainstay of culture at that time. But is also fostered a great revival of civilisation, through the possibility of disseminating cultural goods much more widely - and even the loss of the copyist's art was balanced to some extent by the great upcoming painting schools. But this happened because people have an at least as active intellectual attitude as before, spending their efforts in trying to understand ancient civilisations rather than just copying; and the press was mainly used to disseminate widely the ancient treasures.

- European culture has always thrived on very strong cross-border influences in music, in painting, in architecture, even in literature (the art-form most closely tied to language). This is so true that an account of those would amount to a full Kulturgeschichte of Europe. Many artists and scientists, originating from many different countries, spent major parts of their lives in foreign countries and at foreign courts. Nationalism is only a recent invention, a byproduct of romanticism, that has outlived its time and should by now be outmoded. A lingua franca - a degraded form of latin - dominated everything all through the youth period of our civilisation, and continued to be prevalent until very recently - say around 1800 - in many endeavours, like science and philosophy, as attested by the works and correspondence of major figures. This has in no way been detrimental to the blossoming of national cultures.

To conclude, rather than waging a losing battle fighting technological evolution, it appears more appropriate to spend one's efforts in trying to turn evolution in a favourable direction, and to reap all potential benefits from technology. This same attitude prompted our previous recommendations to go to a competitive pricing system - which is beneficial in se - rather than fighting bypass, and to recognize explicitly as basic rights of the individual liberty and secrecy in telecommunications, rather than to fight a losing battle for control.

2).   Positive policies: Major remedies to the effects on work conditions should aim at keeping people in jobs - to prevent degradation of human capital due to long-term unemployment - and in interesting jobs. Hence they should promote a more adaptable versatile work force, a more flexible labour market to facilitate the adequation of people and jobs of a changing nature.

Only very big firms could possibly try to internalize all required personnel changes, and since we do not want to push for an industry structure consisting only of a couple of giant firms, flexible labour markets are needed in addition to an adaptable work force.

On both these aspects, public authorities can exert strong direct influence. On labor markets' flexibility by an array of already widely discussed measures such as:

-       lifting restrictions on terminations;

-       decreasing the disincentive of unemployed to accept a new low paying job (because incremental income is only salary minus previous unemployment benefits).

-       decreasing the individual's economic losses from job changes (e.g. in pension rights, by having individual retirement accounts as mentioned above; in moving costs, by eliminating transaction taxes in the housing market, replacing them, to be revenue-neutral, by a stiffer VAT on new construction).

The adaptability of the workforce is mainly determined by education policy, and can be improved by measures such as systematic retraining programs for people during their career (evening programs) and when out of jobs (intensive day and evening programs) - probably many of them over network facilities (chiefly for the 'evening' part); developing more curiosity at school, and having TV channels publicising and disseminating scientific and technological developments and their implications, at a high level (say of a non-specialist engineer); - a broader technological and basic scientific education in vocational education and increased requirements of general education and insistence on fundamentals at all levels.

Such measures merge with those aimed at countering negative effects like degradation of language and culture by having much stricter language requirements at school (and in public administrations ?) and a much stronger curriculum in humanities (essentially history and classical literature). Also people are not going to listen more or less to hard rock etc., or view more or less American porn videos according to a more or less restrictive European policy on telecommunications. Anyway, liberalism in such respect is part of our tradition. However, cheap availability of high bandwidth may enable authorities at all levels to offer a sufficiently varied menu of competing, high quality products. Those would then, just as for printed media, limit the influence of low quality and/or foreign TV and other video productions.

Such possibilities include, besides some previously cited ones:

- TV channels covering all major scientific and technical developments, and their implications;
- other channels devoted to national literature, poetry, theater, history, and to scientific developments in humanities (archeology, history, classical and ancient literatures and civilisations, knowledge of ancient scripts and languages, ethnology, linguistics, etc. ...);
- one hi-fi digital radio channel of classical music;
- one channel diffusing high-quality older and more recent movies;
- in addition, some information channels could be organized on a Europe-wide scale - like one broadcasting on a digital TV channel a log of all recent dispatches of major news agencies, accessible by keywords (in the original language) - or like the financial information channel we mentioned before.

If such specialised programs are organized by all nations or major regions, and offered on a Europe-wide scale (in addition to today's major diversified programs), a truly varied and high-quality menu would be available to individuals all over Europe.

Finally, a useful large scale initiative at a European level, stemming from the same idea of using advanced telecommunications to make cultural goods more widely available, but that would also fit in well with next section's insistence on R&D support, especially at the infrastructural level, would be to organize some kind of electronic 'library of congress', accessible to anybody in the E.E.C. essentially at marginal cost.

E.   Industrial policy

In a status quo scenario, probably favoured by most PTT's, network boundaries would be pushed as far as practicable inside CPE, and into value added services. As a result, PTT's would be sole buyers for most of telecommunications equipment, channelling their orders to one or two preferred national suppliers. European firms, in such a scenario, would more or less survive non competitively in captive markets. Most innovations would come from abroad, and telecommunications structure is likely to be highly inflexible to further changes in technology or demand, due to excessive integration of too many functions, all managed by a rigid, centralised bureaucracy. Such a scenario would be highly detrimental mainly to European telecommunications and other high-tech industry, and to intensive users and users with special demands - i.e., essentially to business in general. It might allow somewhat lower costs initially for residential users, but in the long run the costs of higher rigidity, as well as the general pauperisation in Europe that might ensue from the absence of high tech industry (or at least its main sector), would probably more than offset this.

Yet, despite these detriments, such a scenario seems a Nash equilibrium - in absence of specific countermeasures, no participant is likely to find it in his interest to upset the scenario. In particular, customers are essentially powerless and non organised, and would anyway not be aware of other possibilities, neither of the many uses to which they might put those possibilities.

And European suppliers would be cushioned in home markets by preferential national procurrement policies, and locked out of most other European markets by similar policies. So they would have a too small and too uncompetitive home market both to have the incentive to create very competitive products and to play the learning curve and develop sufficient economies of scale to become competitive. They might export a bit here and there, often in semi-political deals, but they would never tackle the major competitive markets for first-rate products. I mean the U.S. and soon probably Japan. The more elaborate equipment required there would mean to start almost from scratch, as a new entrant, in those high risk and highly competitive markets; protected national manufacturers do not have the mentality and are not geared to play that kind of game and take that kind of risk.

Among the specific measures needed to promote a more favourable evolution, we have already considered previously in this report those that dealt with network policy proper (boundaries and function, regulation, freedom and secrecy, etc...), and those dealing with promotion of national cultures and of the quality of the work force and with the flexibility of the labour market.

We now consider the necessary industrial policy measures. It should be noted to start with that, while many of the previous measures, notably those concerning, culture and education, fell naturally within the domain of national or regional authorities, the measures to be considered here would best be europe-wide policies, precisely in order to further a unified, europe-wide market and to avoid national distortions to competition.

We will consider successively the matters of anti-trust policy (1), the more fundamental and permanent measures to be taken (2), and the more transient, trade-related measures (3).

1.   Equipment markets are really global markets, so as long no european manufacturer attains the size of IBM or AT&T (and as long as there remain at least two or three major european firms in the sector, otherwise one should open borders completely to foreign competition), there is no reason to hinder any swaps, mergers, acquisitions, etc... (provided the acquiring firm or the merged firm be still a european firm).

But attention is warranted for upstream and downstream effects. Indeed, oligopoly theory and competition policy focus traditionally on the buyer-seller game, while upstream conditions like wage setting are studied independently in a worker-producer game. It is quite clear however that an upstream monopoly (e.g. in labour supply) may bring all inefficiencies of monopoly provision to an otherwise apparently competitive market (a similair observation is often also made w.r.t. the U.S. network under rate of return regulation). Similarly for downstream conditions: e.g., just the use of a common agency (say a P.T.T.) may have the same effect.

To put the above in the more concrete form of a paradigm - without any pretense to reality - it is not Siemens that has excessive market power in Germany, it is its captive (because of national procurement policies) customer the Bundespost which is the monopolist, marketing Siemens' telephone sets and buying its switching equipment.

In particular, the closest attention by E.E.C. anti-trust enforcement authorities should be given to any trace of preferential national procurement policy. It is true that measures like those suggested in A(6), or any form of privatisation, would substantially alleviate this risk - but would probably not eliminate it completely. In addition, public authorities would remain huge customers of CPE, and might use preferential policies there. In the meantime, as a first step, one might think of something like quotas, both for network switching equipment and for CPE, of at least 50% of all orders from both network management and public authorities, that would have to be attributed (competitively - no compensation agreements or the like) to E.E.C. firms from other countries than the ordering country. In such a way, at least 50% of the european market would be open to full, europe-wide competition and protected from international competition. And at the same time, national governments would still have some fall-back cushion to give, if desired, to their firms when they flaw one design, while they work on another better one. Obviously such a scheme is full of defects - in particular, quotas should always be only transitory measures. But it would be important to implement policies to a similar or better effect.

2.   The project itself of an advanced telecommunications network, and many of the previously cited policy measures, will strongly promote europe-wide services, furthering the demand for telecommunications - and also european integration. Here we want to consider the supply aspects: although firms are in general more responsive to what happens in their home markets than in foreign markets, this effect may not be sufficient to guarantee that european firms really respond and become competitive, and that no substantial part of this demand leaks to foreign firms - possibly under the camouflage of a joint venture with a european firm.

Measures to this effect could take the form of trade measures, but these often provoke international complications and relations. Further such measures are a priori not desirable, and should be considered as transient. If there is one area where Europe should have a competitive advantage, and should not need any protectionism, it is high-tech.

There is however a set of supportive measures, which is valuable in se and typically considerd as belonging to the proper role of public authorities, and which does not invite nearly as much international complications: any measures supporting scientific and R&D infrastructure. In this area, it seems advisable to use mostly policies aiming broadly at the whole infrastructure fist in order to avoid discriminating against small firms and new entrants in favour of the more established firms (the former often convey the fresh blood to the industry); and second in order to avoid targeting already established technologies and missing the next generation. This consideration also implies that any 'goal-oriented' policy should specify a major goal, representing a real challenge all across a broad front of technologies, and specified in terms of the results, the functionality to be achieved, rather than in terms of the specific techniques to be used.

But Europe seems to be not too well equipped institutionally to pursue such 'goal oriented' policies: the size of the scientific establishment needed to bring them to success, and the size of the budgets required to fund them would make any such project maybe unfeasible, probably unjustifiable (why should only one country pay when all its neighbours will also benefit from all spillover effects ?) at the national scale. And the lack of major departments, like a defense department, at the european scale inhibits any such project there - except for the Euratom treaty, which might enable a major project in fusion energy (satisfying thus at the same time the cry for clean energy ...) but this is too remote from telecommunications and electronics to be of much help her. (A major unmanned space program would already be less remote).

Specific policies to further broadly the whole infrastructure are:

- training and education, electronic 'library of congress' - these were already considered sub (E);

- normalisation efforts on a Europe-wide scale. We have excellent national programs in this respect like DIN; it should be a very high priority to let them join forces with other national organizations and change their scope to EEC-wide;

- public R&D money - both as general support to university research centers and as cost-plus funding for public projects;

- a network of public laboratories in Europe (à la Japanese);

- tax favours (immediate expensing) for venture capital and R&D investments;

- matching funds for R&D investments, and/or - in view of the lack of prowess of european firms in bringing new ideas to a market succes - some scheme for delaying the matching funds until market success (e.g. by lowering tax rates on the profits from resulting products for a couple of years, or allowing to carry forward initial R&D investments at more than 100% to offset future profits from the resulting products);

- it is probably appropriate to add to the above that public authorities also have to use some portfolio policy, just like we have seen that private firms have to move out regularly from activities which are no longer strategically important for them, in order to free resources for and to focus management efforts better on new, strategically important activities. This report shows how, just in the telecommunications area, a huge number of new questions require the public authorities' attention, and in many cases intervention. There is no way to keep up with all such new tasks and challenges without at the same time shedding involvement in any area where it is no longer essential, where the market or other mechanisms would do roughly as well (if not much better). Such examples were given above.

3.   To implement policies that aim at avoiding leakage to non european suppliers it would be useful to have a formal (legal ?) concept of a 'european firm', the intent being to mean a firm whose headquarters, know-how, R&D and control are located in the E.E.C. We have already needed this concept in several of the previous recommendations, and there will in addition be many other uses. Some care is needed in the formalization of the idea - e.g. one would want a firm like Philips to be considered as a european firm, despite being fully controlled by a 'Stichting' in the Antilles; on the other hand one would not want the european subsidiaries of a non european firms, except when fully controlled by the european partner and aiming at developing and manufacturing products fully in Europe.

A first policy instrument is an active, europe-wide procurement policy. For network equipment, european networks could set up a common list of specifications, and a common organization could sollicit bids on this from all european telecom manufacturers - with the commitment not to bargain besides the bids between individual networks and manufacturers. Individual networks could then choose among the bids those that suit best their particular circumstances, subject maybe to some additional regulations to prevent undue national preferences. This is also an example of a way to stabilize the market (page 12) which I think would be quite acceptable. For CPE equipment one could think of rules imposing drastic restrictions on purchases of CPE equipment from non-european firms whenever public money of whatever source is involved. One could in addition instruct public authorities at all levels to look actively for possible uses of any new products developed by european firms.

Even more than such procurement policies, the major key for this effort to result in a successful european telecom industry lies in early and good quality european standards - and much prodding and other activity by public authorities maybe required to achieve this. This is so urgent that one should not wait for the establishment of a Europe-wide normalisation and standads organisation, like that which was suggested in the previous paragraph. In the meantime, any good quality standards, whether promulgated by individual firms, or industry associations, or whatever will do. Indeed, we have seen earlier why timing was essential for the success of this project, and standards are one of the very first obstacles on the critical path.

In this respect, the more urgent points concern:

-     level 4 communication over the network (this is the transport level, i.e. the provision of end-to-end communication between terminals on home-LAN's: these are user standards, not network standards, and hence concern CPE manufacturers, not the networks), and

-      standards for home-LAN's, as previously described. In a first stage, just a wiring plan for new homes and how to retrofit old homes would already open the market. This whole proposal intentionally stresses much more the residential sector than the typical strategy of e.g. a U.S. firm would do. This is because the high versatility required say in home-LAN's will more than probably imply standards and equipment which are also adequate for the business sector, and mainly because, as explained before, residential applications imply a mass market, and thus the opportunity to gain from the outset an important competitive advantage by a high volume, experience curve-driven strategy. It may also help avoid a head-on clash right at the start with U.S. competition.

When speaking of good quality standards, we mean among others that they should not be geared towards a specific application, but be of lasting value for a wide array of applications. One should not rely on manufacturers for this, since for them, product-specific standards are often a way to protect the market for a specific product. E.g., standards for digitizing images should evolve towards application-independent standards, applicable as well to TV as to computer graphics and fax, and admitting standard and easy digital interpolation algorithms from passing from lower resolution to higher resolution images and vice-versa; in the long run, portability of files across applications is more important than small additional efficiency gains in each specific application. Similarly for standards for digitizing sound - all the way from 384 Kbit/s hi-fi audio down to 16 Kbit/s voice. Similarly error-correcting codes should depend only on the final accuracy required (given the network's guaranteed accuracy), and not on the application involved, just as the level 4 communication protocols shoud depend only on the type of communication desired. Such aims may even warrant to sacrifice compatibility with some older equipment or standards - e.g., in a transition period, broadcasting could continue to be done as now over the air for the older equipment, and would start being done simultaneously for the new equipment over the network using the new standards.

Finally, this standardisation effort should aim not so much at protecting the european market from foreign competition by incompatible standards as at allowing easy adaptation of european equipment to export markets - thus at providing a great degree of compatibility with likely future standards elsewhere (this is one reason for insisting on the quality of standards). Thus, we should for example, other things being equal, strive for a market structure as similar as possible to the likely future U.S. market structure. (E.g. this is a major reason, in addition to the ones previously cited, for definitely preferring the U-reference point to the T-reference point as a user-network boundary). This attitude follows from the basic aim of this proposal, which is to gain a first mover advantage and quick, high volume production in european markets, to enable european manufacturers to move successfully to competition in the export markets.

GLOBAL COMMUNICATION NETWORKS:
NATIONAL AND INTERNATIONAL RESEARCH AND
DEVELOPMENT STRATEGIES

Jeremy Beale

1.   Introduction

Communication networks form the whole range of communication functions in the processes of inputting, processing, transmitting, switching,
and receiving messages from one place to another. Communication networks are organized at local, trunk, national, and international levels with
the development of networking integration and capability progressing
historically in Europe upwards from the local to the international level.
Traditionally, networks have consisted largely of telephone technologies
in voice transmission, but recent major technological changes have occurred with the introduction of 'information technologies' (IT) which form
in the convergence of telecommunications and computing equipment, to
process and transmit digital data, voice, textual, and visual messages in
the network. This has included innovations in a wide range of both software programmes and hardware equipment, and these promise to continue
for quite a while into the future.
The following discussion will focus on the ways in which these development relate to changes in the general economic and political structure of
national and international relations. In the contemporary era of international interdependence in which huge changes in communication networks
are occuring, national autonomy is highly qualified by a wide range of
international institutions, relationships, and commitments. In considering
the development of global networks in the European Communities, where
a range of actors is involved in the international consultative and decision-making processes established by the Treaty of Rome and developed
since, the specific questions we need to ask are these: How does/will the
position of European states, consumers, capital, and labour in the national
and international political economy structure the research, development,
production, and use of global communication networks in Europe and
abroad ? In what ways can the Member States and the Commission of the
EEC respond to, and act to affect, the development of these networks and
their associated technologies ?
We support the view here that the use of new communication technologies
and global networks by national groups is essential for continued participation in the economic growth of the international economy upon which
national prosperity depends. However, we argue that just **using** the new
communication technologies of global networks within the context of an
open free trade system can result in simply a one-sided loss of national
autonomy for all but the most economically and politically powerful of
countries and groups within nation-states. We will argue that this is
particularly the result of the high costs of capitalisation, and the historical political and economic structure, of the research and development
(R & D) of the 'core' technologies at the centre of these networks. We
argue that for the loss of national autonomy which goes with the use of
these global networks to result in increasing social, economic, and political equality depends upon international cooperation between state institutions and a wide range of social groups within the European Communi-

ties in the research and development of communication technologies which set international standards, especially in the capital intensive sectors of the industry.

We do this in the following manner. First, we consider recent developments in the economic and technological components of national and international communication networks, and the organizational possibilities and changes which these allow - in the autonomy of state institutions and social groups organized at international and national levels in particular. Second, we analyse how these economic and technological developments relate to the general economic and political structures of national and international relations. Third, we consider how the possibilities and problems revealed by this analysis have specifically occurred in past and present national and international R & D strategies for the development of communication networks and technologies within the European Communities. And lastly, we consider the outlines of future strategies which may be pursued by the Member States and Commission of the European Communities in relation to consumers and the representatives of capital and labour in order to achieve progress in the equitable development of communication technologies and networks.

2.   Global Communication Networks: Economic and Technological Outlines

A basic indicator of the way in which the new communication technologies have related to increasingly internationalized economic relations is in the value of the international markets. In 1984, $ 325 billion was spent in telecommunications services and equipment, and $ 125 billion on computers. This is expected to rise to a combined figure of $ 830 billion in 1990, with about $ 540 billion of this being on telecommunications. Revenues from network services in the USA, Europe, and Japan (about 90% consisting of voice traffic, though data transmission is growing faster) came to about $ 200 billion in 1984 - which represents about 85% of all telecommunications revenues in these parts of the world. At the same time, the global office equipment market, which represents 90% of all data communications, came to nearly $ 20 billion (1).

There are, of course, significant national and regional variations in this overall international growth. The biggest market for telecommunications equipment is in the United States, which represents 74% of all telecommunications market (East and West, but excluding the Soviet Union) was expected to grow at a fast rate (6.7% per annum): nearly doubling to $ 20.5 billion between 1980 and 1990. This represents a decline in world market share from 26.8% in 1980 to 23.5% in 1990, though this is still the third largest market sector in the world (after the USA and Asia). Western Europe's share of this regional market is expected to reach $ 16.3 billion in 1990 (2).

Growth in world demand for purely telecommunications equipment is expanding rapidly - having been projected as more than doubling between

1980 and 1990, increasing at an annual rate of 8.1% from $ 40 billion in 1980 to $ 87.5 billion in 1990.

Telephone voice equipment (switching and transmission gear and peripherals for voice) has been predicted as remaining the largest part of this market, growing by 8% annually worldwide from $ 32.5 billion to more than $ 70 billion between 1980 and 1990, according to consultant firm Arthur D. Little. The second largest telecommunications market is predicted to be in telegraph, telex, and data communications, growing by 9.5% per annum between 1980 and 1990. Demand is again greatest in the United States, which constitutes more than 60% of the world market. However, Europe and Asia's percentage in this category compared to others in telecommunications has been projected as growing from 6.8% to 9.7% and from 6.4% to 7.2% respectively - increasing their share of worldwide markets in this area to 32.5% and 39% respectively (3).

Despite overall international growth, the end-user equipment part of this market is predicted to grow only marginally in value in Western Europe though, as large growth in some sectors is offset by the decline in the analogue leased circuit modem market, which accounted for 65% of the data transmission market in 1981. The reasons for this are the fall in unit prices of specified modems and the increasing availability and usage of public data networks (4), especially ISDN, which make modems (which change analogue into digital signals and vice versa) increasingly technically redundant and uneconomic. This indicates that the important technological and economic developments in this area will remain in the core processing and transmission technologies at the heart of communication networks.

The growth in demand for new information and communications' equipment has gone hand in hand with a rapid increase in corporate, national, and international R & D programmes for the development of core digital data, voice, and visual processing and transmission technologies (5) which vastly increase the **mass** and **range** of information which can be transmitted from one place to another and which, combined, change the qualitative **uses** of this information (e.g. long distance monitoring and manipulation in tele-conferencing, manufacturing and extraction, or weapons operation). Micro-electronic chips have been at the core of the development of mechanisms which can package and switch this vast amount of information from one place to another within the process of transmission. The **spatial** capability for carrying the large and varied amounts of information generated by this micro-electronic technology almost instantaneously from one part of the globe to any other has been through the development of satelite and cable (particularly fibre-optic) technologies which therefore form the core of future long distance and global communications networks.

But the effective demand for this equipment has occurred because this technological capability has gone hand in hand with a reduction in the absolute and relative economic costs **for capital** of using micro-electronic, satellite, and cable technologies. This is based on the reduction in average unit costs arising partly from their international use. As the Sola Pool points out:

'The costs of switching, of billing, and of the local loop are by now the greatest part of the costs of a long-distance call (these are costs that do not vary with distance) ..... the savings that will result from new long-distance technologies may not bring total costs down much, but those variable costs that make the price of a long-distance call a partial function of distance are disappearing ..... for example, the advances in coaxial cable and ..... optical waveguides. Each successive generation of carrier has much greater capacity and markedly lower costs per circuit ..... long-distance transmission costs are becoming a minor part of the total bill. It is clear that the marginal cost of transmitting extra miles is a vanishing number and even the average cost (which is the important figure) is 'just pennies', even over such distances as that across the USA. If distance was already a minor factor without satellites, with them it has become trivial. For a signal that travels 22.300 miles up and 22.300 miles down, it can hardly be important whether the base of the triangle is 1200 or 12.000 miles (6).

The general social and political importance of this aspect of the new communications equipment is its effect on the speed and quallity of economic operations and organization within and between firms probably separated by formal political boundaries. The introduction of equipment with the expanded capability of multiplexing telex, facsimile, telephone, slow scan TV, and videophone signals into one digital stream within a global network promises to provide instant processing and transmission of a massive range of economic and political information, and popular entertainment and values across vast geographical distances. Furthermore, given an area of open economic activity, this allows firms, academic institutions, and state organizations to increasingly diversify and combine - irrespective of spatial criteria - operations and activities which were previously restricted to national centres. As we shall consider later, in the case of industrial R & D in core communication technologies this is being advanced by the international collaboration between various private and public institutions in the European Communities organized under the ESPRIT and RACE programmes. Nationally and internationally, this affects (and will increasingly affect) the basic relations of general economic and political power between business corporations, other social groups, and national political authorities, and the general economic environment in which national decision-making is made (7). This suggests that the general economic and political autonomy and utility of national organization is, and will be, greatly reduced.

However, the increase in international power of particular social groups and state institutions which this brings about will in fact depend upon their relative position within the concrete structure of national and international political economy: not all states and groups within states will be affected equally.

How the loss of national power occurs in fact, and how it affects the economic and political power of individual national and international institutions, also depends on **what** communication networks and associated technologies are developed and used for, and **how** they are integrated into existing international and national networks. For whole new **networks** do not appear in one instant in time to replace old ones; rather, existing networks are replaced in **parts** with new equipment. Network change occurs apparently in a somewhat piecemeal process which reflects a range of actors with public and private influence. How overall change occurs reflects, therefore, the political **structure** in the economy of social need, demand, and organization met by the network system. As Gerd Junne has put it:

'All too often, efforts to come to some kind of technology assessment end up this way. First, possible positive and negative effects are listed and then a balance is drawn to see whether the positive or negative effects will dominate. In reality, however, positive and negative effects will not offset each other, because they often affect different groups ..... positive and negative effects will be different for different groups. And since politics deals with the question 'Who gets what, when and how ?', it is the distribution of seemingly contradictory effects of the global grid over different groups which has to be dealt with .....' (8).

What will be crucial in determining this matter will be the relationships formed between national and international state institutions on the one hand, and between them and various social groups on the other.

This brings us to consider **how** the research, development, production, and use of these communication technologies is structured by the framework of international political economy.

3.   The International Political Economy of Communication Technologies

Most of the research, development, production, and use of traditional and new communication technologies occurs in North America, Western Europe, and Japan, which are also the major exporters of communications' equipment to the rest of the world. The use of traditional equipment is now a general global phenomenon, most Third World countries are extending their national networks and integrating them more closely into the international network (this being largely complete in the West with the extensive introduction of international direct dialling), while, as we have seen, a high level of demand for micro-electronic processing and switching equipment is now also largely a global phenomena. A smaller number of countries, however, are taking up the use of satellite transmission and receiving facilities, and a very few are beginning to lay down fibre optic links within and between their own and other country's communication networks.

The ownership of advanced transmission technologies outside a few countries in the West was initially organized on an intergovernmental basis (i.e. through the international public network authorities for cable and, in satellites, through such groups as INTELSAT and INMARSAT). However, it is now incoming increasingly national - with India, Brazil, Indonesia, Canada, Australia, and Japan, joining the US and the major European countries as owners of their own satellites (9) - or regional, with groups of countries forming consortia for exclusive purposes. It is also becoming a more private affair: a huge growth in consortia of private carriers for different groups of international corporations has occurred since the end of the 1960s (10). And individual companies, too, in some cases now have their own satellite systems which completely by-pass the international public communications' networks. General Motors, for example, has acquired its own satellite network for communication between its international subsidiaries (11).

Satellite networks, which at the moment carry around 20 per cent of the world's long distance traffic (12), are vastly cheaper to use than continental coaxial cable, microwave, and new waveguide systems (13). They have facillitated the global spread of international corporations R & D activities, and will eventually allow a range of industrial R & D to be conducted in the intense vacuum and gravity-free conditions of space, possibly through the use of large, multi-purpose space stations, which thus makes them attractive to industrially advanced countries (14). Their use is also in many ways preferred by industrially less developed countries as a means of international (and sometimes national) communication because of their ability to transmit information, and be received, without the need for a large or complex preexisting telecommunications infrastructure.

However, there is an inherent international political tension in the use and development of satellite networks over those of cable. This is because the natural resources utilised by communication networks, and the natural environment in which they operate, is structured partly by natural limitations and partly by the conventions and facts of property rights. The space used for the geo-stationary orbit of satellite communication networks is physically limited and thus needs international institutions for its peaceful regulation, the rules of which are currently made at the World Administrative Radio Conferences (WARCs) of the ITU (15); for cable, on the other hand, the actual physical restrictions are less, with limitations arising mainly from local, national, and international ground rights - something which public telecommunications' authorities have already generally agreed. It is partly because of such complications that most communication networks will consist of a mix of technologies depending upon the structure of power holding between state institutions within a given international, national, and even local (e.g. between Land and Federal governments in the FDR) region.

With the growing ownership of new global communication networks with the technological capabilities outlined in the previous section by private financial, commercial, and industrial enterprises, business corporations organizing capital accumulation on an international basis have developed (16) which create an **international structure** in the operations and growth of national and international economies, and the general basis of prosperity generated by them. As a result, all state institutions and social groups are faced in a competitive world with the choice of either participating in the ownership and use of these technologies or running the risk of forfeiting information and communications which may be vital to their own continued and future prosperity. States and social groups will or will not fall economically behind leading economic nation-states and social actors according to the degree to which they gain the facilities to 'log in' to the information and data flows of global networks. This situation has led many commentators to argue that countries need to enter into an international system of free trade for communications' goods and services as the most efficient way of gaining access to their use.

However, though the use of these technologies increases international inter-dependence this does not in itself prevent the growth of existing national and international inequalities. It has been predicted that over 80 per cent of the new communication services coming into being will be available only in the US, Japan, Western Europe, Australia, Canada, and the USSR (17). This creates a potential danger, as Cruise O'Brien and Helleiner note, that it will be mistakenly assumed that 'telecommunications and information systems will in themselves promote growth and development, and that the only problem is their insufficiently rapid acquisition. The use of high technology in other sectors has frequently produced new forms of dependence rather than enlarging independent capacity' (18). For the uneven demand for these technologies partly reflects their particular uses which, as Dosi has argued generally, are determined by the specific structure and controle of R & D in new core technologies at the original centre of the R & D **process** (19). As we shall now indicate, the structure and control of R & D in core technologies cannot be abstractly separated from general structural inequalities in the international political economy (20).

First, major demand for new communications' equipment comes from large (in particular international) business, with very little overall from private individual consumers. This has become intense with the increasing impact and spread of economic recession from the early 1970s, precisely because - apart from the economies of scale for capital mentioned earlier - large corporations have found a use for communication technologies as a means of cutting labour cost - either in increasing manufacturing and office automation, or through taking advantage of their international capabilities to exploit the economic, social, and political advantages of less developed countries or areas. These technologies and networks, in other words, have been used by many firms to resist the effects of decreasing demand in the economic recession by increasing labour productivity, and thereby profitability, despite any decreasing demand for their goods or services: their lower unit costs also partly reflect lower labour costs in production and servicing. There are programmes for the development of social **applications** of communication technologies by national and international bodies (21). But the dominant trends in the **core** communications' R & D have re-inforced either, in the move in informatics towards technologies in software engineering, man/machine interfacing, and computer aided design and manufacturing (CAD/CAM), this effect on labour costs (22) or, in the move towards ever more highly integrated circuits and parallel processing, military purposes (23).

Second, the traditionally heavy military involvement in communication technologies' R & D also re-inforces existing international inequalities between countries with their internationalization. This has meant in effect that, though most countries want to develop communication technologies on a national basis, the actual development of new technologies has been dominated by the two superpowers, particularly the US. This is going to become even more the case with the centrality of communication technologies in the R & D programme of the Strategic Defence Initiative, despite the Challenger disaster in 1986 (which led to a slackening of the criteria of commercial viability for the Shuttle programma and a return to 'pure science' and military criteria as the determinate of the programme's budget). As long as communications' R & D is governed by these military criteria, its development will be dominated by the West, and predominantly on a national basis by the US.

Third, and connected to the predominance of big business and military interests in the structure of the political economy of communication technologies is the fact that development and production of the major components of communication networks is generally - and increasingly - a capital intensive industry, and therefore necessitates heavy investment costs and a market size larger than that for a consumer goods industry in order for R & D costs to be amortised (24). Under the present conditions of the world economy, the creation of such demand necessarily involves either a very large national market (as for instance in the United States or Japan), or cooperation in the creation of an international one (as in the European Community) - and a high level of capitalization - if R & D expenditure is not to be onerous or impossible for any but the largest national state or corporation. As one report for the Commission of the European Communities has put it:

'In Europe the telecommunications market is more like a patchwork, than like a common market. Almost every member country has a different telecommunications system, with different norms and standards, with the result that most systems are incompatible ..... Due to the higher R & D-investments for the next generation (of) digital exchanges the market should be extended ..... an investment of $ 1 billion needs a market of at least $ 14.3 billion to cover the R & D costs. Nor (sic.) the UK, neither France or Germany has a market of that size (25)'.

Moreover, as a result of the internationalization of the structure of economic activity within which international and national prosperity is generated and which we noted earlier, in many cases national attempts to raise taxes to finance development programmes simply catches nation-states in the kind of fiscal crises which were common in Europe throughout the 1970s.

From this analysis we can see that stressing the imperatives and advan-

tages in the internationalized use of communication networks and technologies is insufficient if separated from consideration of the international
structure of political economy in their research, development, and production. This is pertinent in a critique of those who argue that the use, and
rate of introduction, of IT in industry is itself a significant indicator of
relative economic power, that a country or region can remain/become
powerful by simply relying on service industry to the neglect of manufacturing industry, and that the development of a capability in communication technologies will result simply from a free trade system in communications' goods and services. The research, development, and production of
the major hardware components of communication networks is essential
for creating a greater structure of international equality, though this will
remain on a national basis only for the richest countries in the West. As
has now been realised in the European Communities with the start of
ESPRIT and RACE, co-operation by states in all but the wealthiest
countries is needed not just in building a free trade system in communications' goods and services and the creation of a sizable market for them,
but also in maintaining and building a sizable enough investment base for
international cooperation in the research, development, and production of
communication technologies.

However, the important question which this leaves unaddressed is just **how**
such a productive base is maintained and built. For just as it is of limited
value having the use of communication technologies without the productive capability to determine their development, so is the converse equally
as true. A crucial problem for European producers in improving their
market position has been the lack of leading-edge customers as a result of
a pre-existing synergistic relationship between users and foreign producers (26). A key element in gaining international economic equality in
communications' equipment and networks is therefore keeping producers
abreast with the leading technologies and standars in (particularly) the
capital goods sectors in close consultation with leading edge customers,
and a European strategy must aim at (and, as we shall see with ESPRIT and
RACE, is moving towards) this end. At the same time, in order to guarantee that this does not lead to greater economic, social, and political
inequalities, a wide range of social groups need to be brought into the
relationship between consumers and producers in the research, development, and production of communication technologies and networks. In the
case of those groups who do not already have much economic and political
power, this can only be guaranteed through the power of state institutions.
Some kind of competitive environment may be conducive to ensuring that
such state involvement is a dynamic and forward-looking one (particularly
in the area of end-user applications), but total exposure to international
procurement and international competition (particularly in core technologies) could spell the complete destruction of both a future leading-edge
producer capacity in Europe and a more socially beneficial one. Such
exposure has been historically practiced by neither of today's leaders in
communication technologies - the US or Japan - who have opened their

communication markets not only after decades of public support, whether in the form of spending on military programmes or state-led R & D coordination, which has **now** put them in a position of superiority from which they call for a free trade system (27).

4. National and International Communications' R & D and Policy Formation in the European Communities

The most important and exciting impact on communications' R & D in the European Communities occurs at the moment in the possibilities and initial developments arising from the EEC's ESPRIT and RACE projects. These combine firms and academic and state institutions in different countries in Europe in common research into advanced core communication technologies. In order to evaluate these programmes we now need to consider how they stand in relation to the ways in which the general developments outlined in the previous sections arise as specific problems and possibilities within the context of the European Communities.

Despite continuing national divergences in the exact balance between public monopolies and market services in Europe (28), there has been a general trend towards increased liberalisation in a range of communications goods and services alongside a number of national and European programmes for state support for communications' R & D. However, an economic 'crisis' in the European development of communications' technologies has been growing throughout the 1970s and had become quite extreme by the 1980s, when growing trade deficits in this general sector began to pile up - in contrast to previous surpluses. To some extent the loss of orders has been a **relative** function of the wider international recession as much as any absolute fault of the European IT and communication industries themselves, as a relative international surplus capacity has developed in the industry. Though there have been exceptions, it has in many cases been precisely where European governments have financially helped their producing industries to modernise that they have been most succesful in improving their technological standing. Three such examples are Siemens in Germany (29), the digitalisation programme in France during the 1970s, and the PAFE programme for French industry under the Socialist government in 1981 (which led to the industry growing by 8% - Matra and Thomson increasing production by 20% by 1984 - and the trade deficit in the sector being cut from Ł 720 million in 1983 to Ł 130 million in 1984) (30).

The backwardness of European equipment producers has often occurred precisely where there has been a **lack** of consistent private or state financial support for long-term R & D (most obviously in the case of the UK), and where producers have as a result had to fall back on dependency on captive markets to produce any profits at all, or where there has been institutional conflict and uncertainty (as in Italy and in the UK during much of the 1970s) (31). And though it is true that the strong US market is one in which technological development is something of a 'free-for-all' (32) this has followed, and with SDI is restarting, a period in which US firms receive massive state funding for communications' R & D **indirectly** for civilian development (and therefore less efficiently) through military programmes. Moreover, when compared to the less-subsidised and more privatised European micro-electronics industry, the more general European communications industry is economically more successful (33).

The above points are not meant to hide the fact that a problem exists for European communications' producers but to highlight the fact that this is often a lack of resources, and that unqualified liberalisation and privatisation are not in fact obvious answers for solving this. The problem of funding advanced technologies, which cannot be met within the present limits of national markets and individual nation-state finances, often has more to do with a general fiscal crisis of the nation-state in relation to the growing internationalisation of economic activity, and is just not reducible to the supposed inefficiencies of the European communications' industry itself. In many ways this problem is better solved by producers and PTTs cooperating in common strategies which will rationalise the provision and use of resources in Europe (34) than by privatising monopolies or forcing Europe's relatively small-scale international producers to compete against foreign global giants such as AT & T, who would often be the main beneficiaries in liberalising competition in national markets. This is the area where ESPRIT and RACE make a start and where future effort needs to go, with more rather than less coordination between producers, servicers, and consumers at the international level in Europe in order to reduce waste.

Significant European cooperation in the research and development of communications technologies is just beginning to occur. Throughout the 1960s and 1970s communications and computer R & D programmes in Europe were organized almost solely on a national basis with, for instance, the Unidata experiment in international European cooperation failing to take off in the mid-1970s. Even as late as 1981, following the Japanese announcement of their Fifth Generation programme and the Tokyo conference to discus the possibility of international collaboration in this, no country was prepared to seriously embark on such collaboration, even in the European Community, where ESPRIT and other programmes were already being presented for discussion. Instead, as economic recession hardened, and call for improved services and lower costs in communications increased amongst major business users, European states concentrated their efforts on attempts to collectively increase competition at the Community level in public procurement markets. These inevitably became bogged down in arguments over whether the competition was to be between Community 'producers' or 'suppliers' - i.e. whether to allow firms originating from outside the Community to compete in the liberalised markets on equal terms with those originating from within the Community or not (35). With a major problem for many Community producers being that they had insufficient equity to fund the massive R & D in advanced core technologies which precisely gave US and Japanese firms their competitive advantages (36), it was hardly surprising that straightforward liberalisation proposale would meet stiff and effective opposition within the Community. And after the failure to find major new funds for the national programmes in advanced core technologies which had begun in the early 1980s - with instead mainly existing funds incapable of adequately meeting the declared goals of the programmes being simply reallocated (37) - pressure from key corporations on national governments in Europe for commitment to a European solution to the problem of IT and communications R & D became irresistable (38).

The international cooperation which has been generated by the European Communities' ESPRIT and RACE projects has significant implications for national autonomy. Whether as a direct consequence of the programmes themselves, or more indirectly as a result of the general environment of technological cooperation which they have encouraged, there are increasing cases of transnational collaboration in the research, development, and production of IT and communications' technologies - of importance in the use of communication networks for a range of industries - between European firms. There are two aspects of sifnificance here. The first is the immediate consequence of R & D cooperation in the IT and communication technologies themselves, between people in different firms in different countries, using private communication networks in the process of their actual work. It is hard to see how such collaboration could lead to anything but greater international integration at the expense of national autonomy when the R & D is concerned with basic hardware, and even more so in the case of software. Second, to the extent that such cooperation has led, and continues to lead, to the formation of European joint stock companies which set European - and from there possibly global - standards in software and hardware, the promise of rates and levels of profit being attained which are significantly higher than those of the various national companies seem to be quite great. It is a realistic expectation to assume that, to the extent that such a situation is the case, the national firms themselves will increasingly see - and will increasingly have - their interests in commitment to further international, rather than national, industrial R & D integration. But this loss of national autonomy and international integration is one of greater equality between state institutions and private producers, and of a qualitatively better kind, than that resulting from simply the use of communications equipment to 'log in' to liberalised global networks designed and produced by others.

This still leaves the issue of public participation in the decision making processes leading to these policies for international technological development unaddressed. Industrial consumers of communications have so far been well represented in the development of new technologies in Europe, following the establishment of telecommunication users' associations composed of large national and international businesses throughout the EEC during the late 1970s and early 1980s, which led the call for reduced costs and improved services in networks. Consumers of the actual capital equipment technologies (largely the PTTs and, in the case of the

UK, privatised British Telecom) have also been closely involved in relevant national and European programmes. However, other social groups such as the trades unions have been absent from discussions of the formation of these programmes (39). We can now turn to consider how this situation may be addressed in the future by the Member States and Commission of the European Communities.

5. Future Strategy Scenarios for the European Communities

There are five basic strategies which Member States and the Commission, consumers, and the social partners of capital and labour could possibly adopt in responding to the technological changes underliving the development of international communications' networks, evaluating them in the light of the analysis provided above. These are:
1) Resistance to all change;
2) Exclusively national development of the technologies;
3) A 'Fortress Europe' development of the technologies in cooperation with other Community members but to the exclusion of all others;
4) A total exposure to global 'push' and 'pull' forces in the development of the technologies;
5) A mixture of national, Community, and international development of the technologies.
We will nog briefly review these options in the light of our discussion in the preceeding sections.

In today's interdependent and technologically dynamic world of resistance to all forms of technological change is a feasible strategy for no one, and is supported by virtually no groups in Europe. The 1960s and 1970s European strategy of 'national champions' has also failed in most EEC countries, being replaced by various 'niche' strategies. This national strategy of specializing in a particular area of technological expertise can, if developed in a sufficiently advanced and valuable area, provide a useful bargaining position in a wider strategy of international cooperation.

Given Europe's present relative technological backwardness in IT and communication technologies a solely European strategy of technological development is also not a terrible convincing one for the future as it could well really cover for a regressive strategy of protectionism, also harming the important foreign links of European firms and states. However, the institutions of the European Communitaies may provide an optimum level of formal organization for the development of communication technologies by groups within the Communities as they provide the highest level of statutory control, and through which cooperation with other countries or organizations can be organized on a bilateral basis (40).

An appropriate mix of national, European, and global development of communication network technologies would be one which was done on the basis of a high degree of international specialization, but in which the development of strategic technologies was retained by state intervention coordinated through the European Communities. This is in fact the general strategy presently being followed by nation-states and the Commission in the relations established between the national programmes and those of ESPRIT and RACE. Such a strategy increasingly demands a greater degree of international coordination, and the signs are that Member States are prepared to increasingly move in this direction. As a result, it can be expected that the role of Community institutions in the formation of policy for the development of communication technologies, and particularly the Commission, will increase in the future.

However, the Commission will be unable to make headway in all areas of R & D, and though military cooperation will probably continue to increase, this will be on an inter-governmental basis outside Community institutions. Where the Commission is most likely to make headway is in the civilian application of communication networks where, as we mentioned at the start of this chapter, it is particularly well suited because of the wide range of social interests which it is able to consult under the terms of the Treaty of Rome. It has already developed this with big business under ESPRIT and RACE; it could possibly now expand its activities to cover R & D in core technologies determined by wider social interests. With the spread of network technologies into more and more areas of life it is important that organizations representing a wide range of social interests become involved in - or are created for - the Community planning of R & D if this is to be as efficient, fruitful, and equitable a process as is possible. It is premature to state the exact configuration of relations between producers, users, Member States, and the Commission cannot be determined in general beforehand because of the largely piecemeal nature of network development which we noted earlier. As the process will depend upon the particular level and type of communication technology under discussion (41), more detailed research will need to be done in the future on the question of the institutional structures best suited for developing particular social interests in communications' R & D. But the Commission in this process can build on its experiences with the Round Table group of companies and in the Joint European Planning Exercise - IT which led to the formation of ESPRIT and RACE.

Notes

(1)   Arthur D. Little 1980; all prices are in 1979 values and rates of exchange.
(2)   Ibid.
(3)   Ibid.
(4)   Logica 1982.
(5)   These core technologies are signified by a number of different terms: 'long-lead-time' and 'generic' technologies in the ESPRIT programma, 'pre-competitive' and 'enabling' technologies in the UK Alvey programme. What distinguishes them as core technologies is their multiple application in a number of different industrial, social,

and military uses. There are severe difficulties in constructing usefully precise comperative figures for spending on these programmes. See Arnold and Guy 1986, pp. 11-16, for a discussion.

(6)   De Sola Pool, 1976, p. 34.

(7)   See Cruise O'Brien and Helleiner 1980, pp. 465-469.

(8)   Junne 1986, pp. 30-31.

(9)   Maral and Bousquet 1986, p. 7.

(10)   Cruise O'Brien and Helleiner 1980, p. 466.

(11)   **The Economist,** November 23-29, 1985.

(12)   Maral and Bousquet 1986, op cit.

(13)   Martin 1977, p. 341.

(14)   Maral and Bousquet 1986, pp. 36-38; Pelton 1981, pp. 69-72.

(15)   Pelton 1981, pp. 69-70; Soroos 1982.

(16)   As Cruise O'Brien and Helleiner 1980, p. 466, note: 'Modern telecommunications systems have ..... evolved under US leadership, and specifically in response to the needs of transnational corporations (and defense surveillance) ..... The reduction of non-technical barriers has led to the immense growth of private carriers since the end of the 1960s upon which many forms of transnational enterprices (and business consortia) are dependent'.

(17)   Pelton 1981, p. 133.

(18)   Cruise O'Brien and Helleiner 1980, p. 467.

(19)   See Dosi 1984.

(20)   This is also reflected in the increasing politicisation of issues concerning the international regulatory environment in the ITU. For a discussion, see Soroos 1982.

(21)   For a discussion of some of the projects and theoretical and practical issues involved, see Ancelin et al. 1986.

(22)   This is clearly seen in two statements made to the UK House of Lords Sub-Committee on ESPRIT concerning the overall shift from emphasis on problems of hardware to those of software. As Sir Herbert Durkin of Plessey stated, 'if you look at the projections of costs of computers in a hardware-software ratio, then software is going to be something like 80 per cent of the cost in the very near future ..... What we are looking for is a way ..... to make the software designer's job easier and enable hom ti do it more quickly and, of course, more cheaply'. D.H. Roberts, Technical Director of GEC, stated it as the need to make a standardisable commodity of the skill element in software labour: 'The reason why a lot of attention is being paid to software engineering is to try and get the techniques and concepts that the small number of very good people have in this country and in other countries applied to the whole of the industry. With many people who write software, it is almost an art form and when somebody has created a programme nobody can understand, if that man leaves, you have to start again because the programme is not properly documented. It is not an engineering discipline. You do not finish up with a drawing such that another

engineer could say, 'I can understand that'. That is why attention is being given to software engineering. It is try and get an engineering approach to software' (UK House of Lords 1985, pp. 23, 41).

(23) Melody 1986.
(24) For a discussion of this general point, see Rosenberg 1976, ch. 8; for its specific application to global communications networks, see de Sola Pool 1976, pp. 48-49.
(25) Roobeek 1984, p. 27.
(26) McKinsey 1979.
(27) It is useful to recall that the present US market dominance of, and economic efficiency in, advanced communication technologies has not always been the case and only came about after the massive public spending on R & D in advanced technologies for the military during the Cold War. See Dosi 1984. I am not arguing that European nation states could have done the same thing, or could now by themselves. But as Arnold and Guy 1986 point out in their discussion of the ESPRIT programme, both the US and Japan are much more overtly nationalistic in their R & D support programmes than Europeans have so far been prepared to be.
(28) Morgan and Webber 1986.
(29) Morgan and Webber 1986.
(30) Hills 1985, p. 13.
(31) Dang Nguyen 1985.
(32) Borrus et al. 1985.
(33) McKinsey 1979.
(34) Dang Nguyen 1985, pp. 122-130.
(35) See Beale (forthcoming).
(36) See McKinsey 1979.
(37) See Arnold and Guy 1986 for a discussion of this problem in France. Other reports have confirmed this same problem in the case of the UK Alvey programme.
(38) See Beale (forthcoming).
(39) Trades unions have been involved in negotiations in some countries and corporations over the introduction of communication technologies and networks as they appear in the workplace: see Etui 1982. However, they have not been involved in the discussion of the formation of programmes for their development (this being explained sometimes by both management and unions as an issue for management) though they are, of course, in a number of ways users of the technologies.
(40) See Rallo 1984 for an example of how the Communities have become an actor in this way in the case of the aerospace industry.
(41) See, for example, the discussion in Leakey 1986 for an elaboration of this point in the case of business users.

References

Ancelin, C., Frawley, J., Hartley, J., Pichault, F., Pop, P., and Qvortrup, L. (eds.),
    Social Experiments With Information Technology FAST Occassional Papers of the Proceedings of the EEC Conference on Social Experiments with Information Technology, Odense, Denmark, 13-15 January 1986 (Brussels: Commission of European Communities, 1986).
Arnold, E., and Guy, K.,
    Parallel Processing: National Strategies in IT (London: Frances Pinter, 1986).
Arnold, E., and Guy, K.,
    'A Preliminary Comparison of IT programmes - A Report to the Alvey Directorated' (Falmer, Brighton, England: Science Policy Research Unit, University of Sussex, March 1985) (mimeo.).
Arthur D. Little Inc.,
    World telecommunications Study: 1980-1990, Vol. 1. Cambridge, Mass.: Arthur D. Little, 1979).
Beale, J.,
    'Information Technologies and European Integration', in MacLean, J., and Tooze, R. (eds.), **The International Political Economy of Information and Technology** (forthcoming).
Borrus, M., Bar, F., Cogez, P., Thoresen, A.B., Warde, I., and Yoshikawa, A.,
    'Telecommunications Development in Comparative Perspective: The New telecommunications in Europe, Japan and the US', Paper originally prepared for the Office of technology Assessment, US Congress (Stanford, California: Brie, Stanford University, May 1985) (mimeo.).
Cruise O'Brien, R., and Helleiner, G.K.,
    'The Political Economy of Information in a Changing International Economic Order', **International Organization**, Vol. 34, No. 4 (Autumn 1980).
Dang Nguyen, G.,
    'Telecommunications: a Challenge to the Old Order', in Sharp, M. (ed.), **Europe and the New Technologies: Six Case Studies in Innovation and Adjustment** (London: Frances Pinter, 1985).
Deutsch, K.,
    The Analysis of International Relations (London: Prentice Hall, 1968).
Dost, G.,
    Technical Change and Industrial Transformation: the theory and an application to the semiconductor industry (London: MaxMillan, 1984).

Elliott, F.E., and Wood, P.W.,
'The International, Transfer of technology and Western European Integration', **Research in International Business and Finance,** Vol. 2 (1981).

European Trades Union Institute,
Negotiating Technological Change (Etui: Brussels, 1982).

Haas, E.B.,
The Uniting of Europe: Political, Social and Economic Forces, 1950-1957 (Stanford, Calif.: Stanford University press, 1958).

Hills, J.,
'Industrial Policy and the Information Technology Sector', draft paper to the Greater London Council Conference on technology Strategy, London, November, 1985.

House of Lords,
Select Committee on the European Communities, ESPRIT (European Strategic Programme for Research and Development in Information technology) with minutes of evidence (HMSO: London, 1985).

Junne, G.,
'The Emerging Global Grid - The Political Dimension', in Hamelink, C., and Muskens, G. (eds.), **Global Networks and European Communities: Applied social and comparative approaches** (Tilburg: IVA, Institute for Social Research at Tilburg University; The Hague: ISS, Institute of Social Studies, 1986).

Leakey, D.M.,
'A European Strategy for Equipment Procurement', Paper presented at the ESRC Communications Policy Research Conference, Windsor, England, June 18-20 1986 (London Centre for Information and Communication Policy Studies: Polytechnic of Central London, London, UK).

Logica LTD.,
Telematica 1982: Information Technology Markets in Western Europe, Module D: The Transmission Market Review Report (London: Logica Ltd., 1982).

Maral, G., and Bousquet, M.,
Satellite Communications Systems (Chichester, England: John Wiley & Sons, 1986).

McKinsey & Company,
A call to Action - The European Information Technology Industry (Brussels: Commission of the European Communities, January 1983).

Martin, J.,
Future Developments in Telecommunications (Englewood Cliffs, New Jersey: Prentice-Hall, 1977, 2nd e.d).

Melody, W.,
'Dealing With Global Networks: Some Aspects and Public Policy of International Markets', in **Collected Papers of the EEC Fast COM 8 Conference, 'Dealing With Global Networks',** Tilburg University,

Tilburg, Holland, October 1986 (Tilburg: IVA, Tilburg University, 1986).

Morgan, K., and Webber, D.,
'Divergent Paths: Political Strategies for Telecommunications in Britain, France, and the Federal Republic of Germany', **Working Paper Series on Government-Industry Relations,** No. 6 (Falmer, Brighton, England: School of Social Sciences, University of Sussex, September 1986).

Pelton, J.N.,
Global Talk: The Marriage of Computer, World Communications and Man (Brighton, England: Harvester, 1981).

Rallo, J.,
'The European Communities Industrial Policy Revisited: The Case of Aerospace', **Journal of Common Market Studies,** Vol. XXII, No. 3, March 1984.

Roobeek, A.J.M.,
'Changes in the Structure of the Telecommunications Industry', Vakgroep bedrijfseconomie, Universiteit van Amsterdam: Amsterdam, 1984.

Rosenberg, N.,
Perspectives on technology (London: Cambridge University press, 1976).

Sola Pool, I. de,
'International Aspects of Computer Communications', **Telecommunications Policy,** Vol. 1, No. 1 (December 1976).

Soroos, M.S.,
'The Commons in the Sky: the radio spectrum and the geosynchronous orbit as issues in global policy', **International Organization,** Vol. 36, No. 3 (Summer 1982).

THE EMERGING GLOBAL GRID – THE POLITICAL DIMENSION

Gerd Junne

There is no clear dividing line between the political dimension and other dimensions of the emerging global grid, i.e. the worldwide integration of hitherto distinct services (such as voice, data, facsimile, telex, radio and video) into a global digital telecommunication network. There are at least three reasons for the intrinsically political character of a global grid:

a)   Most large telecommunications networks are state-owned, and public agencies have a monopoly in long-distance telecommunications in most states.

b)   The development of telecommunications technology is closely linked to the development of military equipment. About half of the research and development expenditures on telecommunications are spent on military purposes.

c)   Telecommunication networks have become increasingly important means to influence public opinion in mass democracies. The discussion on the ownership of the telecommunication networks and the control of telecommunication programmes, therefore, is a discussion on the distribution of political power.

In this contribution, I shall concentrate on three issues. I shall first present competing views on the political implications of the global grid. I shall then present a number of arguments in favour and against an exclusively public, a totally private and some form of 'hybrid' telecommunication system. Finally I shall discuss advantages and disadvantages of national, European and international (global) telecommunication equipment procurement strategies.

1.   Competing views of the political implications

Public opinion and experts are highly divided with regard to the political implications of the expansion of existing telecommunication networks into a global grid. Advocates believe that the new media can contribute to more pluralism, more participation, more democracy and more national and international political integration. Scepticists are convinced that the opposite may be the case. They fear that mainstream-views will dominate the commercial media, participation will give way to passiveness, possibilities of manipulation will increase, and power will become even more concentrated. Some of these arguments will be elaborated below. The result of this discussion will not be the simple truth that reality will be somewhere in between the two extremes. All too often, efforts to come to some kind of technology assessment end up this way. First, possible positive and negative effects are listed and then a balance is drawn in order to see whether the positive of negative effects will dominate. In reality, however, positive and negative effects will not offset each other, because they often affect different groups. New telecommunication technologies, for example, can at the same time lead to better access to information and to less access. This is not contradictory, because positive and negative effects will be different for different groups. And since politics deals with the question 'Who gets what, when and how ?', it is the distribution of seemingly contradictory effects of the global grid over different groups which has to be dealt with under the heading of 'the political dimension' of the global grid.

More and less information: The integration and expansion of telecommunication services will provide a larger variety of choice between different audiovisual programmes and direct access to a large number of data banks and information services. In principle, therefore, the amount of information available and accessible will increase, for those who feel the need for it, can formulate their information needs precisely enough, are able to find their way through the search routines, and are able to pay for it.

At the same time, the large choice between different programmes, and the fact that many programmes can be received around the clock will probably increase the inclination of many people to extend the time they spend on consuming television and video programmes. The easy access to diversion can increase passiveness. It can undermine the will to go out for additional information. The additional information available will also remain largely confined to well-educated people, because even data banks with user-friendly interactive programmes can only be used by those who have enough background knowledge to specify and find what they are looking for. The global grid will therefore only increase the access of the better educated to additional information.

For children who spend a considerable share of their time in front of television, it may increase their access to information, but it will reduce their possibilities to gather personal experience. In this way, it may in the long run reduce their individual autonomy necessarily based on their own experience and increase alienation (1).

Political implications of a new organization of work: A global grid will not only make more information accessible (for some), it will also make it accessible practically everywhere. This will have a profound impact on the organization of work. 'Telework' will make it possible to carry out many administrative jobs (and even research work) at home. For some groups, this will provide increasing flexibility to combine work and private life (e.g. single parents with young children), and it may fit well into the life-style of 'yuppies' (young upward-oriented professionals). For those employees, however, who carry out simple administrative activities and have less leeway to define the content of their work, less separation between work and private life may lead to less relaxation and more stress and may even constitute a health hazard. In home-working the risks of isolation and 'hierarchical contact' through central office control are greater than with other forms of work. 'Trade unions also fear (...) that such work may pose a threat to employees' security and rights as it could seriously undermine the trade unions' organisations' (2). Increasing individualization would thus imply a shift in the political balance between capital and labour in favour of the employers.

More or less political participation: Better access to information in principle provides better chances for political participation. Protagonists of advanced telecommunication networks maintain that political participation can also be improved by the fact that the new grid would allow two-way communication instead of the traditional one-way communication between sender and receiver who cannot switch roles. Viewers of a political debate, for example, could at any moment express at the push of a button whether they agree or disagree with a specific viewpoint, or whether they are in favour of one or the other party. Political leaders, as a consequence, could respond much faster to the preference of their constituencies.

Leaving the question aside whether such an instant involvement in political decision making would really improve the results of the political process, it is highly questionable whether this could ever be more than a token participation. It could give people the idea of being able to participate, whereas it would not really. Instead, it might increase the range of instruments for political manipulation.

More of less pluralism: The argument that the global grid may reinforce the instruments of political manipulation can be countered by pointing out that this would only be the case if ownership or use of the new media was monopolized. Advocates of the advantages of the global grid argue that, instead, the chance to receive a larger variety of programmes will automatically increase pluralism. Pluralism would be enhanced as more regional and local programmes could be produced. This, however, is a very open question. Given the financial situation of the public agencies, most of the additional information will come from private enterprises. In order to finance the programmes, they will have to compete for viewers. They will therefore have to adapt their programmes to the mainstream taste. Additional programmes accordingly will mostly offer 'more of the same'. Pluralism could increase, however, as more regional and local programmes could be produced.

International conflicts or integration ? The new telecommunication technology will provide ever more people with the possibility to receive programmes from other countries. This would give them the chance to know other countries better and thus prepare the ground for more international understanding. The possibility to follow foreign radio programmes, however, has not had the same effect in the past. To the degree that foreign programmes are followed at all, they can easily lead to a more pronounced perception of the national differences and can accentuate rather than reduce existing prejudices. Whether international understanding is promoted or undermined by international programmes depends very much on the pre-existing level of understanding.

The actual dominance of American films in national programmes in many countries of the world has shown that the impact on consumption patterns is more important than the impact on political attitudes. Standardization of world consumer demand, to which a global grid certainly would make a contribution, however, would have rather ambivalent consequences for international political relations. It will probably lead to increased imports in countries with a comparatively weak industry. The eventually resulting balance of payments deficit may lead to protectionist measures that may increase international conflicts.

More or less economic concentration: Standardization of consumer demand would fuel the worldwide concentration process, since smaller companies that specialize on the production for national markets with special demands would lose out against international competitors. Economic concentration may not seem to belong to the 'political' implications of the global grid, but since concentration processes are so crucial for the distribution of political power as well, the topic is included here.

Advocates of the new technologies argue that they will help in at least two ways to counteract the tendencies towards increasing economic concentration: (a) The global grid will make many new services possible, a development which creates many chances for newly-formed companies. (b) The intrinsic disadvantages of small and medium-sized companies that are not able to keep a specialized staff for market research and similar tasks, could be balanced by a better access to general data banks that could reduce the backlog of information available to smaller companies in comparison to large corporations.

On the other hand, the new telecommunication facilities provide large companies with much better instruments to control not only their own subsidiaries and affiliates at a distance. They help them also to co-ordinate production of their suppliers. In that way, formally independent subcontractors become more and more integrated into the realm of large corporations that dominate their decisions without having to participate in their capital. Since the new facilities tend to be capital intensive, large companies can make faster use of the new facilities and thereby increase their advantage with regard to smaller companies. While some small new companies may be stimulated by the creation of a global grid and a few others will see their comparative disadvantage reduced, the general concentration process is likely to speed up rather than slow down as a result of the installation of a global digital telecommunication network.

2. Public or private telecommunication systems ?

The telecommunication sector itself has always shown a very high concentration. This is true for the ownership of the telecommunication network, which has been a monopoly in most countries virtually from its inception. But it is also true for the telecommunication industry that produces telecommunication equipment. In most countries, a close symbiosis between the public carrier and a few private equipment suppliers has developed. In this part, I shall deal with the question of ownership of the carrier. Part 3 will deal with the organisation of the equipment industry.

The case for private telecommunication systems: Governments almost everywhere thought that a public monopoly was 'the best way to provide an essential service fairly and universally, with the economic benefits of scale and uniform standards'. Today, however, 'three major countries - the United States, Japan and Britain - have concluded that with technology and user needs growing more sophisticated, competition is the best way to exploit telecommunications in all its burgeoning forms' (3) that become possible as a result of the global grid.

Lack of competition has been seen as a major reason for the slow application of new technologies, and major corporate users of telecommunication facilities have formed strong lobbies that pressured for deregulation. Their main arguments are:

(a)   Deregulation would stimulate technological progress.

(b)   Competition would reduce prices for telecommunication services and consequently would help to fight inflation.

(c)   Lower prices for telecommunication would attract large consumers of telecommunication services (banks, insurance companies) and company headquarters of international corporations.

Reasons to maintain a public system: There are strong arguments as well to maintain a public telecommunication system:

(a)   Deregulation may not lead to more competition but to the replacement of a public monopoly by a private monopoly. British Telecom, for example, 'is still a long way from losing all its monopoly privileges' in spite of privatization in November 1984. Although Mercury Ltd., a subsidiary of Cable and Wireless, 'is now competing for business customers, (...), its market share is unlikely to exceed 3% to 4% by 1990, and others cannot enter the arena until then' (4). The promotion of British Telecom as a 'national champion' in the telecommunication industry is rather inconsistent with moves to encourage competition in the domestic market (5).

(b)   It is true that more competition could lead to lower prices for telecommunication services, at least for some services. Competition will concentrate on the lucrative business (long-range) communication. Prices for less profitable services to peripheral regions, however, may increase as a result. Telecommunication prices probably would decline as a consequence of deregulation, because income from the telecommunication branch has often been used to cross-subsidize other postal services and to contribute to general government income. Lower tariffs for long-range and business communication therefore probably would lead to an increase of charges for postal (mail) services and local calls as well as tax increases. Overall inflationary pressure, as a consequence, would not be reduced. The burden of higher prices would only shift away from business and onto the shoulders of private consumers.

(c)   Increased competition will lead to higher productivity and better services of the telecommunication carriers. The other side of the coin, however, will be that many jobs will be lost. During the three years preceding privatization, British Telecom brought the workforce down already by 15,000, and it is reckoned that continued cuts over the next four years will run at 5,000 a year (of a total of 240,000 in 1985). No wonder that almost two-thirds of BT's workforce opposed privatization (6). Even NTT (Nippon Telegraph and Telephone Public Corp.), which was regarded to be one of the most efficient telephone monopolies in use before privatization on April 1, 1985, is said to have 100,000 employees (out of 330,000) too many on the payroll (7).

(d)   Another argument against privatization is that any duplication of the tremendous investment in telecommunication networks would imply very high - unnecessary - social costs.

Hybrid systems as the most likely outcome: While exclusively public telecommunication systems may provide the best guarantee for equal services at equal price throughout the country, some of the critical arguments against a public monopoly are probably valid. They may slow down technological progress, although this is not necessarily the case. Without public ownership, the large-scale modernization of the French telephone system in the 1970's, for example, would not have been possible. It can be argued, however, that without a public monopoly, it could never have become so backward either as it was before 'the great leap forward'. In order to combine the advantages of public and private ownership and avoiding the disadvantages of both, most countries probably will end up with some kind of 'hybrid' system which could guarantee sufficient competition while avoiding the excessive consequences of cut-throat competition. A hybrid system could mobilize investment from public as well as private sources and thereby speed up the extension of the telecommunication network, while it would guarantee the continuation of non-commercial services.

The highly ideological debate about private v. public ownership of the network probably does not lead very far. The political question, instead, will be how a hybrid system should look like that combines the virtues of both without sharing their vices as well.

3.   National,   European,   and   international   telecommunication strategies

A hybrid telecommunication system would leave more space for private companies, but which companies ? Should only 'national' companies be allowed to participate, or should foreign companies be able to compete on equal footing ?

Preferential procurement from national companies: It is not only the public monopoly of the carriers, it is also their 'too cosy' relationship with a very select number of private equipment suppliers that is blamed for retarding the technical progress of the telecommunication systems. If procurement policies favour national suppliers only, new technologies may be introduced rather late. National suppliers that do not have a large share of the world market, are only able to spent a limited amount on research and development and will not be able to realize optimal economies of scale in production. As a consequence, they will have difficulties to keep up with technological developments, and the equipment delivered will be comparatively expensive. This will have an impact on the prices of new services. Relatively high prices will dampen demand for these services. As a consequence, supply as well as demand may be negatively affected by too strong a concentration on national suppliers.

The development of a new generation of digital switching equipment, e.g.

is estimated to cost about $ 1 billion. If a 'normal' share of seven procent of sales is devoted to research and development, sales of about $ 14,3 billion would be necessary to recuperate R+D expenditures. Even the three largest markets in Europe, however, do not have the volume that would allow to earn the R+D investment back (see figure 1).

Figure 1
European market fragmentation.

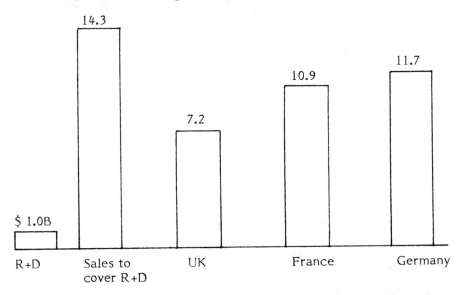

Source: Mackintosh, Telephone Engineer & Management, McKinsey analysis.

The pressures are strong, nevertheless, to restrict procurement to 'national' companies or at least to companies producing in the same country. This would secure employment which might be lost if the market was opened up for international competitors. Some of the domestic firms might even be threatened in their existence, if they were to lose the protected home market, since they would not get any orders abroad, or can only win orders from abroad on the basis of the economies of scale they can realize because of the guaranteed production volume for the domestic market (8).

Opening the market for international suppliers: The same forces that are in favour of deregulation are also in favour of opening up national markets for international suppliers, for the same reasons. Only competition from (or co-operation with) international suppliers would provide access to the most advanced telecommunication technology and would allow the largest extension of new services (which depend on the latest hardware).

In the European case, however, a closer co-operation with American and Japanese companies could lead to increasing dependence on U.S. and Japanese firms. Reliance on technology developed elsewhere would probably imply a reduction of research and development activity in Europe itself. This would undermine the future position of the companies involved and would make them become rather weak negotiation partners.

A closer co-operation with American and Japanese firms may also endanger the future of the European component industry. The European chip industry could decline if more use was made of foreign technology and consequently of chips produced elsewhere.

Ironically enough, the opening up of the market for overseas supplies in some cases is just the result of efforts to create a strong and independent national telecommunication industry. In France, for example, the preference for strong 'national champions' has led to a situation in which only one large telecommunication equipment producer has been left (CIT-Alcatel). In order to avoid dependence on a single supplier, the French DGT (Directorat Général de Télécommunication) had to look for another supplier outside France, and chose APT (AT + T and Philips Telecommunicatiebedrijven B.V.) (9).

A European market for telecommunication equipment: Creation of a European market for telecommunication equipment may be a solution in between which would avoid the shortcomings of the concentration on national suppliers without running the risk to be wound up by international competition. The creation of a European market for telecommunication equipment could be phased in such a way that it would provide companies with a chance to adapt. It would probably also lead to a smaller number of telecommunication equipment producers: of about 12 European companies that have developed digital switching equipment, probably not many more than four would be left (10). But this could be achieved by arrangements among the existing companies that would help to spread the negative effects more evenly.

A certain concentration process is necessary in order to avoid the tremendous duplication of research and development that actually takes place in Europe. If some kind of division of labour could be agreed upon between the different research centers, the same research potential could be used to speed up technological development and to achieve an important technological edge with regard to American and Japanese equipment producers.

Closer co-operation among European telecommunication firms would better fit into a common European technology policy. If most European telecommunication companies gave priority to bilateral co-operation with American and Japanese companies, a European technology policy could hardly get off the ground. Advances in telecommunication technology, however, are crucial for many other fields as well: advances in factory and office automation depend to a large extent on advances in telecommunication technology (that would link 'islands' of automation into integrated systems).

Do bilateral co-operation agreements with American and Japanese companies and a European technology policy contradict each other ? Yes, to a certain extent. The cooperation agreements may render the means of a European technology policy ineffective and reduce the motivation of the companies concerned to participate in European programmes. A European technology policy would no longer increase the relative advantage (or reduce the relative disadvantage) of European firms, because (a) common standards and regulations would be to the benefit of the outside cooperation partners as well, (b) European government procurement and infrastructure investment would imply (at least indirect) orders to companies from the United States and Japan, and (c) the knowledge accumulated with the help of subsidized research and development would leak away to co-operation partners from outside Europe. Furthermore, the motivation of European companies to help to elaborate European programmes may be reduced, because their own bilateral cooperation agreements with American and Japanese partners would already fulfill the needs to which the European programmes would cater. And scarce management time can make it difficult to follow-up both with sufficient energy.

In reality, however, at least the last fear is not borne out by reality. Philips and Olivetti, for example, two companies that both have linked up with ATT, are still ardent proponents of a European technology policy. First, as any other company, they are interested in any substantial outside funding they can get as long as the conditions are acceptable. Second, they may need the European programmes to improve their position **within** their co-operation agreements in order to become or remain an interesting partner and to avoid being pressed into the minor position of a junior partner.

In addition, **only** the cooperation with partners outside Europe may keep the restructuring of the European telecommunications industry within politically acceptable limits. If European companies can share the research expenditures for new systems with outside partners, a lower total sales volume will be sufficient to earn the outlays back. That means that more than only four European telecommunication companies would be able to survive. This would ease the tensions that otherwise unavoidably would create obstacles to a common European telecommunication policy. Besides, only the close cooperation with outside firms may make it possible to continue procurement policies favouring European companies without running the risk of strong American objections. If American firms profit from these policies via their link-up with European firms, trade conflicts may be softened.

General European competitiveness, especially of the ever more important sector of new services, may be supported more efficiently if the most sophisticated telecommunication infrastructure is installed, no matter by whom it is provided. National or European support for the competitiveness of the European equipment producers may be at the cost of support of the economy in general, if this means that the installation of a first class infrastructure is postponed. This, however, does not so much depend on

the level of sophistication of the equipment suppliers but on the investment expenditures by the - mainly national carriers. In order to increase
these expenditures, a strong political backing is necessary. If many of the
orders to be expected go to foreign companies, it may be more difficult to
bring a strong enough political coalition about that would support the
financing of the new infrastructure.

Probably, a phased strategy would have the best chances to succeed and to
combine the advantages of opening up the markets at a European and at a
world scale. A controlled reduction of trade barriers (11) could be combined with synchronic steps of deregulation in different Member States of
the European Community and a common technology policy that would link
advances in telecommunications to developments in other fields. This
could strengthen the world market position of many European producers
not only in the field of telecommunications. It could, however, entail
political conflicts with the United States which certainly would protest
against any opening of national markets restricted to other European
producers. The telecommunication companies themselves probably would
be the first that want to avoid such a conflict, as long as they try to get a
foothold on the American market for telecommunication equipment
which accounts for about 40 per cent of the world market.

The conflict with the United States, however, could be limited if the
opening of the market could be phased in such a way that it would finally
lead to the opening of the market for American companies as well, which
would form less of a problem in a situation in which European companies
have become strengthened by closer co-operation and a better division of
labour.

4.   Conclusion

Three questions have been tackled in this contribution in order to identify
areas for further discussion and research:

(a)   More research is necessary on the possible impact of the creation of
a global grid for different groups of the population. It cannot be taken for
granted that the positive effects will outweigh the negative effects.
Possible negative effects will have to be identified and measures have to
be discussed that would reduce them or compensate for them.

(b)   The discussion of 'private' v. 'public' telecommunication carriers
remains by far too abstract (and by that too ideological). Given the
different national telecommunication systems in Europe and the different
level of deregulation in different Member States of the EC, it can be taken
for granted that the European telecommunication system will be a hybrid
system. The political task is then to define in much more detail the
characteristics of a system that would combine the virtues of both, a
public as well as a private system, without incorporating the vices of both
as well.

(c)   The question of monopoly or deregulation with regard to the telecommunication carriers is closely related to the question of opening the

market for producers of telecommunication equipment from abroad. Whereas a strategy of limiting procurement to national suppliers in a time of fast technological progress may hamper the progress of the national economy more than support it, a total opening of the market may easily have effects that are not welcome either. A gradual strategy of 'Europeanization' of the market for telecommunication equipment may be a feasible strategy in between, which should be formulated in such a way that conflicts with the United States are minimized.

Notes

(1) Cf. Mettler-Meibom, B., **Breitbandtechnologie. Uber die Chancen sozialer Vernunft in technologiepolitischen Entscheidungsprozessen,** Opladen, 1986.
(2) **Commission of the European Communities, Directorate General for Research and Documentation, New Technologies and Social Consequences,** memo, 27 March 1985, p. 12.
(3) **International Management,** April 1985, p. 32.
(4) 'The sole exception to this ruling is Racal Vodafone Ltd., now selling cellular phones in competition with BT, and with hopes of capturing 50% of a market potentially worth up to $ 1.1 billion over the next five years.
The legislative protection enjoyed by BT even extends to the particularly lucrative area of value added networks which allow the movement of information between farflung sets of incompatible equipment. Outsiders cannot use BT lines to offer such services until at least July 1989. Among other things, the breathing space will give BT time to sort out tariff systems that can stave off future competitors'. **International Management,** April 1985, p. 40.
(5) Cf. 'BT as national champion', **Financial Times,** 4 February 1986.
(6) **International Management,** April 1985, p. 33.
(7) **International Management,** April 1985, p. 32.
(8) Cf. Webber, D., **The politics of telecommunications de-regulation in the Federal Republic of Germany,** manuscript, January 1986.
(9) Roobeek, A. and R. van Tulder, **Telecommunicatie: Over grote bedrijven in kleine landen,** manuscript (to appear in 'De Ingenieur', May 1986), p. 17.
(10) Roobeek and Van Tulder, p. 14.
(11) Telekommunikation und nichttarifäre Handelshemnisse in der EG, in: **Die Weltwirtschaft,** 2/1985.

PART 3

APPLICATIONS IN THE PUBLIC
AND CONSUMER INTERESTS

ON SOCIAL SOFTWARE

Gareth Locksley

1.   Introduction

The term 'social' rarely, of ever, appears in the vocabulary of 'computer-speak'. When it does crop up it is usually uttered in the context of the transformation of society for better or worse. Normally, 'social' is juxtaposed with 'consequences'. Circumstances, events and conditions are received as an outcome of technological change and society eventually accepts these. Underlying this course of advancement is the primacy of economic necessity in a harshly competitive global markets such that the social invoice can only be picked-up once the commercial conditions have been resolved satisfactorily. This paper rejects this concept of 'social' and its relation to technology. Here it is argued that as a matter of the highest priority the social usage of the new technologies and the global grids must become integrated with their economic exploitation. That is to say that social objectives must now be given equal weighting with those economic imperatives that have dominated the growth and development of the grids. The case does not rest on any appeal to any moral position or even that tax-payers should get some return for their investments. Instead it is argued that unless the social dimension is planned into the grids their further development will be severely restricted.

Undeniably, the major forces of development in the fields of information and communications technologies (ICT) have been economic because they can express effective demand. The rate of development in the ICT has been exceptional but driven by economic forces a boundary is being approached both in terms of how much further it can go and where they can be applied. The limit of the use of the grids is caused by the restricted availability software. Economic considerations have produced a narrow field of application that has largely been fully exploited. What is pro-grammable has been programmed. The software of 'intelligence' is a sickly infant. Further the risks of additional development are high and unattrac-tive so the child may never reach adolescence. But the calculus of social software are different though the results can be applied in the economic field thereby providing the prospects for a major advance in productivity. It is not just that social software development will enable advances in the economic sphere. If the European Communities build a new electronic super highway there must be uses for it unless it is to go the way of agricultural interventions. Social software will allow all citizens to drive along the freeway making the grids all that more economical to everyone. Without social software the ICT may become the playthings of the few, with social software they may become an instrument of real advance in the commercial and social aspects of European society.

In 1985 France, West Germany, the UK, Italy, the Netherlands, Belgium, Denmark and Spain spent Ł 55.2 billion in data processing with the first four countries' expenditure equivalent to 72% of the total for Western Europe. With the exception of Spain this DP spending amounted to 2.0% or over of GDP (1). For the UK the figure was Ł 12.3 billion or 2.7% of GDP and for France Ł 12.5 or 2.4%.

In 1985 the total market for mobile communications in the same countries (less Spain) was estimated at Ł 300 million or $ 427 million (2). The projected European market for telecommunications equipment for 1987 is $ 17.2 billion at 1979 prices (3). Another estimate puts the total tele-communications market including services at $ 79.4 billion for Europe (or CEPT's membership) in 1984 (4).

These sums largely represent non-household, business and government spending. But the penetration of information and communication technology (ICT) related products has extended from these major centres of application to the home. Together France, the UK, West Germany and Italy, with over 60 million, account for more than 15% of the world's total population of television sets (5). Many households in member states can boast all or some of the following: a telephone, television, video recorder or home computer. Telephone and tv penetration in the UK is over 90% and the rate of VCR take-up is more than 40% whilst around 20% of households have home computers.

There is a rush in the Community to prepare the way for the total linkage of household, government and business use (and investment) of the ICT's and all their various forms of communication from sophisticated com-puter-to-computer-global talk to plain-old-voice-and-watching-the-tv. The ISDN system will offer this prospect and it will herald a new era of communications. Much of the funds for the implementation of the new grids are sourced from the public purse and represent a social investment. There are some obvious questions that follow from these developments. The answers will influence the future course of communications together with the future construction of associated ICT products with knock-on effects for the economic base and social system of the Twelve.

Of the many relevant questions only two are partially considered here. Firstly, what makes all the ICT products work ? And secondly, when they are working, what will they be doing ?

2.   Software and functions

The digital hardware of the global grids are machines. They are so much wiring, plastic and casing or so many printed circuit boards, chips, resistors, connectors, buttons, knobs and bits of metal. The inside of a home computer looks much the same as the inside of a tv or VCR. A mainframe computer is very similar to a telephone exchange when the case is taken off. A cable tv system is almost the clone of a telephone network and both are analogus to a geographically dispersed computer. Even a communications satellite bares a passing resemblance to a solar powered pocket calculator. But these machines are different from the pre-digital machines not only physically but functionally - they do more. The same set of components can be re-arranged or supplemented or enhanced to produce a different machine capable of performing a dif-ferent dedicated function though sharing a common function. An auto-matic teller machine (ATM) in a hole in the wall can perform financial transactions with a customer whilst possessing some of the functions of a telephone kiosk. Alternatively a collection of components can be 'fixed' and then perform a multitude of functions. The general purpose computer can run the payroll of an organisation and/or its stock and/or the machines on the factory floor. It is the Swiss army knife of the digital age. Pre-digital machines have very restricted functions and are unable to perform this re-assembly or become integrated. A lathe cannot become a truck or even a saw, nor would these machines work in conjunction branching from a common root.

The flexibility of digital machines derives firstly from the nature of the material they handle - the common on/off 0/1 electronic impulse. This is a considerable advantage and a 'revolutionary' step. But this is only to say that trucks, cars and aeroplanes run on fossil hydrocarbon. The major advance comes from software and it is this that makes the machines work. Digital machines sharing a common pool of components can carry out their many tasks because software facilitates, instructs and organises their operations. Take away the software and we are largely left with so much wiring, casing, plastic etc. Software provides the flexibility, the usefulness and the 'value added' to digital machines.

All the grids - global, national, regional, local - all their hardware - tv's, VCR's, computers, exchanges - all they collectively do is ultimately a matter of software. This is very obvious with VCR's and tv's where the rented or broadcast movie is software and provides value to the viewer. But it is exactly the same for the computer user where the software now sells the hardware in most instances. Buyers are unconcerned with the technical specification of computers instead they ask 'what will it do ?' meaning what functions will the software perform. Telephone networks provide value by allowing communication. Here an exchange routes the messages and links the communicators. These functions are performed in the digital exchange by software (6). With a value added network service software is again the agent that transforms a communication by literally adding value.

The hardware of digital machines allows the realisation of the function of software - that is its specific purpose. The scope of hardware is defined by the number of different software applications that can be operationalised on an individual piece. A VCR can operationalise an infinite number of pre-recorded tapes of a particular combination of standards (of tape and tv) but its scope is limited merely to this one function and combination. An ATM can perform more tasks in that it has two-way communications facilities but its scope is still limited. In both instances this is a matter of design and their functions are deliberately dedicated though this is not necessary.

The big machines of the global grids can and do carry out a multitude of functions. They can and do incorporate the functions of the ATM and the VCR by design. The general purpose computer, be it a computer per se or a telephone exchange, is built to carry more software and to facilitate more software applications. The central notion of ISDN is more software on more digital machines. Software makes the grids work and software performs pre-designed functions - it 'does' for society. Clearly there is a choice of which functions are performed and with that there follows a choice with respect to the associated hardware which allow the operationalisation of the decision. But there is no technological determinacy to this process because digital machines and software are characterised by flexibility. Whatever the choice process the outcome defines what the grids do and the way they do it.

3. Software genres

Typically software has been categorised under two generic types: systems and applications. The former automatically controls and manages the hardware resources - bringing them into operation when needed with a view to their efficient usage. Applications software is concerned with the specific tasks of interest to the user. Applications are the 'visible' end of the software spectrum whilst systems software is 'invisible'. One important sub-category of systems software is database management systems. With computers this software organises 'whole files or individual data stored in memory, controlling access according to the needs of running programs' (7). A new development of this is the data base query system which 'gives the user direct access to information contained on a data base, according to various criteria and, possibly using instructions close to ordinary language, for which it might make use of artificial intelligence techniques ..... a data base query system constitutes a user interface for data base management system' (8).
It is usual for system software to be supplied with the hardware and to be created by the hardware manufacturer or some contracted systems house. Applications software can be packaged, custom (bespoke) or integrated. Packaged software has achieved a level of standardisation such that it can be reproduced and sold to many different users all with the same task which the package will treat in an identical manner. In such instances the development costs can be spread over a wide clientele. Custom software has been tailor made for the tasks of an individual user so that development costs fall entirely on the single user. Integrated software can be a mixture of custom and packaged software that has been put together by an intermediary along with hardware acquired from manufactures.

4. The software Boundary

Theoretically the limits for the application of the ICT's are very far off but the prospects of attaining this level of applications are constrained by software availability. There is a boundary imposed on the information society/economy and the value potential of the global grid by software - the thing that it works on or that makes the grid work. The source of this boundary is both technological and economic. Though the software sector is recognised as one of the keys to economic progress (9) we know much more about the economics of the brewing industry than of Europe's software sector. As yet there are no regular studies of the sector and only the US government seems interested in economic analyses of the EC's software sector (10). Here only a very restricted analysis of the economic and technological limits to software are presented.

Many aspects of the global grid suffer 'Baumol's disease' of rising costs (11). Here we assume two components are combined to make a final product. With one of them technology is static and with the other it is progressive. In the case of the latter productivity gains from progressive technology provides the basis of falling costs per unit of output whilst there is a relative rise in the costs of the other component. Through time the balance of the total costs of the final product switches irreversibly to those of the component with fixed technology. Frequently the fixed technology component is labour intensive and the costs of the final product rise with those of labour inexhorably. This outcome is, according to Baumol, inevitable whenever there are differentials in the rate of change of technology. For example, theatre has become relatively more expensive in terms of most other goods because there have been no major technological advances since before the time of Shakespeare.

This cost disease is clearly applicable to computers. Baumol argues as such and produces some empirical results based on the costs of computing facilities at Princeton University's computer Centre (12).

The price and size of a unit of hardware or memory has consistently tumbled. The craft mode of production of software has not experienced any technological change so that it has become progressively more expensive relative to the hardware it runs. In the mid 1950's hardware accounted for more than 80% of costs of applying ICT's but by the mid 1980's software made up nearly 90% of such costs (13). The costs of hardware are not holding back the application of the ICT's but those of software. This has an important influence on what the global grids do because this issue reduces to 'where is software allocated ?'.

Allocative mechanisms are well understood by economists. Their model indicates that resources are allocated to those activities that provide the highest returns over costs (risk adjusted). Where the private sector makes these choices the returns will be measured in terms of monetary income. Only public sector decisions on the allocation of software may reflect wider considerations. This places the public sector even closer to the centre of the global grids because the public purse is at the same time the main source of funds for many activities centred on the ICT's.

A technological boundary arises from the nature of computer science. As yet we can only model those activities that can be expressed precisely as a list of logical steps. Such software is analogous to the factory assembly system. The direction of software application has been strongly influenced by this constraint and market forces, which in combination have overproduced in the accounting application and underproduced elswhere. Technological restrictiveness is being eased by developments in the software of artificial intelligence but the focus of software will be guided by market forces.

5. The software focus

Global grids are grids of software which both manages and provides the content of the grids. We can examine software from the demand (user) and supply (creator) aspects. Some users will also be the creators of software but the decision calculus will be the same whatever the organisational arrangement. There are two basic elements of the decision: a) what can be modelled and b) the costs versus the benefits of modelling. A further dimension can be added to the calculus by discriminating between the public and private sectors.

In the private sectors of supply and demand all decisions will be made on economic bases with a view to expanding income through a combination of cost reduction and revenue expansion. In these circumstances software will be applied in order to raise profits. Users will be concerned with cost effective solutions to internal administrative tasks that can be modelled or for which a manual exists. They will also look to software and the grids for solutions to their tasks of dealing with the external world. This could involve marketing, the delivery of services and the collection of information. The decision to make or buy software will reflect the least cost calculus. But the demand for software and associated grids is formly founded on their contribution to private sector income.

The supply side of the private software market will also be focussed on income which can only be achieved by meeting the needs of users. The bespoke mode of software creation is in some ways less advantageous than the packaged mode for the supplier. Firms desire a continuing presence in the market rather than a 'one off' entrance because they prefer income **streams** which are only achieved by a lengthy existance. By definition bespoke software is 'one off' whilst packaged software offers the prospect of continuing sales and income streams. Mass markets now become important to the software creator. This holds for the tv/video programma or filmmaker as well as the computer software company. Gradually they will be attracted to 'niche' markets for industry specific and standardised software but they will be looking for better prices. The same conditions characterise the VANS market where a very large clientele can be served at low prices or a small number at higher prices.

The focus of software in the private sector can be termed 'economic' for it is designed to generate purely monetary returns. Applications are entirely instrumental to this end and systems software is built to ensure the machines and the grid work to realise income for the private sector. As far as this sector is concerned in answering the question: what do the grids do ? They are used to earn income. The global grids of this sector are economic grids of economic software and hardware.

In the public sector the grids perform a similar function along with some additional duties. The public sector may not be driven by the profit motive but it is still parsimonious. Just like the private sector it will look to software to provide least cost solutions to its internal administrative tasks and for its dealings with the external environment. The public sector has many more 'clients' than any single private sector corporation. The largest employer in Europe (excluding the Red Army) is Britain's National Health Service whose clients are the entire population of the UK. The internal and external tasks of the NHS are overwhelmingly administrative and the function of the software is to minimise the costs of these duties whilst attempting to achieve a standard of health care. Many government department have identical software requirements. Duplication of facilities and records frequently arises. The vision of cost saving governments is a completely centralised system capable of meeting the needs of all of its departments. In these circumstances the grids and its software are again economic.

There are some aspects of government where costs are not the primary consideration. Defence is the most important case. Defence has increasingly come to rely on the ICT's and associated software. Frequently the resulting products and services have limited applications elsewhere by deem of their specialisation or for reasons of security.

Aside from the case of defence software, the forces that generate the software of the global grids are overwhelmingly economic. The focus of software is parsimony with the costs of operations or economically functional with respect to creating, maintaining or enhancing market relations. Consequently the software that exists, the hardware that it runs and the content which it provides will reflect the economic position of influential users. Clearly, governments and big business are and will be the best served by the global grids so that we now have big user economic software. Their interests could come to dominate the use of the grids.

6. Economic intensification

When the plans of member states for ISDN are realised the grids of the EC will have an enormous capacity. To this must be added the satellite capacity from France, West Germany, Luxemburg, the UK, Ireland and others capable of tv transmissions and additional forms of communications. It is pertinent to ask again, what will the grids do ? Their current focus is economic and largely comprised of intra or inter corporate, intra government and corporate: government communications. Though individuals and households form the largest segment numerically of users their economic contribution is limited. For example the biggest 300 customers of BT make up 33% of its revenues with its other millions of customers contributing the rest.

It is also pertinent to ask whether those users of the grid that value it most will have constructed or hired their own private systems in advance of the public ISDN installation. If their requirements can be met by dedicated grids specifically designed for relevant functions, there will be an economic argument to follow such a solution. The implications for the public grids is to remove traffic and push up the unit costs to the remaining users. A rational response by public grid operators is to forestall such developments by striving to meet the specific needs of these users and compete with private networks, that is to enhance the economic nature of the new grids.

Consequently, our question reduces to: is there enough economic software to utilise the capacity of the grids ? But if the new grids become more intensely economic and are primarily directed to the biggest users there follow issues related to the other goals of the EC with respect to competition policy, small firms, regional problems, social policy and European integration because such a strategy would accentuate the heavily skewed distribution of economic power. We should also note that there have been failures in the market for economic software over the grids. In September 1986 the US corporation Federal Express abandoned its ZapMail electronic document transmission service which had been a big drain on its profitability since its inception in 1984. Federal Express wrote-off $ 190 million after tax and a stock broking analyst described the move as 'enormously positive' (14). In its first issue of 1987 the **Financial Times** reported 'A much vaunted joint-venture to bring a new range of sophisticated electronic information systems to the US financial services industry has been abandoned after fewer than three years by IBM and Merril Lynch, respectively the world's largest computer company and stockbroker ..... A recent IBM-initiated study of IMNET (the service) concluded that the venture 'would not be profitable for a long, long time and might never be profitable at all" (15). Trintex a videotex service set up by IBM, Sears Roebuck and CBS is also in a parlous state and CBS has withdrawn. IBM has previously withdrawn from Satellite Business Systems (SBS) which when introduced appeared a significant market entry to the global grid market. These are only indications of the problems of successfully operating economic software in markets but the involvement of IBM should be salutary.

7. Social software

The ordinary citizen and household have played no part in the foregoing analysis yet they may be needed to use the grids. Because access to grids is provided through economic market mechanisms the individual's involvement is limited to his/her disposable income. There are services, exant and in development, that are concerned with the household and the grids. On offer are tele-shopping-banking-betting-alarm and dial-a-disk-weather-share price-guru. But the central feature of these services are that they remain firmly economic, they ease the relation between the householder and the economy or are market relations **per se.** Essentially they deal with the economic needs of the household or banks and retailers. Households have needs besides the economic though these needs can have economic repercussions. Individuals and communities of various sizes are concerned with their non-economic life in matters such as housing, comfort, health, education, leisure, enlightenment, self-expression, communication, transport, culture, and the environment. Similarly they are concerned with the various agencies and levels of government. For some the social services are particularly important. Needs are related to an individual's characteristics: age, sex, health, disability, religion, race, marital status, economic status, family circumstances, proximilty to work/family/medical care/educational establishment/seat of government/mode or transport.

In essence the needs of people are related to their social condition. Given the flexibility of the grids some of these needs could be served by the ICT's. The crucial software designed to meet these social needs would be social software and its function would be to enhance the non-economic life of citizens. This is not to say that such activites on the grid would not involve economic considerations but rather that these activities would be primarily concerned with needs arising from being a person rather than an economic unit. Naturally serving these needs would use resources, though perhaps only to a limited extent, and some form of charge system may operate. For example, a doctor's visit, even when money changes hands, is not an economic activity but is related to social needs, nevertheless there are economic ramifications to the visit.

The concept of social software is founded on the principle that there is a non-economic aspect to life that would benefit from the application of the ICT's. The global grids could provide advances for people just as they do for organisations. Information and communications can be just as useful to individuals as individuals as it is to legal entities - it is a matter of the appropriate software directed to the appropriate functions and tasks.

There is however a problem of articulation. A legal entity like a company or government agency can articulate its needs for information through the market of by fiat. It is aided in this process because it can formulate its requirements since it has clearly defined objectives and because in the market there are other entities interested in specifically meeting these needs. This is the nature of economic software. But for individuals there is an economic constraint on articulation derived from the very nature of the social need. Further, people have ever changing needs between the cradle and the grave and do not live their lives under some clearly defined objective. Due to the essential non-economic nature of many of these information requirements people are frequently ignorant of what they need, what is available and what could be available. This will hold even where there are social services and software in operation. Parsimonious government agencies may be less concerned with the take-up of services than to meet financial targets.

These special problems for social software of articulation and formulation of needs are particularly challenging. But any solution to them will not only improve social conditions but will have direct beneficial affects on the economic software sector. The following sections provide an example of social software and draw out the implications for research and product development that ensue.

8.   'Helpline 1000'

For the foreseable future the dominant form of communications between people will be voice. This has not gone unnoticed in the commercial sector. Recently Barclays Bank undertook an expensive campaign of tv commercials. Set in a futuristic hi-tech society its simple message was 'I just want to talk to somebody !'. Print, on paper rather than screen, is likely to remain an important form of communications. Brian Winston observed '..... although every word on this page has been in the clutches of various computers, from my personal word processor to the publisher's more elaborate devices, what you hold in your hands in a user-friendly, portable, randomly accessible retrieval device half a millenium old and of a design elegance unmatched by any of the vaunted machines of the 'information revolution' - a book' (16). We have already moted the penetration of the products of ICT's in the household. Any socially oriented information system should be built from this collection of household hardware, be based on voice and the printed (paper) word and be driven by social software. 'Helpline 1000' is a project that takes account of these principles.
The central features of 'Helpline 1000' are:
-    it is based on the telephone network;
-    it uses a single telephone number - 1000 - or some other appropriate number;
-    it is voice based, that is information is transmitted to the user by another person;
-    it is designed to provide information to and receive information from users and to 'match make' into;
-    the range of information that can be managed is without limit but is determined by users;
-    it addresses the information needs of the community and requires easy and universal access in the designated community;
-    it is comprised of a 'front office' and 'specialist' offices which handle all inquiries;
-    the 'Helpline 1000' system of one community can be linked to that of another;
-    it can be extended to a printed word system, again using the telephone.

At its simplest, initial phase, 'Helpline 1000' works as a clearing house. There are a very large number of organisations, many of them voluntary, in many cities which provide mostly non-economic information to ordinary households. The impact of these organisations is limited by their difficulty in reaching all those in need of their specialist information. In the UK a campaign to get a telephone number known costs about $ 200,000. The promotion of the single number '1000' for all such help and information providing organisations would represent a considerable saving and would require only small volumes of repeater campaign funds. In this system 'Helpline 1000' front office is acting as clearing house or central contact point for all the voluntary and statutory 'help' agencies.

However it is very likely that a caller will not know or be unaware of the appropriate help organisation or the range of assistance available. Equally the nature of the caller's request for information may involve more than one organisation and probably in a sequential manner. Further, the caller may be unable to articulate their exact needs or be unable to express them in a way that maps into organisations. Overcoming these problems would be a suitable task for social software.

A 'Helpline 1000' system would then work as follows. The caller rings the front office '1000' number requesting information which is not clearly defined or expressed in a fashion that does not translate to an obvious and unique help organisation. The call is answered by the 'Helpline 1000' operator in the front office whose function is to illicit the precise nature of the caller's requirements and to provide responses to these by voice. Operators are equiped with a collection of hardware and social software which will assist the operator in discovering the needs of the caller and linking these to the specialist help organisation. A series of diagnostic questions will appear on the operator's screen but he/she will talk these over the line to the caller. Extra help in the operator's task can be provided on the screen for any individual question so that the operator can express the questions in a form comprehensible to the caller. The answers to the questions will lead to another set or the best sources for the particular request. Where there are 'competitive' sources of information the choice between alternatives would be left to the caller, though he/she might ask the advice of the 'Helpline 1000' operator. All conversation between caller and operator has been spoken while the operator has been accessing the 'Helpline 1000' system and its social software. The final information provided will depend on the configuration of the 'Helpline 1000' system. The front office operator may merely pass-on another telephone number and the name of someone or the details of a form etc. Alternatively, the front office may form the entrance to a Local Area Network. Here more specific information may be provided by a specialist operator, a specialist diagnostic and data base (17).

The format outlined above is a one-way form of information transfer - requests from the public are answered. But information could also be deposited by households for access by other households and organisations. By changing slightly the social software of 'Helpline 1000' with the operators again asking some pertinent questions, people could lodge information that others will use. It may simply by 'I have an unwanted refrigeratory in working order for anyone who wants to pick it up'. Or the message could be 'I'm forming a group to organise visits to pensioners during the cold weather' which would be of interest to like minded people and pensioners. Such a facility would be especially useful in the formation of groups with common interests whose potential membership are spread throughout the community and would normally face considerable difficulties in locating each other and coming together.

The 'Helpline 1000' system with appropiate social software could also be used to 'match make' information. In these circumstance someone with an unmet information need will lodge this with the front office whereupon it will be stored in the match make basket. When an overlapping call is received it will be connected with the original and a match will be made between the two. For example a disabled person may have an interest in the theatre either as part of the staff or part of the audience. This data is lodged on record in the match making basket. At a later date a theatre group may lodge that they are interested in performing for disabled groups or are seeking disabled players. Now these two items of data can be connected and the two callers put in contact. In this way communications has been created and enhanced with the problems of articulation largely overcome. The match make process allows users to design the contents of the information stored and acts as a check on areas of where people have information related concerns that are not covered by agencies yet allows self-solutions to such deficiencies. The match make solution would be very useful for the timetabling and routeing of community bus systems. Clearly it would be possible to extend the geographic spread of the 'Helpline 1000' system by linking the individual community-based 'Helpline 1000' into a network.

Obviously there will be many instances where the information required is too much and too detailed for voice communications and a printed record will be needed. The document may be a form or medical information and records. For example, a claim form for a state benefit or housing application would be unsuitable for voice transmission. Similarly warnings about the possible side effects of a drug on certain patients, up-dates on treatment or even news of an emerging wave of a particular strain of flu and its likely victims are best communicated in printed form. A screen delivery system would not be the best response, especially if it has to be copied. However if these forms or news were stored digitally they could be dispatched through the grid. Low cost printers in conjunction with the 'Helpline 1000' network could provide a feasible solution to this type of socially demanded information. As yet it may not be economic to provide every household with such a device though it may be practical for every doctor's surgery. Printers could be installed in public libraries and the like where people could pick up their specific forms. Much depends here on the design of low cost (probably low speed) printers and on achieving suffi- cient economies of scale to bring down their cost to the point where every household could have one.

The 'Helpline 1000' system outlined here is an example of the social use of the ICT's and the need for social software. Clearly it can be introduced to support social policy. It would directly benefit people in the non-economic aspects of their lives and would represent a visible pay-off to the funds they have contributed via the tax system to the development of the ICT's. But there are likely to be secondary advantages to the economy in general as well as the health of the grids themselves.

A large scale 'Helpline 1000' system would stimulate usage of the global grid whose capacity for such application is not in doubt. The demand generated in this fashion may have a beneficial effect on the whole economic calculus of the grids by spreading their costs over a wider body of usage. Certain collolary affects would follow directly from the introduction of the 'Helpline 1000' concept. There would be numerous highly skilled jobs created in the front office and other establishments of the network for the operators. There would also be an increase in the software jobmarket for the high skills of creating the necessary diagnostic questioning routines that are important in establishing the nature of the call and the information transfer or creation. The necessary hardware would also have to be manufactured and installed. In combination this brief list of side effects amount to an economic pay-off to the social investment envisaged in the 'Helpline 1000' concept. Only a trial project and a thorough costing exercise would reveal the full scale of these.

9.   Implications for research

If has been argued here that the focus of current software and its associated hardware is economic (i.e. that it is linked to cost savings or income generation). Further, that the expansion of grids is intensifying these trends but there is a boundary to an unlimited extension of software application. The research that lies behind this focus will similarly pursue the economic bias with an emphasis on efficiency defined in economic terms. Though the range of available software, both systems and applications, is wide this body shares certain key functions. Most software is capable of handling very large volumes of data at very high speeds where there are very frequent updates and ideally tasks should be easy to model. The systems software organises the machines so that they are capable of receiving and/or delivering information from or to dispersed members of the facility. It also organises data files that are changing rapidly and providing access for change or retrieval. Applications software is designed to operate in this high speed environment and make selections from the data set on which particular tasks are performed. Security is also considered as an important aspect of the grid's software. So is the ability to communicate quickly with any member of the grid, which is equivalent to a constant update routine. All of these common functions must be performed in an economic manner which is related to the value of the particular tasks carried out. These features form the parameters of software research. But they are much less relevant to the social software concept.

'Helpline 1000' can be used to illustrate the differences and suggest certain implications for research.

In contrast to the global coverage of economic software, that of social software starts with the community - a narrow geographic concept - with the possibility of links to other communities. This would imply that Local Area Networks (LANs) are much more relevant to social software. The community-based nature of social software also implies communal access to the grid rather than any restrictions. Following this through, the hardware needs to be widely dispersed throughout the community whilst the necessary social software can be held in the front and specialist offices in the case of the 'Helpline 1000' project. In turn this introduces a cost parameter for the community's hardware, especially if it is to be available to the widest possible memebership. It also follows that the cost of use is an important consideration in the research programme to support social software. Economic parameters therefore enter into any proposal for social software but there are other features of social software that ease this constraint in comparison to those binding in economic software. However there may arise steady demand for communication beyond the immediate community and its neighbours. It is quite natural that in the European Community there will a need for social communication between widely dispersed groups with common interests. Consequently there will be a heirarchy of 'Helpline 1000' faciliteis covering ever more encompassing groups. Clearly it is essential that compatibility is achieved throughout the entire system if it is to deliver its full potential by joining communities together.

Speed is not a primary consideration for community-based grids because the time frame of communication, input and output isn ot the millisecond of the economic grids. For a household an information inquiry under the current regime may involve a days work. A bus journey to, say, the local government offices can be followed by one or more interviews, the completion and return of forms and the request for more detail from the authority - even when the individual knows his/her exact information needs. A system that can respond in minutes would represent a sizeable time saving to the user but in terms of the costs of developing such a system, slow response allows for sizeable cost savings. There are also implications for the software of routing the communications transfer. Whereas packet switching and other optimalisation techniques will make efficient and speedy use of the grids for the commercial sector, the messages of social software can be optimalised to produce least cost outcomes and utilise 'off-peak' capacity. This is especially the case when documents are sent to households. The implications for research are for slow speed hardware and software which should be less expensive to develop.

The social software of 'Helpline 1000' is not concerned with the same type of updates that obtain for economic software. Rather than a potential update of all records the 'Helpline 1000' system is likely to accumulate information and to change information far more infrequently. A form is unlikely to have its format changed weekly nor is much socially relevant information likely to change from day to day. Therefore the emphasis rests more with the ability of the system to store large volumes of data rather than to continuously change selected files.

However the special features of the 'Helpline 1000' project are the diag-nostic software of the front and specialist offices together with the match make tasks of the system. The former are far complex and match making can be conceived as a form of search procedure on key words. To determine these keys the original front office software will have to guide the operator to the appropriate classification and storage. Consequently the heart of the 'Helpline 1000' example of social software is the screen guidance given to operators which allows them to relate to both the caller and the machine. This software is a form of expert system since it will be providing 'reasoned' questions and answers initiated by itself, the operator and the caller. Its most important task will be to define ill-defined and poorly articulated information needs and to connect these to the correct sources. The initial part of the operation represents a difficult form of modelling. This software would be a combination of a data base query system and an expert system. It would be the most difficult and expensive element of research in the social software mode.

10.   Economic considerations

Fundementally there are two general lines of implications for research involved in the concept of social software. The first emphasises hardware and software of slow speed, measured in terms of its storage, retrieval and transmission times, and low cost, measured in terms of usage and production. The speed factor is at variance with the dominant line of research in the EC for the ICT's. At the same time any high speed requirement raises the costs of usage and production. The dominant line of research brings the manufacturers of the EC into head to head competition with those of our major economic opponents, the USA and Japan. This 'triad' are producing very similar products in and for the global grid often involving some collaboration but ultimately in opposition. It would seem that the research implications of social software do not support the EC in the process of economic competition. Yet the products of the economic global grid are not those that will appeal to all consumers either in terms of costs or functions. Always to emphasise the new frontiers of the ICT's is to ignore the breadth of market left behind by the advancing leading edge. The dominant line of research is producing 'elite' economic software which has a numerically small clientele. However, the products that would spin-off from research in social software being slow speed/low cost, would achieve mass markets as a matter of design. Additionally they would appeal to low income countries and regions which have largely been passed over by the ICT's and their applications. Consequently, low cost/slow speed transmission, storage, access, and processing devices plus cheap printers capable of receiving messages over the telephone, together with appropriate software would find markets in these economically poorer countries and regions. The export or technology transfer potential of the social software line of research is sizeable and a dual track approach of fast/slow and cheap/dear to the ICT's would be beneficial. Interestingly, Peru, a country not known for its technological contribution has recently won an export order to supply 100,000 IBM-compatible personal computers to the Soviet Union, an order worth over $ 450 million (18).

The second implication follows from the need for the expert system that drives the 'Helpline 1000' concept. Expert systems are very relevant to economic software because they can expand the range of applications and the number of personnel that use the global grids. Theoretically, expert systems should be able to encapsulate and reproduce the skills of workers that have been gained from a lifetime of experience and they represent a feasible route for escaping the software boundary. In many areas the boundary has been already reached so that further potential productivity gains have become limited. Given the economic forces experienced by EC firms in the global market, the development of expert systems would appear to be a high priority objective. However there are factors that retard privately gunded research of them. These are related to risk.

The problem for private funders is that there is no known 'production function' for research especially where basic research activities are involved. Resources go into the process but the 'outputs' cannot be forecast, in fact it is quite feasible that the output is irrelevant or non-existent. At any stage in the process, research activities may require additional injections of resources with again no foreseeable or measurable output. Clearly, this represents a high risk for the private sector. Expert systems, being on the frontier of knowledge in the ICT's, are a particularly risky subject matter.

The degree of risk is considerably deepened with expert systems due to the potential costs of failure. Normally an expert system would be used to replace or enhance existing procedures. Given the costs involved only the most 'expensive' procedures would attract the committment of funds to expert systems, those involving the scarcest skills and resources. Functionally those performed by these resources would be high-level decision making where the costs of failure are the highest. Consequently, where complex modelling is involved, with the risk of technical deficiences, and the costs of any 'mistake', in terms of the economic viability of the corporation, are high there are strong factors working against the development and implementation of such software. These factors combine to produce a boundary to the application of economic software with repercussions on a wide range of economic activities.

The expert system that drives the social software of the 'Helpline 1000' project suffers from the same technical modelling problems. It would be a major achievement to define the informational needs of someone who has difficulty in expressing them or is in some way ignorant, and then matching these needs to a previously defined data set. The unknown production function characterises research in social as well as economic software. But the risks of failure, though present, are not so binding on the client. Mistakes in the economic sphere are frequently irreversible because we cannot turn back the market and because there are others in the market that are looking to punish any mistake. This is not the case in our non-economic lives. We are moving much more slowly, the instant is of no concern, the stock of data changes only gradually, we are not striving to outdo or punish, we are more co-operative than competitive, and mistakes can be rectified.

Research in the field of social software is inherently less risky than in the economic field. Yet the products of the research are applicable to economic software - there is a positive spin-off and a consequent outward shift in the boundary and potential productivity gains. The techniques of 'Helpline 1000' could just as easily be used by the manager of an industrial corporation, insurance company, travel agency or government department. A 'Helpline 1000' system in operation would act as a fitting experimental test-bed for users and when it has proved itself in this context it would certainly be transferable elsewhere.

Palpably, the implications for research in the field of social software whilst providing benefits to individuals and households, simultaneously produce advantages for the economy of the EC. Two have been suggested here. The first involves a dual track approach to products with those appealing to the household also offering potential export markets. The second emphasises the less risky test-bed of developing software for the social sector which is then transferred to the economic sector.

There are other implications which are extremely important but are briefly mentioned here. They revolve around the role of the public sector. In terms of research funding the economic conditions associated with software development do not favour private sector leadership in the expert system and basic research suggested here. Similarly, the public sector is likely to take the dominant role in the segment of the dual track approach aimed at the providing low cost/slow speed products. On both counts public funds will be required. But the financial repercussions of the social software concept extend to the grids. It would be wasteful to develop social software if conditions were such that people could not use them. The limit to use will be economic either because households cannot afford to be connected or could not meet the expense of use or hardware. The unit costs of the latter can be reduced by socialising consumption - with the public sector buying in bulk. This would have the secondary effect of making exports cheaper. But the fundamental problem will remain that of achieving and then maintaining universality for the networks and affordable tarrifs. These conditions are becoming unfashionable under the pressures of de-regulation and intensifying competition. Yet the household remains important to the grids. Paplably there is a key role to be assumed at the European level to ensure both the harmonisation of national grids to facilitate inter-community social communication and access to the services of social software. Whilst the grids are increasingly assuming the characteristics of private networks there is in fact a new rational for an extension of public involvement and some of Community-wide regulation to strengthen the household sector. From this will follow economic benefits for all. If, as has been claimed, ISDN means integrated services nobody wants the huge electronic highways will need to attract household usage if they are not to be another expensive example of EC over production.

157

NOTES

(1)   Compiled by **Computer Weekly,** December 4 1986.
(2)   **Financial Times,** May 6 1986.
(3)   **Financial Times,** January 6 1986.
(4)   The **Economist** Telecommunications: a survey. November 23 1985.
(5)   **Screen Digest,** Ocotober 1985.
(6)   It is frequently observed that 70% of the development costs of a public switch are due to software.
(7)   OECD **Software an emerging industry** ICCP 9, 1985, p. 23.
(8)   Op. cit.
(9)   See for example ACARD **Software a vital key to UK competitiveness** HMSO 1986.
(10)   See International Trade Administration **A competitive analysis of the US software industry** US Dept. of Commerce, 1984.
(11)   See for example W.J. Baumol & W.G. Bowen **The Performing Arts: The Economic Dilema,** Twenthieth Century Fund, 1966.
(12)   W.J. Baumol, S.A.B. Blackman & E.N. Wolff 'Unbalanced Growth Revisited: Asymptotic Stagnancy and new evidence' **C.V. Starr Centre for Applied Economics,** New York University, 1984.
(13)   OECD op. cit.
(14)   Reported in the **Financial Times,** 30 September 1986.
(15)   **Financial Times,** 2 January 1987.
(16)   Brian Winston, **Misunderstanding Media** Routledge and Kegan Paul, 1986.
(17)   Clearly operators will require special training and perhaps the hardware will require special shut-off devices to deal with 'nuisance' callers and others who might abuse the system.
(18)   See the **Financial Times,** 9 January 1987.

THE CHALLENGES OF TELEMATICS: SOCIAL EXPERIMENTS, SOCIAL INFORMATICS, AND ORGWARE ARCHITECTURE

Lars Qvortrup

1.   The Hardware Fascination and the Orgware Challenge

The word 'telematics' comes from the French télématique, which is intended to describe the growing integration between data transmission and data processing and storage.
Through the development of many different techniques, such as fibre optics and micro-electronics, it has become possible to increase long-distance intercourse between people, between people and computers, and between computers themselves. Possibilities have thus been created for point-to-point communication and mass communication by means of a single network, and the possibilities have been greatly enhanced for the automatic acquisition, storage, processing and retrieval of information.

One major current problem is that the development of new I.T. is so impressive: anybody can give you a selection of 'big' names in hardware, being familiar with the details of high-definition VDUs, of capacities of fibre optical networks, of different kinds of floppies, etc., etc. Still many people are capable of discussing the pros and cons of software - the advantages and disadvantages of the various word-processing, accountancy, CAL or CAT of computer games programmes available at the market. But in contrast to all this, they seem to know remarkably little about the organization of I.T. systems, either on the theoretical or practical level. And yet, compared with hardware and software, the social organization constitutes the most significant element of any I.T. system.
This 'hardware dominance' is found again in the theoretical fields of I.T. For example, the fundamental theory of information is still dominated by the approach of Shannon, saying that 'information' should be treated like a physical quantity such as mass and energy. This approach can be compared with the classical paradigm of for example Peirce, according to whom the basic element of social communication is the sign, conceptualised as '...something which stands to somebody for something in (...) reference to a sort of idea'.
In the theory of Shannon, the definition of 'information' is implicitly derived from I.T. as 'information machinery'. Shannon's theory is a hardware based theory of information. According to Peirce, however, any theory of information should be based upon a social definition of 'sign'. Peirce's theory is a socially based theory of information.
A similar problem is found in most current information system theory. Theories of information systems are still based on the classical paradigm of cybernetics developed by Norbert Wiener; so-called 'man-made systems' are defined as subsets of 'natural systems' (cf. for example the textbook of Robert G. Murdick on Management Information Systems). One of the qualities that differentiates a 'social system' from a 'natural system' is, according to the classical 'politics': 'The most we can hope for is to limit the effect of disruption due to politics. Structured Analysis approaches this objective by making analysis procedures more formal'. (Tom DeMarco, 1979, p. 13). Once more it is obvious that the theory is based on technology and only subsequently applied to society.

The Priority of 'Orgware': We have seen above that hardware dominates in the practical as well as in the theoretical fields of I.T. But why is this really a problem ? Why should the organizational aspects be given first priority ? Let me answer these questions first by giving an example. In the following sections I will elaborate a more general answer.

A couple of years ago the idea of 'telehouses' was elaborated in Denmark. A 'telehouse' is a centre where telecommunication and data processing equipment is placed at the disposal of the citizens of a rural village community, so that communal use may be made of the facilities available. The first 'telehouse' was established in Sweden in September 1985, and today ($1\frac{1}{2}$ years later) 18 telehouses have been or are being established in Sweden, Norway, Finland, and Denmark. The success of the idea (to offer communal access to telecommunication facilities, and to combine access with training and information services) has been obvious.

In some respect, the 'telehouse' expresses the reality of telematics: living in a rural village community, you have access to national and international databases. But more important is it that the 'telehouse' experiments have demonstrated the importance of the organizational aspects of I.T. implementation. I.T. alone is useless, unless it is integrated into, and used within, a specific organizational network. The basic issue concerning I.T. today is not hardware, nor software: it is orgware. Orgware refers to an organization of human beings, in which information technology (viz. a system of computers and telecommunications networks) is integrated into, and subordinated to, the organization's social network.

Furthermore, the experiments of the Nordic telehouses have demonstrated that orgware - the design of the optimum organization of I.T. - is an issue on which the users are the experts: you have to establish a close collaboration between technical expertise, social expertise and the 'everyday expertise' of ordinary users, if you are to have any hope of designing advanced orgware products.

But the Nordic telehouse experiments have clearly demonstrated that orgware is a critical factor. We all know that you have to be very careful with hardware: it designates complex and sensitive systems made up of the finest integrated circuits, whose reliability depends on a high degree of technical accuracy. And we know about the complexity of software: the vast memories, the sophisticated programs, etc. But what do we know about the social organization making use of I.T., what do we know about orgware ? Almost nothing ! Normally, the specific organization considered is considered to be a 'natural' datum, preceding the requisite technicalities. Fallaciously, however, all the emphasis is placed on the latter. But from office automation research we have learned that the dominant reason for shortcomings in the implementation of I.T. in offices is not defective hardware, nor defective software, but user-resistance - which is not 'the effect of disruption due to politics', but which is the effect and the expression of 'defective orgware'. And this is the case in many other attempts to implement I.T. within social organizations. In comparison with hardware and software, orgware is certainly the most sensitive and the most complicated factor.

The Integration of Technology and Society: One of the fundamental trends within the field of new information and communications technologies is the increasing integration of technology and society. Neologisms like 'telehouse', 'smart building', 'intelligent city', etc. reflect this trend.

In these neologisms, words referring to technology are casually linked with words referring to aspects of our social organization. Yet what is really interesting is the fact that the words referring to technology are the words with spiritual connotations - 'smart', 'intelligent', etc. - while the words referring to aspects of the social realm in effect refer only to its physical realities - 'building', 'city', etc. We find ourselves, in other words, in a kind of ghost-world, a world in which all that is truly social is represented by dead things, and all that is technological seems to be animated by human intelligence.

Compared with traditional analyses of the artificialisation of social life - Karl Marx's analysis of the subsumption of labour under capital, or Max Weber's analysis of the 'dead machinery' of modern bureaucracy - what, then, has changed ?

I think that we have to add two further aspects to these traditional analyses. Firstly, not only the power, but the very nature of bureaucracy has changed. Take, for example, a modern hospital. If you want to understand the nature of a modern hospital, it is not sufficient to analyse it as a health-restoring institution, nor as a bureaucratic institution (reproducing a specific societal relationship between the 'expert' and the 'man in the street', and a specific methodological definition of 'health', 'hygiene', 'efficiency', 'progress', etc.). A modern hospital is also an audio-visual network - and, as such, it constitutes a symbol-generating institution. Already when the patient arrives at the hospital, he is re-clothed: a new visual representation of the patient is created. And during his stay at the hospital a number of textual and audio-visual pictures are filed: case records, x-ray pictures, body scans, cardiograms, medical certificates, etc. This system of symbolic representation is subsequently referred to by the patient's general practitioner, his insurance company, etc., etc.: when the actual flesh-and-blood patient leaves the hospital, he leaves behind him a complicated system of symbolic representations: a symbolic patient. It is, in fact, my hypothesis here that all modern institutions, besides performing their literal functions, produce, store, and communicate, their own specific symbolic representations.

Consequently, in our analysis we must answer at least three questions:
- what kind of health does a modern hospital produce (qua functional institution ?);
- what kind of bureaucratic oppression/control does a modern hospital exercise (qua bureaucratic institution ?);
- what kind of pictures - symbolic representations - does a modern hospital generate (qua symbol-generating institution ?).

Secondly, the process of subsumption is expanding: today, we cannot talk only about the subsumption of labour, or about the subsumption of public administration. We have to analyse the subsumption of our total everyday lives under information technology.

For example, the vision of the so-called 'intelligent city' is a vision of totally artificialized social life. What is the social significance of the 'intelligent city ?' It is a vision or a myth, of course, but every vision is an extension of an already existing tendency. Consequently, this vision represents a specific aim and a specific way of thinking, which is current among contemporary architects, town planners, and the like. An intelligent city is not, primarily, an accumulation of buildings and people. It is, first and foremost, a network, a large, artificial nervous system, with its nerve centres and nerve fibres. It represents, in other words, a new phase in the artificialisation of human life, in which our social interaction is totally electronically mediated and/or regulated: one thinks of human interaction via networks, computer-aided traffic regulation, etc., etc.

In the early 1860s, Karl Marx coined the concept of the 'real subsumption of labour under capital', emphasizing the fact that workers didn't just sell their capacity for work, but that they became both physically and psychologically subordinated to the means of production. By analogy, today we may claim that the 'intelligent city' may constitute the 'real subsumption of citizens' everyday lives under information technology', which, in relation to Marx and Weber, would thus represent a third phase of subsumption.

But Marx also emphasized the duality of the process: the 'great civilising influence of capital'. Similarly, we must understand the potential dual impacts of I.T.: more sophistication of social life, and more control and alienation.

Social and Scientific Challenges: What, then, are the most significant social and scientific challenges which have been generated by this tendency towards the further integration of society and information technology ? I would like to deal with three specific fields of action:
- social experiments with information technology;
- social informatics; and
- orgware architecture.

2. Social Experiments with Information Technology

The man in the street must be given direct influence with regard to the implementation and development of new I.T. Firstly, because he himself is directly influenced by new technology in his everyday life. And secondly, because he has the most relevant qualifications for optimizing the development of new I.T. A particularly promising instrument for maximizing public influence on new I.T. is the Social Experiment with I.T.

The designation 'Social Experiments with Information Technology' originated in France in the early 1980s - as 'Expérimentation sociale en télématique' - and at that time it referred to such R. and D. activities as the interactive videotex programmes known as Télétel 3V around Paris, CLAIRE in Grenoble, and TELEM-Nantes, as well as the integrated broadband network project in Biarritz. At the present time, however, there is urgent need for a more general, normative definition of the concept, since

it has been employed differently in the various different E.E.C. countries, and since it has been used to designate activities reflecting very different societal interests:
-    grass-roots activities involving new information technology, such as Folkedata in Denmark, and the I.T.E.C.s in England, have on occasion been designated social experiments with I.T.;
-    governmental initiatives to develop national I.T. services on the basis of specifically delimited local community pilot projects, such as Bildschirmtext in West Germany, have also on occasion been designated social experiments with information technology;
-    private firms' strategies for socially-oriented product refinement and/or marketing, such as value added network services based on videotex, have also on occasion been designated social experiments with information technology.

How can 'social experiments' be defined ? According to Craipeau/Kretz (1987, p. 224) social experimentation is '...an action exerted by society on itself'. A more specific definition of social experiments with I.T. was elaborated by a number of European researchers within a network organised by the European communities' FAST Programme.
According to the output of this network (Anceling et al. 1986. pp. 14f), social experiments might best be defined if one starts with a conception of them as specific forms of implementation of new information technology. Generally speaking, any implementation of new I.T. is a kind of transformation process involving two variables: **human users,** on the one hand, and **the specific I.T. system under consideration,** on the other. The human users will undergo a change (be it positive or negative) effected by changes in their employment or general social conditions - changes involving a demand for new qualifications, necessitating educational and re-training activities, awareness and acceptance campaigns, etc. And the I.T. systems will undergo changes effected by the demands placed on them for modified hardware (demand for improved telecommunications networks, improved display units, key-boards, etc.), and for modified software (demands for improved accessible information, improved search structures, file organiziton, format, etc.).
The really decisive question then becomes: what is the primary aim of the implementation process ? Is it the production of new technology or is it the production of new forms of social organisation ? In the former case, it would clearly be a misconception to describe the experiment as a 'social' one, in any immediate or generally accepted sense of the word.
A further decisive question is: who is the primary subject in the implementation process concerned ? Is it a hardware or software manufacturer (representing the 'interests' of the information technology under consideration ?) Is it a third party (for example an organisation or public authority offering information services ?) Or is it the users involved in, or affected by, the development of the I.T. system concerned ? Depending on the answer to this question, it becomes necessary to distinguish strictly

between two types of social experiments with I.T.: 'participatory work-shops' (in which the users are the primary subjects), and 'social laborato-ries' (in which manufacturers or third parties are the primary subjects).
The definition of the concept of social experiments with I.T. thus becomes the following: Social experiments with information technology are specific forms of implementation of I.T.
- in which the primary aim is to establish new forms of social organi-zation using I.T.;
- in which the activities and the resulting socio-technical products can be used as models for a more widespread - though necessarily contextually-modified - implementation of similar I.T. systems;
- and in which, to this latter end, independent researchers describe and evaluate the implementation process concerned and its results.
Social Experiments qualify as 'participatory workshops' if all the parties involved in, or influenced by, the development of the I.T. system concer-ned, participate on an equal footing in decision-making with regard to the social organisation and application of the I.T. system in question. If not - that is, if the main subject is a hardware or software manufacturer or a third party - the social experiment may more appropriately be designated a 'social laboratory'.
What are the major benefits of social experiments ? As the result of the study conducted by the members of the FAST network mentioned above, the following summarized evaluative hypotheses were developed (ibid. p. 3): social experiments are socially relevant because they are processes in which society as a whole (and not just the companies directly involved) can promote socially beneficial ways of utilizing new I.T. Social experiments are economically relevant because they are rather promising instruments for the production, evaluation, and refinement of socially advanced information systems. Social experiments are processes that influence - rather than merely predict - the future because they generate social awareness and catalyse societal learning process regarding new I.T. Therefore, social experiments should be organised as mutual learning processes in which the endusers can have influence on the organisation of new information systems, and in which a close collaboration between social and technological expertise is established.
It should, however, be noticed that social experimentation is a very complex social process. In the words of Craipeau/Kretz (1987, p. 195):
'Social experimentation, fundamentally bound up with social change, es-sentially combines contradictory logics, those of scientific objectivity and of social action, and is always a project for the merging of ethical, political and economic factors'.
'The product of a changing society, the project of social experimentation is always centred on three poles, those of knowledge, of power, and of the social aspect. Because of its knowledge component, social experimenta-tion aims to retain the scientific model and the effort to achieve objecti-vity and neutrality; from the power aspect, social experimentation deri-ves its strategic objectives and its purpose of influencing society; its

social object is to promote collective participation and the greatest possible support. It acquires its symbolic effectiveness from its ability to blend these three logics into a single event, embracing a combination of concrete social exchanges in - as it were - a spiral movement in order to incorporate them in a new code'.

'Social experimentation is, furthermore, both a procedure, as a method of administrating innovation, and a social process, as a place and dynamics enabling the strategies of the social actors, partners and users to be confronted'.

3.   Social Informatics

It is becoming increasingly obvious that I.T. cannot be regarded merely as a subordinate branch of traditional natural-science-based technology. What has to be fundamentally reconsidered by researchers is precisely: what is the 'nature' of I.T. ? Some answere to this question are already being elaborated within the field of Social Informatics.
Technology - as has been generally understood ever since the earliest formulations of Critical Theory - has both primary and secondary objects. The primary object of traditional technology is the natural, or physical, world. Technology has, in other words, been primarily developed with a view to manipulating and exploiting the natural world and its products. Developing more or less consciously, however, as a result of this primary ambition, a secondary object for technology has emerged - human beings and social organisms. Technology processes the human being and his social organism as if he were merely another piece of animate physical nature in its traditional sense.
This realization is by no means one which I would wish to challenge. But it is my claim that it is essential for us to distinguish between the various different sub-categories of technology. For Information Technology differs fundamentally from traditional, natural-world related technology in that both its primary, and its secondary objects are at one and the same time human beings and social organisms. The function of Information Technology is not to manipulate and exploit nature or its physical, chemical, or biological products: the function of Information Technology is to manipulate and exploit human beings, their cognitive products, and their social organisms.
One of the things inevitably follows on from this fact is that Information Technology trends to have, or will tend to have, even more far-reaching consequences for the functioning of our social lives than traditional technology has had. At the same time too, however, it means that one can make quite other and more far-reaching demands on Information Technology that one can on traditional technology, with regard to its functioning withing the social realm. And there is the more fundamental consequence that there is clearly an urgent need for the systematic refinement of those pure sciences - and here I am thinking particularly of the social sciences -

on the basis of which Information Technology is - or ought to be - produced. Incidentally, it may perhaps be relevant to recall that there is nothing strange about the chronology here. Just as the steam-engine preceded Thermodynamics, so Information Technology will have preceded Social Informatics. Social Informatics is a field of social science. Its basic aim is to discover the fundamental nature of Information Technology, and to establish an Information Theory based on human and social science.

Three fundamental hypotheses within traditional information theory must be criticized. Firstly, we must critically change the hypothesis mentioned above that Information Technology is a subordinate branch of traditional technology. I.T. is not a tool for manipulating nature of natural products; I.T. is a medium for manipulating human beings, cognitive products, and social organisms.

Secondly, we must criticize the assumption that information is a physical quantity and that information theory therefore is a subordinate branch of thermodynamics. 'A basic idea in communication theory', Shannon wrote in **Encyclopaedia Britannica**, 'is that information can be treated very much like a physical quantity such as mass or energy...', thus suggesting '...deep-lying connections between thermodynamics and information theory'.

Finally, the specifica differentia of social organisms must be analyzed. According to traditional theory, so-called 'man-made systems' form a subset of natural systems. This hypothesis was established in the classical theory of cybernetics, and it still forms the basis of current theories of system design, management information systems, etc.

Within traditional information theory it is theoretically impossible to distinguish between deterministic natural and technical systems and voluntaristic social systems. Traditional information theory (and its derived hypotheses regarding the nature of I.T., of information, and of social systems) therefore merely reflects the ghost-world mentioned above, in which all that is social is represented by dead things, and all that is technological seems to be animated by human intelligence.

4.   Orgware Architecture

One of the fundamental problems within the 'Communication Society' is the structural incompatibility of information systems and social organisms; of deterministic and voluntaristic systems. The different taste of integrating these structurally incompatible systems is the challenge taken up by the new applied science of orgware architecture.

Orgware is the designation given to the interlaced totality of a technical information system and a human organization within a social organism (for example: a computerized office; a 'smart building'; an editorial network using a computer conference system; a system of electronic libraries; an 'information society'). Orgware refers, in other words, to an integrated totality which comprises an information system and a human organization.

A basic problem is that even though social organizations and information systems are increasingly becoming functionally interlaced, they remain fundamentally structurally incompatible. A technical information system is essentially a deterministic system, while any social organization is - as a network of human interaction - intrinsically a voluntaristic system.
Furthermore, it is important to realize that computers or communications networks are not just 'private' tools for single individuals. At first sight, a computer, or an access terminal, seems to be a visible concrete tool by means of which a human being produces a text or, more generally, processes data. But, in reality, a computer, or any access terminal, sets up an invisible kind of communication, on the one hand between the programmer and the user, and, on the other, between the user and the subsequent receivers of data which have thus been processed by user and programmer in an 'unconscious' partnership. Therefore, very few, if any, of the multitude of problems arising from the fundamental incompatibility between information systems and social organizations can be solved - or properly analyzed at all - on an individual man-machine-interface level. Fundamental problems of this kind have to be analyzed and elaborated first and foremost on the organizational level.
It is this kind of awareness which has given rise to the applied research discipline of Orgware Architecture. Orgware Architecture, then, is a field of applied sociology, with the object of optimally integrating deterministic information systems and voluntaristic social organizations. Orgware Architecture comes out on the side of adaptability, in Mey's distinction between a concept of 'adaptability', where information systems are adapted to human organizations, and a concept of 'adaptivity', where human beings are adapted to Information Technology (Mey, 1986). But the precondition for successful Orgware Architecture is the elaboration of analytical tools which - identify the human information and communication needs and processes within social organisms, - specify these organizational information and communication needs in relation to Information Technology, and - reveal I.T.'s potential adaptability, i.e. its specific functional flexibility.

Note

This article is based upon my contribution to the conference 'Europrospective' in Paris April 23-25 1987.

REFERENCES

Ancelin, C., J. Frawley, J. Hartley, F. Pichault, P. Pop, L. Qvortrup (1986),
   Social Experiments with Information Technology in E.E.C. Countries. Executive Summary. CEC, FAST Programme.
Craipeau, Sylvie and Francis Kretz (1987),
   'Methodological Analysis of Experiments with Communication Ser-

vices', in: L. Qvortrup, C. Ancelin, J. Frawley, J. Hartley, F. Pichault, P. Pop (eds.), **Social Experiments with Information Technology and the Challenges of Innovation.** Reidel Publ. Comp., Amsterdam.

DeMarco, Tom (1987),
  Structured Analysis and System Spectification. Englewood Cliffs, New Jersey.

Marx, Karl (1857-58),
  Grundrisse der Kritik der politischen ökonomie. Frankfurt a.M.

Marx, Karl (1863-65),
  Resultate des unmittelbaren Produktionsprozesses. Frankfurt a.M. 1969.

Murdick, G. Robert (1980/1986),
  MIS, Concepts & Design. Englewood Cliffs, New Jersey.

Qvortrup, Lars (1987),
  'Electronic Village Halls - Teleports for Rural Village Communities'. Online, Hamburg.

Shannon, C.E., and W. Weaver (1949),
  The Mathematical Theory of Communication. Illinois 1964.

Weber, Max (1922),
  Wirtschaft und Gesellschaft. Tübingen 1972.

Wiener, Norbert (1948),
  Cybernetics; or Control and Communication in the Animal and the Machine. Second edition, Cambridge, Massachusetts 1961.

PART 4

METHODOLOGICAL AND CONCEPTUAL
CONSIDERATIONS

THE COURT OF TECHNOLOGY

Some philosophical questions concerning the limits of technological power

Jacob Gruppelaar

1. Introduction

Were someone to get lost in our time and ask: 'What is happening here ?'
we might answer: 'Technology is happening'. If that stranger asked: 'Show
me the way out of here ?' we would be embarrased and say: 'Sorry, but this
is our home and there is no way out'.
Technological innovation or, in general, the development of technology is
a very complicated process. Many of its problems can be reduced to a lack
of theory. We need an accurate analytical model, concepts and methods to
describe the development of technology (1). By means of this article I will
make some suggestions, I present some preliminary - and therefore rather
formal - investigations of the context of change. My strategic starting
point is that nowadays we live in a technological home, a home used to
rapid changes. These changes are technology induced.
The hypothesis of this article is that the power of modern technology is
the paradigm of our social system. I try to make a draft of the culture in
which technology takes command and I try to make explicit the theoretical presumptions of this description. I am interested in the force of this
command and the obedience to it.
Technology is not viewed as a force sustaining human life, but as an
institute that creates and distributes a way of living. In reference to the
studies of N. Elias I call this institute The Court of Technology (2). The
description and theory of this court is peculiar, compared to other social
systems, because the high fashion is technological change, innovation. It is
useless to talk about a technological society if it is not possible to identify
the context of innovation. The grip of this system must be extensive or it
could not survive the pressure of its own innovating forces. Were this grip
weak every innovation would cause a crisis. It should be remarked that this
search for the context of technological change is a part of a theory which
stresses that there are limits to technological power.
A conclusive theory of the context of innovation (the paradigm of technical change) makes explicit the structure and principes, the tendency and
rhythm of the innovation process. The most interesting part of this theory
deals with the moments of crises, because they are the true test-case of
the technological system. It would be interesting to evaluate also the
economic theories on technological innovation, because they try to vizualize both the change of a context and the context of change (3). Here I
restrict myself to the context of change. I concentrate on the institutional
aspect of change.
It is a conceptual study, it elaborates the idea: 'context of change'. The
question is how a society can be committed to the development of
technology, how the change-identity of our 'Industriekultur' is to be understood. Therefore this text contains few if any direct references to telecommunications and information technology. However few the direct
references to the other contributions in this book, I think that the problems they treat, have directly to do with a search for a context of
change (4).

The problem of technological power is that it controls and disturbs the context in which we live. My question is how this power of technology is to be understood. My thesis is that the development of technology is to be understood in terms of the technological commitment (paragraph 2). As committed to technology man himself does not own his power. The development of technology is not an anthropological fact, but a socio-historical phenomenon. The power of technology is bound to a socio-historical context and limited because of this context. The theoretical implications of the 'Bound Prometheus' are treated in paragraph 3 and 4.

2. Technological power and society

Historical phenomena are sometimes closely related to certain technologies. Because of the application of new techniques changes occur in agriculture, architecture, warfare, transport and communication. The impact of new energy-recources, new products, new ways of production and organization, on the structure of society and the habit of man, give technology standing as a factor in historic explanation. Some authors even hold that technology is the basic historical category (5).
I prefer to stress the distinctive elements of modern technological society. Therefore I distinguish between technology as a general historic category ('technological involvement') and the technological paradigm that pertains only to modern, Western society ('technological commitment'). A technological involvement is a part of every society, but a society that is committed to the development of technology is extraordinary. The development of technology is not characteristic for every culture, but distinguishes our's from other cultures. The importance of this distinction will bedealt with later. For my argument this distinction is decisive.
a.   **The technological involvement:** in pre- or non-modern (Western) societies technological facts have a limited context because they are separated with respect to each other and an 'un'-limited context because they are part of a non-technological context. It is therefore possible that techniques that change architecture, do not change agriculture: technologies are locked up in their application. These technologies are not part of the development of technology. New techniques develop architecture, not technology.
b.   **The technological commitment:** A systematic development of technology presupposes a certain autonomy of technology, a technological context. Within this context the autonomous power of technology is invented, explored and developed. Technology emancipates as 'plein pouvoir' and forces other developments. All kinds of facts appear within a technological grid. Technology itself decides what is validated as fact, it controls the pertinence and impertinence of what occurs. Technology defines the human situation and, nowaydays, perhaps even the human condition.
Because of this specific quality, and therefore quantity, of the influence

of technology on modern society, one can say that this society became committed to the development of technology. It is said that in modern time the pace of change accelerates, but decisive is the necessity of change, not the multitude of changes. The password of modern society is innovation. There is permanent pressure of innovating forces on the orthodoxy of this society.

The question arises how a society can survive such pressure. How can a society be committed to the development of technology ? How can it contain the dynamism, the unbound power of technology ? A culture or society seems to derive its identity from a historical solidarity. The traditions confirm the patterns of solidarity. What, then, is the identity of a culture that systematically pursues change ? How is this change-identity to be understood ?

I will try to give answer these questions by means of an experiment of thoughts. The aforementioned force loosed by the development of technology puts pressure on the orthodoxy of a society, but, on the other hand, this society generated this dynamism and so must control at least some of its conditions and consequences and apparently this control is strong enough. Technology is not a disintegrating, but a constituting force of modern society. Without technology this society would collapse. I therefore propose to describe technology as the innovation-institute; technology has the function of differentiating and integrating the society (6).

I named this innovation-institute The Court of Technology. In the technological society the development of technology not only has its own 'technical' context and strong influence on a social-cultural context, but also creates, differentiates and integrates, a fresh network of relations between culture, science, education, economy, politics. Of course, technology-development has to do with specific activities such as industry, business, science, but it also penetrates, immediately, the whole realm of society, it pertains to institutions, social behaviour, individuality and identity. Technology is not only a good deal of facts in modern history, it also appears to be the dynamic power, the vehicle of that history. Because of its specific powerful character technology-development can reallocate the parts of a social complex: technology as such discloses energy, it potentializes, mobilizes and capitalizes.

Technology is the institute that contains, forms and controls heterodoxy. Therefore one can say change is prefabricated: not mere change, but only a certain kind of change is possible and pertinent, namely the one contained within this institute. When this institute becomes almighty any other kind of change (and of growth) will be, as such, out of proportion. The development of modern society tends to secure and perfect the stability of change and technology is threatening because it stabilizes. In fact, changes do not just occur anymore, they are implemented. The landingstrip of future things is thorougly secured. Change is institutionalized as and produced within a technological framework, a configuration of science, industry and politics. In summary: the dynamism of technology does not result in a dislocating permanent revolution, but is altogether

contained within a thoroughly organized, highly disciplined, stable society.
In our time technology creates and validates changes. This Court of Technology shapes the appearance of a world, as well as the identity of man, his needs and volitions. Man is committed to a social system in which the technological perspective dominates. This perspective pertains to what appears and to whom it appears. The coincidence of what is seen and who is seeing, this double constitution, will be dealt with later. At this court arises a new way of living. This court forms and governs the behaviour, moods and awareness of its subjects. A socio-geographical ('Lebenswelt') approach of technology should describe this government. What happens to Man when a technological perspective becomes dominant ? How is this dominance to be understood ? Is there a codex of technology ? How does the obedience look ? What about disobedience, crime and punishment ? How does good citizenship look in this technopolis ? Who is the favourite subject ? What is his competence ? Which are the conditions of entry to this court ? How to approach the sovereign ? How to please him ?
It will certainly be a problem to give an accurate description of the way of living in technopolis. At the same time it is hardly possible to exaggerate the penetrating sovereignty of this court, the vastness of its dominions. The spirits of mastery and control, of profitable enterprise, suffuses or at least suppresses many other forms of human activity, even our leisure, our love-life, our praying has to be efficient, profitable. The air of efficiency is everywhere. Our own life is experienced and regarded as a project, that pays or not. We want or have to live and die in an efficient way. There is not much place left for what Cicero called 'Otium cum dignitate', leisure with dignity.
Should not philosophers and social scientists contemplate and investigate the modes and moves of businessmen, the businessman in each of us, in order to understand our time ? Have not their selfconsciousness and energy, their cool and arrogance, their audacity become exemplary features ?

3. The technological fallacy

In this paragraph and the next I will try to elaborate the theoretical presumptions of the Court of Technology. I introduced this 'Court' as a model to describe the development of technology. The notion 'Court' features the grip of a social system on its own dynamism. It is especially relevant to conceptualize and vizualize this hold with regard to a society commited to the development of technology. A dynamic development can only exist as a powerful manifestation of something and someone when and in as much as it is solidified and therefore we have to look for the borders (embodiment) of the power of technology and for the position of Man within this ambit. A non-solidified dynamism is just loose energy.
When it is true that the dynamic force of the development of technology is drawn up within the societal bounds called 'The Court of Technology' then

it should be explained in what sense this societal power is related to human willpower. In the last paragraph I dwelled upon the societal reality ('Daseinsmacht'), even the omnipresence of technology in our time, now I argue that with regard to the foundation of this power, its reality also is deceitful. I need this thesis of 'the technological fallacy' in order to detach the era of technology from history in general. A discussion on the limits of technological power, of the legitimacy of its dominance, can, perhaps, be reduced to the question whether the development of technology is a period in Western history or a basic historic category.

Often the history of technology is identified with the history of mankind. Because of the, indeed, dynamic character of technology several authors have been seduced to identify historical change and human activity as such with technological innovation. This identification presupposes an anthropological view of history and a naturalistic view of Man (7). I want to confront this with a cultural-historical view of technology.

The anthropological-naturalistic view presents the development of technology as progress in the process of hominization, civilization. Man is thought to be human because and in as far as he is technical: Man is - according to the definition of Benjamin Franklin - 'a tool-making animal'. To illustrate this view I quote the Encyclopedia Brittanica. In regard to technology it says:

'Especially since the 19th century, the progress of invention and industry has been considered a key index to the progress of civilization.

'If technology may be defined as the systematic study of techniques for making and doing things, then the history of technology encompasses the whole evolution of Man.

'By virtue of his nature as a tool-maker, Man is therefore a technologist from the beginning, and the history of technology encompasses the whole evolution of Man'.

Technology is conveived as Man's capacity to modify his environment and ultimately Man is made responsible for evolution. This view identifies the technological development and the cultural process in general.

According to this view history is an exposition in time of Man's innate essence. Technology is the objectivation and externalization of the truth of the human body; technology reveals the truth of nature and clarifies the laws of nature. It is Man's profession and destiny to master nature, to overcome the vicissitudes of his environment, the hindrances of time and space. Man has to control his situation and ultimately his condition.

The identification of social change with human rationality is attractive. We are accustomed to admire the dynamic character of technology and the same admiration affects the explanation of the rationality of historic processes. Is not history the sum of human activities ? Why should we not identify history with the history of technology if the development of technology exposes the ultimate truth of these rationalized, purposeful enterprises ?

The cultural-historical view of the development of technology criticizes the idea that Man makes history. Instead of the heroic-optimism of the idea of made-history and self-made Man, technology is treated as a secondhand activity. In the context of a non-naturalistic view the 'homo faber' is understood as a socio-historic phenomenon (8).

The vantage of the cultural-historical view is that Man is not a natural being and therefore has no natural purpose; Man is a cultural being and can only be understood in the context of his culture. His activities are not the neutral means to an objective, natural truth. On the contrary, they are as such prearranged, preordained. Culture stipulates beforehand the domain and context of his activity. Even Man's questions, his so-called final questions, are answers with regard to the claim of this predisposition. The development of technology then cannot be understood with reference to a natural disposition of Man (his so-called needs); it is culturally predisposed as a specific form of activity. Not all cultures have predisposed this development or, at least, not in the same way. For that reason the transfer of technology is, as such, a problem, a translation problem.

If we adopt this view then the development of technology should be questioned as the offspring of a certain culture. We should ask what are the features of this culture, of this cradle of the development of technology ? Where, when and how did this development happen ? Who did it, who was committed to it ?

Important, and perhaps decisive, is the question concerning the power of technology. According to the anthropological-naturalistic view the power of technology indicates that technology is an adequate representation of the laws of nature. Not without any foundations, technology claims a universal validity. Technology is scientifically founded and we cannot just 'culturalize' science. We cannot just smuggle away its claim for objectivity, but however well the claims be founded, nevertheless it is necessary to investigate the cultural background of this universalism and this objectivity. It is also important to validate the fact that initially technology became a way of living only in certain parts of the Western world, in certain layers of its society and at a certain moment of its history. Perhaps it is only because of the agressive, dominating nature of this way of living that it could obtain a monopoly position and pervade more and more areas of Western society and become powerful enough to Westernize other societies. Perhaps this claimed universalism is not only the foundation of the success of the process of modernization and Westernization, but also the ideological veil, the justification of this pretentious process and the legitimation of its merciless ascendency.

4.   The cultural disposition of technology: the time of technology

In the previous paragraph, I confronted an anthropological-naturalistic view of technology with a cultural-historical view. According to the first technology reveals the capacities of Man and the possibilities of nature, both founded in laws of nature. The second view attaches importance to the fact that technology has become a social constituent only in a certain culture at a certain moment of its history, because and in as far as that culture generated technology, that is, development of technology. Then, this development is not the promise of history as such, but an era in the history of a certain culture. Then, it is not the most adequate form of human activity and as such longed for, and not at all necessary, but a more or less desired possibility within a certain culture.

The reason that technology (its development) cannot be the most adequate form of human activities, is not that another form is more adequate, but that the idea of adequacy as such is inadequate: Man is no natural being, Man has no nature, no definite needs that can be adequately represented and satisfied. In fact, ideas like that of adequacy and necessity are the products of the time of technology, and not the other way around.

Therefore, the cultural-historical view is interested in the cultural disposition of the development of technology, in this cradle of technology in the same way as e.g. Weber was interested in the cradle of Capitalism. I want to propose that social scientists might do some investigation on 'der Geist der Technik', 'the spirit of technology'; philosophers might question the specific mode of being of Man that generated ideas like adequacy, causality, necessity, efficiency, independence, will-power, decision etc.

This thesis of disposed technology has far-reaching consequences for the validation of its development. If it is not a decisive and final act in the history of mankind then its domination, its universalism has to be questioned.

According to the cultural-historical view of technology, the time of technology is an era in Western civilization. In this period man is considered to make history, to realize his ideas. This power and independence is questioned when the development of technology is related to a certain cultural disposition. Not the effectiveness of this power is doubted, but its foundation, its legitimation and therefore ultimately also its effectiveness.

Let us return to the Court of Technology and inquire after the theoretical presumptions of disposed technology. The development of technology is not a mere anthropological fact. Technology is culturally predisposed. How is this disposition to be understood ? What does it mean that identity, behaviour and environment are predisposed in a certain way ? What does it mean that this technological way of living is disposed, that the independence that seems to be the promise of technological progress depends on a cultural disposition ? Did perhaps technological progress itself become a cultural disposition ? Does our independence depend on a spirit of independence ?

In order to understand the idea of a disposition I shall make use of Heidegger's main thesis, the so-called 'ontological difference' (9). I shall transfer and translate this thesis into a more sociological context. The question concerning technology then runs as follows: Man's commitment to a world became technological, how is this commitment to be understood ?

Let me first introduce Heidegger. Heidegger did not think about technology among other subjects. He argued that the spirit of technology dominates Western thought, a domination that became manifest in this century. Technology is not a more or less preferable object of thought, it is the essence of Western thought. Heidegger asserted that the history of Western thought as such evolved to technocracy (10). Western thought is typically a will to power. The intention of this willpower is to safeguard and secure Man's situation, Man in his situation. Modern technology is the summit of Western history and according to Heidegger the limit: in the end Man not only controls his situation, but also his condition, his own being. He can decide what or who he will be. This unlimited, unbound power characterizes the so-called age of nihilism.

According to the thesis of disposed technology Man is in a specific way committed to a world. This specificity pertains to Man himself and to the appearance of a world. This commitment has two dimensions: it constitutes the specificity of what is seen and of who is seeing. Commitment has to do with a double constitution, it relates someone to something in a specific way. The persons and things related have an existence and identity only within the relation and as related. This specificity is not the product of someone's intention, neither the reflection of what a thing as such is. In other words: one can be committed to something - or to someone else - but one cannot commit oneself te something. Commitment cannot be done, it happens.

Therefore, the activity within the commitment is always bound to, reactive, receptive, passive with regard to the initiative activity, that is the commitment itself. I repeat: as committed to something one can really be active, one is active because of the commitment, but one cannot be active in respect of the commitment itself. The commitment is the initiative act, that doesn't belong to anyone. It just happens.

With reference to the technological commitment these remarks on the activity, reactivity and passivity of the one committed are decisive. As who and as what are persons and things constituted within a technological commitment ? Heidegger conceived these dimensions of the technological commitment as the process of subjectivation and objectivation: Man is constituted as a subject, the world is constituted as the objects of this subject, that is for the good of this subject. The subject is producer, consumer, the object is material or product. These two parallel dimensions are produced, followed and exhausted by the development of technology (11).

Heidegger argued that Man's subjectivity and the objectivity of the world are constituted within a historic process. Subjectivity, traditionally conceived as self-consciousness, is not the origin, but the product of history. The objectivity of the world is not the solid foundation of our representations, but the result of a specific way of representing, namely the presentation of the world as objects, things. The subject and the object do not exist in themselves, but only as related, they are not original, but originated, they have emerged within a specific history as origin and fundamental. They are, one can say, both subject to the technological commitment. Of course, this subject and object have a reality of their own: this subject is indeed powerful within a world of objects. The power of this subject is effective and perhaps ultimately perfect with regard to its technological environment, but this power as such can never be his property. There would not be any objects without this subject, but they can only appear as and be produced as objects within a technological context; this context is not produced by subjects because they are themselves products, subject to this context.

Therefore I propose to describe the technological era as a court that arranges Man and his world, i.e. his institutions, behaviour, identity. This specific arrangement should not be treated as Man's self-deployment; on the contrary, Man should be treated as competent only with regard to this specificity. In the case of the technological commitment Man is competent in as far as he subjects, in as far as he is a producer. However, in this subjection he himself is subjected to the technological commitment.

Here reappears the forementioned dependent independence: Man is subjected to this subjection. As a subject of technology, Man is not active, but receptive with regard to his own willpower, he cannot control his willpower, he cannot master his control condition, because he himself is subjected to it. Man cannot handle his power; the need for and the end of this power is more power. More power indeed is always needed in order to arrange and compromise the productive and destructive output of this power-process.

5.   Concluding remarks

I have made a distinction between 'technologies' and 'development of technology', between a technological 'involvement' and a technological 'commitment'. I have argued that this development of technology should be studied as a cultural-historical phenomenon, i.e. the subject-matter of a particular socio-geography. I have argued that because of the fact that a development of technology is culturally disposed, its 'objective' power is an ethical problem. Technology is a way of living. Therefore, I think that studies on technology should concentrate on the cultural dimension of the development of technology. One should e.g. ask: For what reasons are technologies developed ? How are these developments introduced in society ? What can be said about the structure and rhythm of the innovation-process ?

The power of technology is bound to cultural values and ideas. It is necessery to map out the cultural limits of this power, limits already trangressed or not. Also important is the question how it happens that the development of technology can transgress limits, even its own limits. When technology is conceived as culturally disposed, it is evident that the idea of the unlimited power of technology is nonsense. Yet, it will be a problem to restrict this power. What kind of power do we need to restrict the power of technology ?

I hope I have made clear that the idea of the unlimited power of technology is not compatible with its being disposed by a certain culture. The development of technology does not realize the truth of the human nature. It only mobilizes one range of human possibilities and capacities. Many other ranges have been suppressed by the development of technology. Perhaps the revaluation of other human possibilities and capacities will help solve problems that are now unjustly treated as technological problems.

NOTES

(1)   See e.g. G. Ropohl, **Eine Systemtheorie der Technik, Zur Grundlegung der Allgemeinen Technologie,** München, Wien, 1979; F. Rapp, **Analytische Technikphilosophie,** Freiburg/München, 1978; H. Stork, **Einführung in die Philosophie der Technik,** Darmstadt, 1977; Durbin Paul T., Rapp. F, eds., **Philosophy and Technology (Boston studies in the Philosophy of Science, 80).** Dordrecht, 1983; Mitcham C., Mackey R., eds., **Philosophy and technology. Readings in the philosophical problems of technology,** New York, 1983.

(2)   N. Elias, **Uber den Prozess der Zivilisation: soziogenetische und psychogenetische Untersuchungen,** Bern, 1969; NB New introduction.

(3)   See e.g.: R.R. Nelson, S.G. Winter, Neoclassical **vs.** evolutionary theories of economic growth: critique and prospectus, in: **Economic Journal** 1974 (84), p. 886-905; --, Growth theory from an evolutionary perspective: the differential productivity puzzle, in: **American Economic Review,** may 1975 (65), p. 338-344; --, In search of a useful theory of innovation, in: **Research Policy,** 1977 (6), p. 36-76; Chr. Freeman, The determinants of innovation. Market demand, technology, and the response to social problems, in: **Futures,** 1979, p. 206-215.

(4)   Cf. the problems with the implementation of new technologies, e.g. with the definition of the use-function or with standardisation.

(5)   See e.g.: E. Kapp, **Grundlinien einer Philosophie der Technik,** Braunschweig, 1977; F. Dessauer, **Philosophie der Technik,** Bonn, 1927; A. Gehlen, A. philosophical-anthropological perspective on technology, in: P.T. Durbin, **o.c.,** Vol. 6, 1983; A. Huning, **Homo Mensura:** Human beings are their technology-Technology is human, in: P.T. Durbin, **o.c.,** Vol. 8, 1985.

(6)   The concept 'institute' as it is used in this text has been elaborated by A. Gehlen **(Urmensch und Spätkultur, Philosophische Ergebnisse und Aussagen,** Wiesbaden, 1986[5]; **Moral und Hypermoral. Eine pluralistische Ethik,** Wiesbaden, 1986[5]). See also: Th. S. Kuhn, **The structure of scientific revolutions,** Chicago, 1970[2]; M. Foucault, **Les mots et les choses. Une archéologie des sciences humaines,** Paris 1966; **L'ordre du discours,** Paris 1971.

(7)   Cf. footnote 5.

(8)   Cf. e.g. M. Weber, M. Heidegger; cf. also footnote 6. These authors have in common a non-humanistic vision on Man, i.c. on the **homo faber.** They argue that the structure of Man's consciousness is the product, not the producer of history. History seems to be Man-made, in fact his willpower is a secondhand activity. Heidegger e.g. argued that Man does not master, nor ever will master the development of technology. Although, this development is certainly Man's own activity. Certainly, this is a strange thing to say. It is very strange because technology is rationalized action, action that has to be effective, profitable, **ce n'est pas un acte sauvage** and Heidegger argued that this mastery cannot be repaired by any kind of emancipation.
I shall elaborate Heidegger's thesis on Man's powerless power, on Man's necessitated will, his passive activity, his forced subjection. In addition to Heidegger, and so to speak, as a sociological implementation of his thesis I shall make use of the analyses of M. Weber, N. Elias and M. Foucault.

(9)   See M. Heidegger, **Die Technik und die Kehre,** Pfüllingen 1962; -; **Der Satz vom Grund,** Pfüllingen 1978[6]; - Die Zeit des Weltbildes, in **Holzwege,** Frankfurt am Main, 1980[6].

(10)   See e.g. M. Heidegger, Nietzsches Wort 'Gott ist tot', in **Holzwege,** Frankfurt am Main 1950, 1980[6] p. 251: 'Das Wesen des Bewusstseins ist das Selbstbewusstsein. Alles seiende ist darum entweder Objekt des Subjekts oder Subjekt des Subjekts.... Die Erde selbst kann sich nur noch als der Gegenstand des Angriffes ziegen, der sich als die unbedingte Vergegenständlichung im Wollen des Menschen einrichtet. Die Natur erscheint überall, weil aus dem Wesen des Seins gewillt, als der Gegenstand der Technik.

(11)   Cf. footnote 10.

GLOBAL NETWORKS: SPACE AND TIME

İ. Gökalp

Introduction

Large-scale technological systems have always been closely interrelated with the type of social organization in which they evolve. These systems, whether they be transport systems, such as railways, or energy distribution systems, such as electricity grids, have exerted a powerful and lasting influence on all levels of organization of modern societies. Naturally these systems themselves are social constructions too. They are modelled by existing social forms which shape both their technical structure and their social application. That is why analysing the interaction between social forms and technological systems is a difficult task for which neither the causal or determinist approach nor the voluntarist approach is wholly satisfactory.

The analyst's task is made all the more difficult when it is a matter of giving his opinion on an evolution that is already taking place, global telecommunication systems being a case in point. However, it is quit clear that all the risks of social analysis are these: how can one assess a trend that is taking shape without stepping over into the realm of futurology; in other words how does one make an enlightened 'guesstimate' operational ? Taking this approach to the problem of global networks raises a number of methodological issues. Some of these issues are more general, relating to the sociology of technology as a whole; they arise because of the lack of sufficiently sophisticated conceptual and analytical tools in this field. Other issues are more specific to the study of global networks and relate both to the technical characteristics of these networks and their social implications.
Some of the problems connected with the current thinking in general on relations between technology and society have recently been identified by Fischer (1985). One of these problems is the over-frequent use of bold metaphors, which are not really justified and which abound in most of the works on the social implications of technology. The new information and communication technologies have provoked metaphors such as 'shock', 'wave', 'global village', 'digital society', 'cable society' and so on. Another underlying hypothesis which crops up in discussions on technology is one which sees technology as having a homogeneous effect and argues that all technology influences society in the same direction, that all the consequences of a particular technology point in the same direction and that all social groups are influenced in the same way. Yet another hypothesis that is implicit in and closely related to the former assumes that all the effects of technology are linear and cumulative. Consequently, this type of analysis does not accept that the impact of a particular technology can be influenced by the time factor, in other words by the evolution of the social environment, or that a particular technology, in a later stage of its development and diffusion, may produce the opposite effect from those observed during its earlier stages. There is also another school of thought, just as widespread, which equates the specific properties of a particular

technology with the characteristics of its social consequences. The use of metaphors borrowed from the language of technology reinforces this line of thinking, making it impossible for those holding such views to conceive of a social shaping of technology.

The problems raised by the specific nature of the subject, i.e. communication and information technologies and their social consequences, are of several types. Firstly, the advent of these technologies has broadened the scope of sociological thinking to include new topics such as social communication or the relevance of information and its circulation, aspects which hitherto have never been the subject of systematic sociological study. The effect on this conceptual void proved to be all the dramatic when it became clear that the technological changes brought about by new communication technologies and information technology were taking place at a speed unlike any of the changes wrought by earlier major innovations. Similarly, these new technologies have also penetrated all social levels of contemporary society at a far faster rate and to a far greater extent than anything seen in the past. It is therefore in this context of a conceptual void placed under stress by intense changes, both real and potential, that the discussion of interactions between society and new communication/information technologies has been invaded by a plethora of metaphorical interpretations. These superficial interpretations have also often done a disservice to serious scientific approches to the subject, leading them astray in their haste.

The multi-dimensional nature of the changes wrought by new communications technologies and information technology and the speed with which these various dimensions interact is yet another factor which has confronted scientific communities rent by rivalry between disciplines and unprepared for positive interdisciplinary collaboration/confrontation (Gökalp 1985). This difficulty in gaining a simultaneous overview of the various aspect of the changes in progress thus opens the way to simplistic interpretations, that are often determinist and unidimensional. Lastly, these new major technological and social trends have rekindled old, unresolved but latent controversies over general concepts such as social change, technical change, transition, social and/or industrial revolution and so on. One attempt to deal with this was to interpret the new changes by analysing them through these existing concepts, forgetting in the process that these concepts, whether they be theoretical or empirical, are themselves social constructions, strongly influenced by the particular configuration of the social, technological and cognitive shape of human societies.

Others became increasingly dissatisfied with these conventional approaches and launched themselves on the perilous venture of forging new conceptual tools and applying them both to the present day and to earlier periods of the modern era so as to lend them the necessary universality. These endeavours, which are dispersed and uncoordinated at the moment, follow three different lines: the first is to give a detailed account of technical evolution in new communications technologies and information technology and of their social consequences (Guile, 1985). The second is a diachronic analysis of the social consequences of other technological systems that have already taken root, such as railways (Weber, 1976; Price, 1983), the telegraph (Pred, 1973), the automobile (Flink, 1980), the telephone (Pool, 1983) etc. The third line of approach is to attempt to introduce some new theoretical ideas on to concepts such as the nature of technological knowledge (Laudan, 1984), the social shaping of technology (MacKenzie and Wajcman, 1985), on the one hand, and the standardization of time (Zerubavel, 1982), the nature of space (Kern, 1983), the relevance of a network approach (Gökalp, 1983) and boundaries (Raffestin, 1986) on the other.

In this text we will endeavour to examine current developments in the field of new communications technologies and information technology and their social implications from these three different angles. To fully understand the technological changes being wrought by NCT/IT, but also their future potential, we shall use the most recent accounts by specialists as a background (see, **inter alia**, Mayo, 1985). Armed with this technical knowledge we will be devoting the first part of the study to the network aspects of NCTs. Indeed, as the very title of this collaborative research suggests ('network research' in Community-jargon), new communications technologies are expected to constitute the technical basis of the new communication networks (NCNs). To support the concept of communication networks we shall attempt to identify their general characteristics on the basis of a study of other communication networks that have had a pronounced influence on the structure of contemporary social organizations. Perhaps we should say at this point that this approach is distinct from the 'historical analogy' approach (Mazlish, 1965; Masuda, 1981) and merely sets out to test the conceptual validity of certain ideas in different historical situations. On the basis of this definitional and taxonomic study of communication networks we will then be able to propose a classification of large-scale communication networks and appreciate more clearly where new communication networks fit in.

In a second part of the text we will look in more detail at the general characteristics of large scale communication systems by relating them to the global characteristics of the type of social organization in which they exist, putting particular emphasis on their impact on the spatial and temporal components of human activity. The third part of the study will take a fresh look at the general characteristics identified in part 2 based on the specific characteristics of new communication networks, emphasizing in particular their multi-dimensional character. In the fourth and last part of the study, we shall explore (via the spatial changes generated by new communications networks) the complex and rapidly evolving relationships between the emergence and consolidation of NCNs and the territorial and organizational dynamics of the nation-state.

1. Definition and taxonomy of social communication networks

Interpreting human activity in terms of networks, at least in modern and contemporary times, is perfectly feasible. Indeed, the fact that we are living and working increasingly in networks or within systems having the characteristics of a networks has, over the last few years, attracted the attention of researchers from various backgrounds to the study of the network concept. This recent interest differs from the already long-established application of that same concept to mathematics, biology, crystallography or data-processing. The concept of a network is suddenly becoming attractive both for the social sciences and for as yet unexplored areas of the exact sciences.

Naturally, some qualifying remarks must be made about this diversification of the applications of the networks concept. This is because in these various applications the epistemological status of the concept of a network is not clear; it might even be said that we have barely begun to ask the right questions. And yet, if this is a concept that is susceptible of generalization, there ought to be no lack of such questions. For instance, we ought to be asking whether the concept of a network is a general representation of that which is common to several entities and what are the essential characteristics of this concept. We might also be interested to know whether it is possible to have a complete understanding of the concept in order to define it and reflect on the level of abstraction of a network and to what extent it can be broadened and generalized. In other words, the essential question boils down to whether one can give the notion of a network the force of a distinct **a priori** concept, by analysing its constituent characteristics or whether it is to be regarded as a sub-concept of some other, more abstract concept.

Any attempt to give precise answers to these questions will entail a theoretical effort (1) to comprehend the term network (2) to be capable of identifying or recognizing a network (i.e. of distinguishing it from a non-network) on the basis of a certain dynamics that has not yet been fully realized and (3) to understand the nature of the network and identify the universal and essential properties (i.e. non-accidental or non-contingent properties) that characterize the concept of a network.

In order to undertake such a classification of the epistemological status of the concept of a network it is necessary, to distinguish, first of all, between natural networks (i.e. as found in crystals, etc.) and artificial networks. We can define the scope of a network even more accurately by confining our attention to artificial, material and social communication networks (which we shall refer to by the term AMSC networks). This therefore excludes from our investigation artificial and material networks which do not have a social communication function, such as diffraction gratings or electrical networks (not to be confused with electricty distribution networks). The concept of social communication also calls for certain clarification. It means that AMSC networks intervene in social communication sphere, which can be defined as all social interchange supported by social relationships make up the fabric of any society. This sphere can be perceived on two levels: first, on a physical, spatio-temporal level, refering to the literal meaning of the concept of communication as contacts or exchanges or exhanges between various material or non-material fluxes. Secondly, the social communication sphere can be defined on an abstract level, as an interface at the boundary of other social spheres, e.g. economic, political, ideological, stategic etc. and possessing certain unifying and structuring properties. Clearly these two levels that make up the social communication sphere are not independent and the concept of AMSC networks enables us to relate them to each other on a more concrete level. This is because the concept of AMSC networks can also be perceived on two levels: first, on a level refering only to the structure and dynamics of the networks grid, to the various fluxes conveyed by the network etc.; and, secondly, on a more global level which correlates the previous level with other social levels. To express this latter approach to the concept of AMSC networks we shall use the term network-sector ('secteur reseautique') which we will elaborate on in due course.

A taxonomic analysis of the evolution of the definition of the word network enables us, firstly, to list all the artificial and material entities to which the term network has been applied and, secondly, to identify those elements of the definition that are constant or new. This study, for which we consulted dictionaries and encyclopedias, shows that the scope of the concept of network has been constantly expanding. The original Latin world means 'little net' (according to L. Apulelus); in the Dictionnaire Universel of Antoine Furetière (1690) it is applied for the first time to weaving; it was applied in particular to railways in the Grande Encyclopédie of the 1890s and has now acquired a multitude of meanings in modern encyclopedias.

As for the individual elements that make up the concept of a network, they have always included the essential idea of lines (strings, lines) interlaced to form a mesh (intersections and openings); later it was used to describe a set of lines converging towards a single centre (as in the case of the telegraph network which is a collection of lines ending at a single centre, the electricity distribution network which is a collection of lines having a single power source, the railway network which is a collection of tracks belonging to a single administration, etc.). The term was also applied to a collection of intercommunicating points (as in a collection of interconnected electrical circuits or networks of computers). A point which emerges from these definitions is that the emphasis in some cases is on the lines of the network and in others on the nodes or intersections.

The mathematical theory of graphs is often applied to the quantitative study of the structure and dynamics of communication networks (Garrison and Marble, 1962; Kansky, 1963). The graphic representation of a communication network is a convenient simplified method of illustration, reducing the network to a collection of nodes and links, and of demonstrating the structure of certain macroscopic elements of a real network. A graph makes it possible to define certain structural parameters, such as the number of the autonomous closed network or the index of connectivity of a network, and to monitor the trends in these parameters over time. It is also a quantitative means of comparing the structure of different networks, both at national and at international level. However, the application of graph theory can under no circumstances claim to be a substitute for the detailed study of the individual history of each network. The formalism of graph theory is only useful and interesting, in our opinion, if it is accompanied by a detailed socio-historical study of the network to which it is being applied.

Other aspects should also be tāken into account in a definitional study of AMSC networks, besides their structure. These include the nature of the fluxes transported (material fluxes - persons or material goods - or information fluxes) and their speed of circulation, which are crucial factors. One example of a classical analysis emphasizing these aspects is that of Pred (1973), which shows how the generalized spread of telegraphic communication altered the economic geography of the United States. Another definitional aspect in the study of AMSC networks is the concept of the boundary of a network. This is because the various AMSC networks of a single nation may cover different portions of the national territory; in other cases several AMSC networks may, indeed, be superposed. Similarly, some networks are less meticulous respecters of national boundaries than others, as in the case of networks carrying transfrontier data flows. We will look in more detail at these problems of correspondence between the boundaries of an AMCS network and territorial frontiers in the chapter dealing with the relations between the development of new communication networks and the dynamics of the nation-state.

One of the key elements in describing the dynamics of a network is the identification of its different phases or periods. It appears that an AMSC type network can be periodized into four phases (Gökalp, 1983): the section phase; the accelerated development phase; the stabilization phase and the decline phase. We will illustrate these various phases using the example of the French rail system.

The period from 1823, the date of the first railway concession, namely the line from Andrézieux to Saint-Etienne, to the 'Basic law on railways' of 1842 in which separate lines were built without an overall plan, is a perfect example of the 'section' phase of an AMSC network. This was also a period of intense debate on the merits and demerits of the new network; moreover, this debate involved comparison with existing networks (remember the rivalry between road, canal and rail).

In the accelerated development phase, the usefulness and superiority of the network have been recognized and it develops and fills out in accordance with a general plan. Thus, in France, the length of the rail network increased from 1931 km in 1850 to 4 100 km in 1860, 17 400 km in 1870 and 23 600 kim in 1880. It is during this phase that the new network takes the place to a very large extent of the old networks. For instance, rail accounted for 3% of all land-based goods transport in France in 1841/44 and 10% in 1845/54; this share rose to 38% in 1855/65 and to 68% in 1875/84 (Salini, 1982).

In the period of stabilization of the development of an AMSC network, the rate of development is slower than in the preceding phase and the trend is towards a maximum extension of the network grid, while still improving the overall productivity of the network. In France, the total length of the rail network increased by less than 80% in the 40 years from 1880 to 1920 - an insignificant increase compared to the 324% increase which took place between 1860 and 1870. During the stabilization phase the network's share in the various economic activities also stagnates. For instance, between 1875/84 and 1925/34 rail's share of land-based of goods transport stabilized around the 70% mark. However, during the stabilization period, owing to technological and organizational improvements, the productivity of the network can continue to be in step with the general economic indicators. In France, there is a perfect correlation between the tonne-kilometre index for rail transport and the index of industrial production until 1955; after that date these two indices took totally separate paths (Salini, 1982).

The period of decline of a network which then follows is characterized, firstly by the diminishing importance of its grid and of its involvement in various activities, but also by the beginning of its replacement by a new network. In France, for example, the closure of certain rail lines proceeded in parallel with the accelerated development of the motorways. Similarly, motorways, which accounted for only 10% of land-based goods transport in 1921/24 increased their share to 50% in 1971/74, while the percentage carried by rail over the same period fell from 72% to 40% (Salini, 1982).

This idealized subdivision of a sector into phases is naturally subject to the fluctuations characterizing each social organization through which the network in question passes and on which it leaves its mark. Particularly in the accelerated development phase certain sub-periods appear which punctuate the major political and economic events of the society being studied. However, notwithstanding these deviations, the picture which emerges is one of a similar average trend representative of the long-term behaviour of each AMSC network corresponding to the four-phase model outlined above.

On the basis of these various definitional aspects of an AMSC network, we could venture a general classification of such networks. The first AMSC networks of the modern era (roads, canals, railways, telegraph) can be described as extensive networks, having a low density and high permeability. In other words, these networks are characterized by the fact that the distance between the intersections of their grid, which is not dense, imposes a structural rigidity which prevents them coming any closer beyond a certain limit. This rigidity is primarily due to the technical characteristics of the networks in question. There is a second group of AMSC networks where this structural rigidity is less pronounced. Telephone, audiovisual, data-processing and telecommunication networks, for example, are intensive in nature since they are capable of forming more and more dense grids. Therefore they are more solid, or alternatively less permeable.

This bimodal classification can be expanded to include a third, intermediate, type of network which could be called an intensifiable extensive network. The road system is a good illustration of this type of transitional network, where the intensification of an initially extensive network is essentially implemented via changes in the characteristics of the vehicle of the network. The telephone system is a further example of a transitional network which from being extensive in its establishment phase changed into an intensive network in its later phases. Hence, the intensification of a network may take place via several types of changes which may involve the vehicle, its power supply, the nature of the flux carried or the speed at which it is carried.

If we apply this proposed classification to new communication networks, they would appear to fit perfectly into the intensive network category, having all the necessary characteristics. In the following paragraphs we will look first at the general characteristics of AMSC networks and go on to examine the characteristics specific to new communication networks (NCNs).

2.   General characteristics of AMSC networks

A comparative study of major AMSC networks reveals, besides the identification of their essential definitional elements, a number of general characteristics relating to their structure, the relationships between different networks and the way in which they influence the social fabric, not forgetting the manner in which the social fabric is reflected in the networks themselves.

One of these general characteristics is particularly prevalent during the phase in which the networks are becoming established. During this phase, the new network often uses the grids of already established networks as a support. Naturally it is in the 'section' phase that the conception of superposition is most marked, illustrating the dependence of the idea of the new network on that of the old. The early stages of the advent of the railways are a case in point, as shown by this account from that period:

'It was in England that this railway 'craze' was born; in 1827 the British nation was as if in the grip of a railway fever to the point where they were even considering tilling in the canals and laying the railways in their place' (Lamé et al. 1832).

To grasp this superposition of ideas mose fully one need only look at the engravings of the period which show railway wagons built like stagecoaches or steamships built in the style of sailing clippers. Examples of super position abound, not merely in terms of ideas but also in terms of the establishment of networks. For instance, in pre-18th century France, roads on the plain are sited as close as possible to the line of the river: from Paris to Reims, for instance, the road runs successively alongside the rivers Oise, Aisne and Vesle. The first railways also ran alongside the major trunk roads and canals. Later, inter-urban telephone wires were attached to the same poles as the telegraph cables following the railway; urban telephone cables, on the other hand, were installed (in Paris) in the sewer network. Lastly, to give a contemporary example, the French telematic services network has also made use of an existing mixed medium, namely the telephone/television network.

It should be added, however, that this phenomenon of superposition often goes beyond mere imitation; it also satisfies a need for complementarity by means of ingenious combination. This is true, for example, in the case of the rail/telegraph combination, the formers transporting 'space' so to speak, while the latter transported time, the standardization of which had become essential for the proper functioning of the former network.

The periods of stabilization and decline of an AMSC network are likewise characterized by another general tendency. During these phases in which the old network is in retreat and a new triggered by a new technology (for example, energy) is taking over, the old network absorbs the new technology and adopts it while passing through a new section phase. However, in this transformation, it is the domination of the new network and its technology that is being affirmed rather than any revitalization of the old network. This is because the new network, in many cases, before establishing its hegemony, begins to dominate the old network or networks and uses it or them as a kind of testing ground.

This was true, for example, of the railways which, after abandoning steam locomotives, first of all went over gradually to diesel engines and then connected up to the electricity grid. Nowadays, the French railways are once again passing through a 'section' phase with the launching of new high speed lines (TGV) which are controlled more and more by the new dominant technology, namely microelectronics and its networks. The same comment could also be made in relation to the automobile industry which is also becoming increasingly computerized, both in terms of power (microprocessor control of combustion) and in terms of its network (computer-aided signalling and traffic control).

One of the key characteristics of AMSC networks is also the fact that they are structured in close correspondence with a dominant industrial sector. As we shall attempt to show further on, the specific character of the network sector stems from the fact that its development is the result of the combined action of a number of determinants which maybe economic, politico-institutional, military, strategic, and even ideological and symbolic. Consequently, the impact of the network-sector penetrates to the very roots of the social structure and is intimately bound up with the re-shaping of social relationships and the organization of society in general. At the same time this means that the specific characteristics of each network sector determine the global characteristics of a given phase in the socio-economic history of the industrial age. In other words, there is a correlation between a network-sector and a given phase in the life of industrial societies. Looking forward for a moment to the arguments that will be set out in the coming pages, this correlation seems to be based on the fact that the network-sector impinges on the two essential components of human activity at the same time, namely its spatial and temporal components. We therefore believe that the network-sector serves to structure and standardize the social time-space sphere by imposing an average reference communication speed on all the social fluxes that cross the social communication sphere.

We shall identify here three network sectors that best fit the characteristics described above. These are the rail, motor vehicle and data-processing sectors. We shall endeavour to elaborate in this chapter on the concept of the network-sector on the basis of the first two examples, leaving the discussion of the last to chapter 3.

To illustrate the multidimensional character and formative role of a network sector, let us look again at the example of the railways. In the case of France, the multidimensionality that characterizes the railways can easily be seen from the speeches of the time on the subject, particularly in its initial phases. The role of the railways as a driving industrial force was predicted, for example, by the deputy Berryer in 1838:

'You will therefore understand the immense advantage in the eyes of your committee of linking all industries, all interests, to the rail industry and interest, of associating and combining all social actions with the action of the railways; that is what has led the committee to recognize that the railways should not be considered apart. We must not consider the rail industry in isolation but all the industries that may join with it' (Blondeau-Patissier, 1979).

This quotation perfectly sums up the economic hopes placed towards the middle of the 19th century in the railways sector, which the Saint-Simonians called, 'the most powerful instrument of civilization, that man's genius is capable of creating after printing'. Studies now show that in all of the industrialized countries of the old and new world these hopes proved to be well-founded and the railway network sector left its imprint both on the dominant production process, the process of appropriation of the market and the social structures of its time. In fact, it was the influence of the railway network that led to a deepening of market relationships in two respects. First it was through the development of the railways that production processes on an industrial scale invaded all areas of production, both as a consequence of purely economic factors (such as the reduction of transport costs and the possibility of access to natural resources that were difficult to exploit without an efficient and cheap mean of transport) and by encouraging various other economic activities (such as the iron and steel sector (Fremdling, 1977)) but also on the agricultural sector by making possible an extension of both the domestic and external markets (Price, 1983).

Secondly, the structuring role of the railways can also be detected in the structural changes it introduced in the regulation of the economy. It was the Saint-Simonian, Michel Chevalier, one of the most ordent defenders of the railways, who instigated the Treaty of January 1860 between France and England (known as the Cobden-Chevalier Treaty) which marked the end of the ban on imports of certain manufactured goods into France. This treaty had become essential primarily because of the inability of the French metallurgical industry to meet the overwhelming demand for rails from the rail companies (Smith, 1979). As a result, the opening of certain lines had to be delayed because of the shortage of rails; the rail companies therefore brought all their influence to beat to secure a revision of the tariffs, despite resistance from French ironmasters.

The railway network-sector was also responsible for other institutional effects, such as the introduction of the new method of management of large companies. A detailed analysis of this process is provided by Chandler Jr. (1977), based on the example of the American rail companies. The author's conclusions demonstrate the scale of the change:

'The railroad and the telegraph provided the fast, regular and dependable transportation and communication so essential to high volume production and distribution (...). As important, the rail and the telegraph companies were themselves the first modern business enterprises to appear in the United States. They provided the most relevant administrative models for enterprises in the production and distribution of goods and services when such enterprises began to build, on the basis of the new transportation and communication networks, their own geographically extended, multi-unit business empires'.

Another key institutional change was the advent of a new type of collective organization of the labour force, initiated by the appearance of workers' trade unions of which the railway workers were the first modern version. According to Litch (1983), who studied the changes brought about in the organization of labour in the 19th century by the growth of the railway companies, 'the railroads comprised the first enterprises in America to undergo full scale unionization and to develop institutionalized means for arbitrating employee-management disputes (...). In the way in which work was structured and managed, the railroads introduced principles and techniques which were unique for the day. For men who had worked on farms, in homes, small work shops or even textile mills, to enter into hire in a railroad company was to encounter an entirely new kind of work situation'.

The role of the network-sectors as prime movers in industry is also seen in the case of the motor vehicle sector, the growth of which led to a finer re-appropriation/recomposition of the market on an increasingly close-meshed grid and which, from the early decades of the 20th century onwards gave rise to new methods of organization of work (Taylorism) and new forms of workforce management (Fordism). These new forms were to spread later to all branches of industry creating a new combination of production and consumption standards for all industrialized countries.

Turning to the data-processing sector (in which we include all uses of microelectronics technology from telecommunications to robotics), it is without doubt the advent of this sector that has endowed the concept of multidimensionality of a network-sector with its full force, since a single

sector has come to dominate all the branches of production by computeri-
zation/automation/robotization of production units and processes and at
the same time is preparing to provide the infrastructure for Man's non-
material and non-commercial activities, from education to leisure. We
shall come back to this new ubiquity in the next chapter.
A study of AMSC network-sectors also reveals a close correlation
between a given network and a particular type of political and ideological
thought/practice. It would appear, for instance, that since the early
decades of the 19th century the ideology and practice of national unification which dominated not only Western Europe but also the United States
of America is intimately linked with the advent and spread of the railroads. The Saint-Simonians in France highlighted this link from the beginning of the rail era. Michel Chevalier set the tone in 1832 in his 'Système
de la Méditerranée':
'The large-scale introduction of railways will be not merely an industrial
revolution but a political revolution. Through them and with the aid of
other modern inventions, such as the telegraph, it will become easy to
govern most of the continents bordering the Mediterranean with the same
unity and instantaneity that we have today in France'.
According to the Saint-Simonians 'the railways lent an impetus to the
organization of industrial labour by opening up outlets for the products of
the provinces through which they passed (...). They influenced the civilization of countries by facilitating interpersonal relations and extending life
by saving time (...). More frequent relations will establish stronger links
between men. Southerners and Northerners will begin to understand each
other and it is then that we can truthfully say that the Pyrénées have
ceased to exist' (Gökalp, 1984).
In 1837 a report by the committee set up to study the projected Lyon-
Marseilles line, strongly underlined the unifying role of the railways:
'The railways do more than simply assist industry and provide profits for
the private sector (...). Nothing could re-establish the links of our national
unity more effectively than the major railway lines, these marvellous iron
rails which, because of the speed of the journey, encourage people to mix
and to interchange the produce of their territory and the fruits of their
labour. The furthest corners of France will be closer and more united'
(Gökalp, 1983).
Other descriptions of the role of the railways as a national unifier in the
case of France abound in contemporary interpretations such as those by
Vincenot (1975) or Weber (1983).
The railways also played a very important role in consolidating the administrative power of the American State, when one thinks of the impetus
they gave to civil administrative reform, to the reorganisation of the
army, in other words, the establishment of a national global regulation
(Skowronek, 1983). There is perhaps no better illustration of this interaction between the railways and the appropriation (standardization) of a
territory than the synchronized evolution of the conquest of the American
West the spread of the rail network from east to west.

In the latter decades of the 19th century, once the territories of the Western countries had been demarcated vis-à-vis the outside and standardized within, the railways were also the preferred channels for the colonization of the East, serving as the physical embodiment of the message from the civilizing West. Likewise, during the era of decolonization and formation of nationstates elsewhere than in the West, these new states in their turn sang the praises of these 'tracks of iron' as a unifying and civilizing influence (Gökalp, 1983; Huenemann, 1983).

In an attempt to explain these close relations between an AMSC network-sector and the various other social levels, one could argue that the existence of these links is due to the fact that these networks impinge directly on the two essential components of human activity, namely its spatial and temporal components. In other works, this hypothesis suggests that the AMSC network-sector has the effect of structuring and standardizing the social space-time by imposing a reference communication speed on all the social fluxes crossing the social communication sphere.

The structural impact of AMSC networks on the spatial component of human activity can be clearly recognized when one appreciates that the conquest of space, its appropriation and reorganization in various forms, such as nation-states, national and international markets, is made possible by the continual stirring of many fluxes (of men, goods, information, ideologies, etc.) which are conveyed by the various communication networks.

The end result of this process is, of course, the growing unification and standardization of the spatial matrix of human activities, both within the various nations and internationally.

This process is accompanied by a process of standardization of the temporal reference at a supra-local level which is also conveyed by the AMSC network-sectors. Looking again at the example of the railways, whose role as a national unifier has already been underlined, we could also show that this same network-sector was responsible for the first standardization of measured time.

Stengers and Gille (1983) have studied this process in the case of Belgium where, at the beginning of the 19th century, each town had its own local time, regulated approximately according to the rising and setting of the sun. But, they say, all this would change with the advent of the railway: 'The need for a single time over the whole network raised the issue of a common reference. Quetelet was to draw the meridians for the whole of Belgium so that, at any point in the network, railway time, i.e. Brussels time, could be deduced from the longitude of the point and the mean solar time. This monumental exercise was to be reduced to nought by the telegraph whose lines, from 1845, followed every railway track. From then on, Brussels time could be transmitted instantly to all stations. On 1 May 1882 Belgium adopted a statutory standard time, that of the Greenwich meridian, on a proposal from its Minister for Railways'.

The French situation can be illustrated by some passages from Vincenot (1975):

'The first salaried railway worker came to this profession with highly flexible concepts of time (...) it fell to the railways to teach the French all about this subject. Not only the railway workers but also rail travellers. 'If we all manage, throughout the entire network, to be punctual to the second, we will have endowed humanity with the most effective instrument for building the new world'. This bold statement came from Audibert, that enthusiastic graduate of the Polytechnique who had just been asked by Paul in Talabot to organize the Exhibition and to educate the public (...). This rigorous programme assumed that a single standard time and punctuality could be achieved on every line in the network'.
We can also quote the conclusions of Zerubavel (1982) concerning the United Kingdom and America:
'It was not until the introduction of railway transportation, that the need for introducing a uniform standard of time at a supralocal level became crucial. It was railway transportation that, together with the rise of the factory, was primarly responsible for spreading the significance of punctuality and precise time-keeping among the general population'.
The structuring of the social space-time by the automobile sector was equally strong, effective and internalized (Dupuy, 1979), and therefore we need not discuss it in detail. As for the new communication networks (NCNs) which are gradually reorganizing this social space-time by exponentially increasing the speed of circulation on theses intensive networks and multiplying the fluxes they convey, we shall look at those in the following chapter.

3.   The characteristics of the new communication networks

In Chapter 2 we identified certain characteristics common to AMSC networks in general, notably on the basis of a study of extensive networks such as the railways and intensifiable extensive networks such as roads. These same general characteristics can also be identified in new communication networks (NCNs) which are networks of the intensive type. In this chapter we shall be looking afresh both at the definitional elements and the general characteristics of AMSC networks based on observations of the current state of development of NCNs. It goes without saying that what we have to say about emerging and maturing NCNs will be guided by the general characteristics we identified in Chapter 2.
New information technologies, including new communications technologies and new communication networks are supported by simultaneous developments in integrated circuits, computing technology, software and photonics. The steady increase in the potential of integrated circuits, which seems guaranteed to last at least for the next decade (Mayo, 1985), will enable their performance to be improved in terms of both the number of functions a single silicon chip is capable of performing (the component density limit, as it is perceived at present, is put at 100 million components per chip of 1 000mm^2) and in terms of the speed with which it performs these functions. One of the major consequences of the increase

in the capacity of electronic chips is a parallel increas in the computing power of micro-computers, i.e. those using a single electronic chip. Indeed, the capacities of micro-computers seem to be gradually catching up those of the biggest computers, currently amounting to some 10 million instructions per second.

The design of software, the productivity of which is now well below that of hardware components, is also being subjected to the positive influence of the two developments mentioned above. Computer-aided software design allows the introduction of new automatic techniques for the creation of standard software. Lastly, developments in the field of photonics, that is to say the combination of a laser beam and an ultra-pure glass fibre is opening up new possibilities in the transmission of information in digital form. Now, thanks to this technology, it is possible to convey 2 million bits over a distance of 125 km without any amplification. From today's viewpoint, the limit of this technology could well be of the order of 1 000 million megabits per second per kilometre (Mayo, 1985).

These technical developments which we have briefly summarized are based on shortterm projections of the capabilities of existing technologies. Therefore it is more than probable that they will be achieved. Other developments are also expected, involving major changes in the present technological limits such as the introduction of integrated circuits based on an individual molecule, the increase of the usable surface of each silicon chip, the transition to integrated optics, i.e. the replacement of electrons by photons, and so on. All of these medium- or long-term developments now fall within the realm of the possible and therefore warrant a discussion of the social consequences both of existing capacity and future potential of new communications technologies and NCNs.

Given their existing and potential technical characteristics, the distinguishing features of NCNs are therefore their intensity, their instantaneity and their ubiquity. The integrated circuits formed by the silicon chips can be seen as the nodes of these new communications networks because it is they that are responsible for emitting, receiving and processing the various communication fluxes. The structure of these nodes, including their interconnections, or in other words the mesh of the NCN is such that there is no structural limit to their further intensification. Similarly the speed with which these perfect examples of intensive networks circulate and process communication fluxes is several orders of magnitude greater than that of other AMSC type networks. Lastly, these new networks are capable of transporting a large number of fluxes of various kinds, destined to have a bearing on a wide range of human activities, from material production to leisure.

The combination of these three technical features - intensity, instantaneity and ubiquity - has important implications for the structure and functioning of existing networks. That is because NCNs infiltrate into the existing networks and completely alter their structure. In the case of land-based transport networks, for instance, it is not difficult to demonstrate how NCNs are beginning to generate profound changes both in terms of vehicle design and of the structure of the network grid or the management of transport movements.

This infiltration by NCNs into existing networks also encourages a greater degree of interconnection between them. In the Paris region, for instance, it is due to the intervention of NCNs that three separate land transport networks - underground, bus and suburban trains - have been interconnected to form a single network known as the 'Carte Orange' network, which in fact is a general transit network rather than a particular mode of transport. In this way the intervention of NCNs increases the scope for complementarity and solidarity between various existing networks whose boundaries, once clearly defined, are becoming increasingly blurred, thus working in the minds of network users and managers towards a globalization of the embodiment of the network concept.

Another equally important consequence of the penetration of NCNs into the fabric of existing networks is to initiate a process involving the gradual elimination of direct human intervention in their operation. This can already be seen both in the above mentioned transport networks and in various distribution networks.

Besides their intensity, instantaneity and ubiquity, another feature of NCNs is their multidimensionality, since they are required to intervene in all spheres of human activity. In the economic sphere, for instance, NCNs and their underlying technology are increasingly dominating the various phases of industrial production, from design to the finished product. Similarly, the distribution of finished products is run increasingly by NCNs. They also have considerable influence in the fields of banking and finance.

In scientific areas, to take another example, researcher's working methods are in the process of being radically changed both as a result of the introduction of computers as a powerful working tool, but also of the new possibilities of almost instantaneous communication of scientific results from one researcher to another or from one laboratory to another. Hence, NCNs are now influening the networks of scientific communities, transcending certain barriers between disciplines and communities which up to now have been difficult to cross. Still in the field of science, NCNs also help to blur the boundaries between basic and applied research by accelerating the interchange between the two communities and helping each to understand the other's problems.

NCNs are likewise having a visible and growing impact in the political and administrative fields, either in the form of computerized networks for administrative management or opinion polls to seek or form public opinion. In these areas, too, NCNs have a twin role. On the one hand they make the boundaries between various spheres of social activity more permeable, as for example between the administrative/state sphere and the financial/private sphere (which are also in the form of networks) a concrete example being the automatic deduction of taxes; or alternatively between leisure and participation in politics, which are now able to meet in a single medium, namely television made interactive by NCNs.

On the other hand, NCNs have the effect, at the same time, of transforming certain existing structures of social regulation which precisely performed this link function between the various levels. Even though this process is still in the early stages, it is time to reflect on the future of social institutions such as trade unions or political parties which were introduced in another configuration of the social space-time dominated by other types of AMSC networks.

One can add to the number of examples of the influence of NCNs simply by thinking of the changes already in progress or in the pipeline in the fields of education, leisure or culture. Similarly, NCTs/NCNs modify and restructure, as the dominant AMSC networks did before them, relationships between the developed countries and the developing countries. In economics, for example, the gradual introduction of the first automated production processes, controlled by microelectronic and computer technology, requiring less and less direct labour input, has ended the equilibrium that had been established between these two poles, where the immigration/emigration of unskilled labour acted as a social regulator both for the developed countries and for those supplying the labour. The end of this process has altered the direction of the fluxes and certain developing countries have taken over, on the one hand, old industries that are difficult to modernize and, on the other, new industries born directly of the technological changes in progress, a prime example being the manufacture of electronic components. Some non-Western countries, such as those of South-East Asia, have therefore changed their industrialization strategy - which had been based hitherto on import substitution of consumer durables and thus oriented towards their respective domestic markets - and have launched into an industrialization strategy oriented to exports, in which the manufacture and assembly of electronic components is the driving force. This new phase of industrialization in certain developing countries, encouraged by all international agencies, has led to major social transformations within these 'newly industrializing' countries, particularly by putting onto the labour market female labour which for a number of reasons, is much in demand in the electronics industry.

At the same time the spread of new communications technology within the developing countries themselves has had a very great cultural impact, particularly through the spread of television which is the new preferred vehicle for the introduction of Western culture into these countries. The socio-cultural impact of this process has not yet been properly studied and deserves to be, particularly from the point of view of the mismatch between the levels of socio-economic development of these countries and both material and institutional references but also spatio-temporal references, to which they are exposed through this cultural transfer.

For those developing countries which have not yet achieved national homogeneity, particularly as a nation-people, new communications technologies are the preferred tool for creating a new standard of cultural reference. Thus, after the era of the railways and the automobile, new communications networks and their technology are now seen as having taken over in the process of establishing contacts between the various cultures and hence of disseminating global or worldwide references.

There is no doubt that the most fundamental of these references are those relating to the spatial and temporal components of human activity which are being fundamentally affected by NCTs/NCNs. Like all AMSC networks, these new networks are drastically altering the relationships between the place of work and non-work, working time and non-working time (leisure). In other words, once again it is the spatio-temporal boundaries between these various compartments of human activity that are being upset by the advent of new conditions of social communication. This new dynamics is fundamentally different from that which was generated, for example, by the railways and which influenced the social space-time by a more distinct demarcation of those boundaries, clearly separating places of work and non-work. On the contrary, this trend is being reversed, with the various types of human activity being concentrated back into a single place thanks of course, to those technical characteristics of new communications technologies and networks which we identified earlier.

On a more global level, new communications networks are also altering the relationships between the places where production tools are designed and the actual production manufacturing process, and the place where the distribution of the products and the human resources employed in the production process are managed. In this way, by redistributing Man's various activities in space and time, NCTs/NCNs are introducting new scales of space and time, re-defining the concepts of proximity in space and time and, in the long term, serving to change the way in which Man perceives space (or distance) and time (or duration).

One of the most important social edifices of modern times, namely the form of macro-social organization known as the nation-state, is likely to be heavily influenced by these spatial and temporal changes. In the following paragraph we shall examine the complex relationships between the emergence and consolidation of NCTs/NCNs and the dynamics of nation-state.

4.   New communication networks and the nation-state

Since the early 1970's, various observers (including experts from international bodies, academics and politicians) have referred increasingly to a 'growing interdependence' between nations and at the same time 'an increasingly clear awareness of that interdependence' (Hart, 1983; Kierans, 1984). Attempts to explain this twin consistently put forward two main reasons. Firstly, these observers maintain that the 1970's were marked by an increase in the density and intensity of all types of fluxes, but they place particular stress on the rapid growth of international trade, maufacturing activity, foreign investment and the dissemination of technologies know-how; at the same time particular emphasis is placed on the role of transnational firms which are seen as forming the basis of this growing interdependence (Fry, 1983; Safarian, 1982). The second reason they mention is the 'oil shock', which is said to have helped to bring out the complementary relationship between nations and the interdependence of their respective economies (Collard, 1977).

We should call to mind the development strategy for the Second United Nations Development Decade, which affirms that:

'Prompted by a spirit of constructive association and cooperation based on the interdependence of their interests and seeking to favour a rational international division of labour, and also anxious to demonstrate their political will and collective determination to attain these aims and objectives, the governments, individually and collectively, solemnly proclaim their resolve to adopt and implement the measures set out below'.

Similarly, the lima Action Plan, adopted by the Second General Conference of UNIDO in 1975 stated that 'Universal interdependence has become a reality'. Kurt Waldheim, at the Third General Conference of UNIDO, also underlined the need for a 'new global strategy, based on interdependence, community of interest and cooperation between states'. The world therefore has to be considered 'as a system the parts of which are organically linked' (UNESCO, 1976:21). People are even beginning to speak of the world as a 'global community', a 'planetary village' or even 'a global village' (Malmgren, 1977). The idea of a global strategy 'on a planetary scale' already put forward in the Meadows Report (1972) is therefore gaining ground within the international organizations. All the offices and specialized agencies of the United Nations are concerting forces to act as the framework of this interdependence that is taken shape (Luard, 1977) in a global system, with a view to achieving 'global change' (Gati, 1983; Jacobson, 1979).

Clearly the emergence of this theory of international interdependence and its promotion by international governmental or non-governmental bodies ties in with the developments in the field of new communications technologies and networks in two ways. Firstly, at the level of the ideologico-political presentation of the anticipated changes in the type of macro-social organization, both nationally and internationally, it is impossible to ignore the strong ties between the changes brought about by the international organizations and those stemming from the academic sphere and concerning the 'future communication society or information society'. It is enough to say at this point that, as demonstrated by Lyon (1986), the ideas on this hypothetical society are now seen as an extension of the theory of post-industrial society and originate from various sources. They are the result of work either by government bodies, such as the Canadian report on 'Planning now for the information society' (Canadian Science Council, 1982), the Japanese report 'The plan for information society: a national goal toward the year 2000' (see Masuya, 1981) and of course the French report 'L 'Informatisation de la Société' (Nora and Minc, 1978), or the work of 'social forecasters' following in the steps of Bell (1974, 1980), such as Stonier (1983) and Masuya (1981).

Irrespective of who is propounding these ideas, one of the characteristics common to all of these proposals is that they predict a new spatial organization of human activity under the influence of new communications technologies and networks. Tama New Town in Japan, the Telidon programme in Canada, the Terese poject in Sweden are quoted as examples of this spatial transformation. Consequently, one may argue that close correlations exist between the discours on planetary interdependence and the potential of new communications networks and technologies to weave the fabric of new types of interdependence which will not necessarily require the territorial support of the nation state.

At present the nation-state is the dominant type of macro-social organization. It is generally accepted that the formation of a nation-state is a process of homogenising/unifying of certain elements regarded as constituting the nation: territory, language, historical and cultural tradition, and so on. Naturally this process of homogenization presupposes the enclosure of a space which it is proposed to unify. The exact configuration of this territory will depend on a whole set of historical and economic factors. What is important to us here is the appearance of these boundaries. However, boundaries and national territory are not necessary prerequistites for the unification of that which they enclose; in other words there is not first of all something within the boundaries which must then be unified. The nation-state does not confine itself to completing national unity, it has been constituted by building on that unity, that is to say a nation in the modern sense. In others words, it is the State that demarcated the boundaries of this space by the action of unifying and standardizing that which is within those boundaries.

The conquest of this 'interior' that has been thus demarcated takes place via a process of homogenization, assimilation and unification of differences and 'smoothing out of the terrain' within the national territory. In addition to this process of homogenization of the national territory and of the nation-state, in which communication systems and networks of all kinds have been involved to good effect, the second essential characteristic of the modern nation-state is that it is not an isolated entity but, on the contrary, a form of social organization that takes part in world trade and interchange form the position it occupies at that particular moment in the hierachy of international relations. In other words, the mere fact that a social entity has undergone internal unification/homogenization is not sufficient on its own to describe that entity as a nation-state if it is completely isolated (Poulantzas, 1978).

So the idea that we have just summarized of the dynamic force behind the constitution of nation-states dirsectly challenges what we have said about the new communication networks. There is no reason, according to this approach, why new social communication spheres should not be formed as a result of a spatial and temporal reorganization of the various spheres of human activity; supported, of course by the new communications technologies and networks. In actual fact this new dynamics works in two ways, involving both the permeabilization of existing frontiers (territorial and other) and the establishment of new frontiers. The dynamics of regionalization in Europe are in fact a fine example of this twin movement whereby the establishment of new regional boundaries in each of the states that had previously unified is accompanied by the increasing flexibility and even eventual elimination of national frontiers.

The current debate on regionalization (and also the merits of centralization as against decentralization) was triggered by the anticipation of major changes in the spatial and temporel scales on the social communication sphere. We shall confine ourselves here to three scenarios of the decentralization of a social organization of the size which concerns us, namely a nation-state (Gökalp, 1986a).

Sub-entities can exist within a national entity. Clearly it is the geographical regions that convey certain specific characteristics due to their particular ante-national history, or to their specific socio-economic development during the national period. One can therefore imagine that a social flux emanating from one of these sub-units may have a certain relevance for all of the points of this sub-unit which would lapse when it reached its borders. The same may apply for all the sub-units. However, if one of these sub-units maintains a specific power such that the fluxes it emits are relevant to the territory as a whole constituted by all the sub-units taken together, it is necessary to take into account the intersecting of regional fluxes and the centralizing fluxes in each of these sub-units. That is the scenario for regionalization as it is understood today.

However, if there is no centralizing sub-unit or region and if the relevance of the fluxes emanating from each sub-unit lapses at their respective boundaries, there will be as many autonomous entities as there are sub-units. This scenario, which is reminiscent of the social organization during feudal times, is now known as the local-based scenario. The most complex scenario is that in which the fluxes emanating from each sub-unit maintain a certain relevance beyond the boundaries of these sub-units and therefore intersect with all the fluxes emanating from all the other sub-units. In that case allowance would have to be made for multiple cross-correlations between these fluxes from diverse sources. This last scenario resembles an advanced state of decentralization and also underlines the heuristic limits of the decentralized organization scenarios that are on a strictly territorial basis and militates in favour of the idea of new aterritorical spheres, both of socialization and conceptualization.

Can this process be considered as the first phase of a structural change leading to a generalized compartmentalization of social communication, enclosing more and more local areas in which an advanced stage of homogenization can be reached ? These new spheres will be transfrontier spheres by definition and could be formed around a common aterritorial matrix.

The sort of communication sphere which would result from such a development will naturally differ markedly from that with which we are familiar today. The concept of belonging to a community or the concept of identity would be considerably modified as a result. Moreover, the very concept of a frontier will tend to evolve from a linear concept, i.e. a limit, towards a zonal concept, possessing a structure and allowing of multiple

intersections, since a single individual could belong to more than one sub-sphere. In other words, a new social recomposition, in which there would be only the deliberate choices of individual opting for the various sub-spheres in which they wish to evolve, could become a possibility.
This could lead to the birth of multiple 'communities', structured around different types of affinity, relating to all the spheres of Man's activity. The community (European Community if one wished to restrict the analysis to Europe) would therefore be made up of superposed sub-spheres which would be no longer national/territorial but related to specific multiple activities/affinities/allegiances. Naturally this presupposes the removal of all barriers to communication and trade between the members of these sub-communities, beginning with language and the universal economic equivalent. It is not difficult to see new communication networks as potentially being capable of playing this role of 'multifunctional translator'.

Acknowledgments

This work has greatly benefited from the scientific and administrative possibilities offered to me by Cléméns Heller, Administrator of the Maison des Sciences de l'Homme at Paris. I wish equally acknowledge the indispensable help of the library of the MSH. I wish to thank also Lusin Bagla-Gokalp who authorized me to use part of her sources on the discourse of UN agencies on 'international interdependence'.

References

Bell, D. (1974),
The coming of postindustrial society: a venture in social forecasting. Harmondsworth, Peregrine.
Bell, D. (1980),
The social framework of the information society, in Forester T. (Ed.) The information technology revolution. Oxford, Basil Blackwell 1985.
Blondeau-Patissier, J.F. (1979),
La difficile naissance d'un réseau. Rapport non-publié.
Chandler, Alfred D. Jr. (1977),
The visible Hand: The managarial revolution in american business, Cambridge, Mass.
Collard, D. (1977),
Vers l'établissement d'un nouvel ordre économique international. Notes et Etudes Documentaires, La Documentation Française, nos. 4412-4414.
Dupuy, J.P. (1978),
Communication au Neuvième Congrès Mondial de Sociologie, Uppsala.

Fischer, C.S. (1985),
  Studying technology and social life in, Castells M. (Ed.) **High technology, space and society,** Urban Affairs Annual Reviews, volume 28, Sage Publications.
Flink, J.J. (1980),
  The car culture revisited: some comments on recent historiography of automotive history. **Michigan Quarterly Review,** 19 (4) - 20 (2): 772-781.
Fremdling, R. (1977),
  Railroads and German economic growth. **J. Economic History,** 37: 583-604.
Fry, E.H. (1983),
  The politics of international investment. New York, McGraw Hill.
Garrison, W.L. and Marble, D.F. (1962),
  The structure of transportation networks. Technical Report 62-11, US Army Transplantation Command.
Gati, T.T. (1983),
  The US, the UN and the management of the global change. New York, The New York University Press.
Gökalp, I. (1983),
  Réflexions sur la notion de réseau artificiel. **Bulletin de l'Idate,** 13: 154-163.
Gökalp, I. (1984),
  Espaces de communication sociale et réseaux; in **Le CNRS et la Communication,** Editions du CNRS.
Gökalp, I. (1985),
  Quelques notes sur le programme STS français. **EASST Review,** 4 (3): 8-11.
Gökalp, I. (1986),
  Reflexions sur les origines du réseau ferroviaire en Asie Mineure. **Actes du Deuxième Colloque International d'Histoire. Economies méditerranéennes: équilibres et intercommunications,** Volume 2, pp. 357-375, Athènes.
Gökalp, I. (1986a),
  Centralité, Décentralité et Réseaux. **Actes du 5è. Congrès national des sciences de l'information et de la communication.** Université de Rennes, Haute Bretagne, pp. 9-16.
Guile, B.R. (1985),
  Information technologies and social transformation. National Academy Press, Washington D.C.
Hart, J.A. (1983),
  The new international economic order, New York, St. Martin's Press.
Huenemann, R.W. (1984),
  The Dragon and the iron horse. The economics of railroads in China, 1876-1937. Harvard University Press.

Jacobson, H.K. (1979),
   Networks of interdependance: international organisation and the global political system. Random House, New York.
Kansky, K.J. (1963),
   Structure of transportation networks. Relationship between networks geometry and regional characteristics. The university of Chicago, Department of Geography, research paper no. 84.
Kern, S. (1983),
   The culture of space and time, 1880-1918. Harvard University Press, Cambridge, Mass.
Kierans, E. (1984),
   Globalism and the nation-state. Toronto, CBC Massey Lectures, CBC Enterprises.
Lame, Clapeyron, Stépaphane et Eugène Flachat (1832),
   Vues politiques et pratiques sur les travaux publics en France. Paris.
Laudan, R. Ed. (1984),
   The nature of technological knowledge. Are models of scientific change relevant. D. Reidel Publishing Company, Dordrecht.
Licht, W. (1983),
   Working for the railroad, Princeton.
Luard, E. (1977),
   International agencies: the emerging framework of interdependance. The Royal Institute of International Affairs.
Lyon, D. (1986),
   'From post-industrialism to information society: a new social transformation ?'. **Sociology,** 30: 577-588.
MacKenzie, D. and Wajcman, J., Eds. (1985),
   The social shaping of technology, Open University Press, Milton Keynes, Philadelphia.
Malmgren, H.B. (1977),
   Managing international trade; in Wallace D. Jr. and Escobar, H. (Eds.) **The future of international economic organisations.** Praeger Publishers, New York.
Masuda, Y. (1981),
   The information society as postindustrial society. Bethesda MD: World Futures Society.
Mayo, J.S. (1985),
   The evolution of information technologies; in Guile (1985), pp. 7-33.
Mazilish, B. (1965),
   The railroad and the space program. An exploration in historical analogy. The M.I.T. Press, Cambridge, Mass.
Meadows, D. et al (1972),
   The limits of growth. New York, New American Library.
Nora, S. et Minc, A. (1978),
   L'informatisation de la société. La Documentation Française, Paris.
Poulantzas, N. (1978),
   L'Etat, le pouvoir et le socialisme. PUF, Paris.

Pred, A.R. (1973),
> Urban growth and the circulation of information: The United States' system of cities, 1790-1840. Harvard University Press, Cambridge, Mass.

Price, R. (1983),
> The modernization of rural france. Hutchinson University Library.

Pool, I. de (1983),
> Forecasting the telephone. Norwood, New Jersey Ablex.

Raffestin, C. (1986),
> 'Eléments pour une thèorie de la frontière'. Diogène, 134: 3-21.

Safarin, A. (1982),
> Gorvernments and multinationals: policies in the developed countries. Washington D.C., British-North american Committee.

Salini, P. (1982),
> Présentation générale des transports de marchandise. La Documentation Française, Notes et Etudes Documentaires, no. 4684-4686.

Smith, M.S. (1979),
> Proceedings of the Annual Meeting of the Western Society for french history, 6: 327-335.

Stengers, I. et Gille, D. (1983),
> Temps et représentation. Culture Technique, numéro de février.

UNESCO (1976),
> Moving towards change: some thoughts on the new international economic order. Paris.

Skowronek, S. (1982),
> Building a new american state. The expansion of national administrative capacities, 1877-1920. Cambridge University Press.

Stonier, T. (1983),
> The wealth of information. London, Thames Hudson.

Vincenot, H. (1975),
> La vie quotidienne dans les chemins de fer. Hachette, Paris.

Weber, E. (1976),
> Peasants into frenchmen: the modernization of rural France, 1870-1914. Stanfors University Press, Stanford, CA.

Zebrubavel, E. (1982),
> The standardization of time. A sociohistorical perspective. American J. of Sociology, 88: 1-23.

SYNTHESIZING CONCLUSIONS

The growing literature on telecommunication developments has been extended by eleven important contributions. They show how global telecommunication networks are changing international economic and political power structures. They show the limits and possibilities for national action by European states. They stress the necessity of supranational, and especially European, scenarios for political action and technological development. They identify a number of networks and services which are focussed on public and consumer interests. These networks and services, this 'orgware' and 'social software' has to be developed as a countervailing power to the private interests of transnational corporations connected with the electronic highways of new digital networks, as an alternative for a race towards Technotopia. Networks and services which focus on public and consumer interests are a legitimate objective of supranational, and especially European, scenarios.

The articles in this book certainly expose a continuous and continued need for research. The development of telecommunication networks, new services and societal change mean the exploration of a terra incognita, vaguely identified by terms like the post-industrial society or the information society. These happen to be the promising and threatening domain of risky investments. The need for research is institutionalized by national, supranational and corporate Research and Development expenditures. The preparation of this book has been part of it.

We stress now the necessity for the kind of research which has been undertaken by the contributors. It has been called strategic analysis. It is a field of applied and comparative research to forecast and assess developments like those with regard to global telecommunication networks and their influence on national and international economic, political, technological and cultural power structures. Forecasting and assessment are undertaken from a special perspective, namely that scientific appraisals and reports serve policymakers and public opinion formation. Policymakers can make better choices when they are sustained scientifically to understand actual trends, evaluate expert expectations or reassess public needs. And choices are unavoidable, e.g. on standardization matters, prerequisites of future networks, tariffs and prices, investments in consumer apparatus or new services, the social and educational consequences of information technology, and so on. These all are difficult choices, which play at many levels of policymaking. Corporate policies and private interests are concerned, but so are households, public institutions, local communities, nation states and supranational organizations like the European Community serving threatened public and consumer interests. Strategic analysis serves the difficult tasks of policymakers and of all those who play a role in public opinion formation. So, it does not forecast and assess an unchangeable future exactly, but enlightens possibilities for changing nondesired trends, expectations and needs or to reinforce those which are really desired. It serves a mouldable future. In that sense it is critical and responsible research. It is the possible contribution of a number of political economists, innovation economists, comparative researchers, policy researchers and game or negotiation researchers, all being members of the social science community. We continue to stress that strategic analysis must be an integrated part of national and European Research and Development programmes. Especially at the European level they should be charged to do concrete and comparative research into social, economic, political and cultural indicators of telecommunications and their trends. They should reassess comparatively the relations between new services and public needs, evaluate experiments. They should be able to propose new solutions for services which may meet public needs as has been done, for instance, by proposals for social software or social experiments with telematics. They should be ready to propose new ways to organize public and consumer interests being alternatives for state (or suprastate) regulations and the 'bureaucratic arthritis' of West-European welfare states. They should translate policy problems with regard to international negotiations into research questions and models to be tested or explored. These negotiations can deal with standardization policies, tariffs and prices, the integration of existing separated networks (satellite, CATV, telecommunications), etc. Further, there is need for a technology-oriented philosophy and social science. We have stated that the dominant interests of philosophy and social science are not facing this orientation, on the contrary. It is urgently needed as a scientific discourse and body of knowledge stimulating researchers in the field of strategic analysis to develop new ideas, supporting them at the conceptual and methodological level and identifying unavoidable ethical questions of the legitimacy of new technologies and their applications in society. Researchers doing strategic analysis and the few philosophers and social scientists who raise relevant conceptual, theoretical and methodological questions must be encouraged to extend the prologomena for a technology-oriented philosophy and social science as they are, for instance, part of this book. Certainly at the ethical, legitimacy, level programmed research efforts are of direct interest for policymakers and public opinion formation. So, it is a useful part of continued research programmes with regard to information technology and telecommunication developments.

BIOGRAPHICAL NOTE ON THE CONTRIBUTORS

Jeremy Beale (1957) has a BA in Government and American Studies from Colby College, Maine, USA, and an MA in International Relations from the University of Sussex, England, where he is currently completing a doctoral thesis on technical innovation and European integration. He has taught undergraduate courses on international political and economic relations, and has acted as a consultant on the development of information technologies within the European Community, and on US/EEC economic and political conflicts. Relevant publication "Information Technologies and European Integration", in John MacLean and Roger Tooze (eds.) **The International Political Economy of Information and Technology** (London: Allen & Unwin, forthcoming).

Iskender Gökalp (1951) is Chargé de Recherche at the CNRS (Centre National de la Recherche Scientifique). From 1983 to 1986, he participated in the CNRS programme on 'Science, Technology and Society'. His major research interests are situated in the interdisciplinary space between the natural sciences and the social sciences, one research theme being the dynamics of large-scale technological systems.

Jacob Gruppelaar (1958) studied philosophy in Nymegen (The Netherlands) and Louvain (Belgium). He is researcher at IVA, Institute for Social Research at Tilburg University. His major research interests are: philosophy and technology, philosophy and the social sciences. He participated in the EEC Com-8 project on global networks. Currently he is researching the rationality of technological innovation processes. Publication forthcoming.

Gerd Junne (1947) studied political science, law and economics at the Free University of Berlin and at Geneva. He wrote a Ph.D. dissertation on the Euromoney market. He is professor in international relations at the University of Amsterdam. Besides, he served as a consultant for the U.N. Centre on Transnational Corporations. His major research interests are: multinational corporations, changes in the international division of labour, impact of new technologies on international relations. Relevant publications: (with Rob van Tulder) **European Multinationals in the Telecommunications Industry.** Pilot Study for the Institute for Research and Information on Multinationals, Geneva, 1984; (with Rob van Tulder) **European Multinationals in Core Technologies,** (Chichester: Wiley) 1987, forthcoming.

Gareth Locksley (1948) is a lecturer in Economics at the Communications Policy Centre of The City University, London. Previously he was a member of the Centre for Communications and Information Studies of the Polytechnic of Central London and worked for the Greater London Council (GLC) on the economic issues of new technology. He has also been a consultant with the European Commission for whom he has produced three studies, one each on the computer, telecommunications and motor car industries. He has carried out research in Australia on its new technology industries. He has published widely in Europe, the US and Australia. Currently, he is researching the new media of satellite and cable.

William Melody is Director of the new initiative of the Economic and Social Research Council on implications of the information and communication technologies, a position he assumed in August 1985. He is on leave from an interdisciplinary Faculty of Applied Science at Simon Fraser University, Vancouver, Canada, to assist the Council in the first two years of its new programme. He has carried out research on communications economics, the effects of government regulations, the impact of changing technologies, and the evaluation of policy alternatives. He is the author or editor of many publications, including, **Communication Technology and Social Policy, Information and Communication Technologies: Social Science Research and Training.**

J.F. Mertens (1946) studies in physics, mathematics and economics. Ph.D. in mathematics (cum maxima laude). In 1971, he was appointed professor at the Université Catholique de Louvain. He has lectured in Heidelberg, Jerusalem, Berkely and Bielefeld. Major scientific interest: game theory. He is editor of the International Journal of Game Theory.

George Muskens (1944) has studied sociology and mass communications at the University of Nymegen. He is head of the division of Cultural Studies at IVA, Institute for Social Research at Tilburg University. Research and publications on content analysis (dissertation), cultural professions (journalists, writers, visual artists, teachers), cultural policies, new information networks, and public information services.

Lars Qvortrup (1950), 'mag art' in Linguistics (similar to PhD), associate professor at the Telematics Project, Odense University (Danmark). His major research interests are communication policies and social informatics. Relevant publications: **The Social Significance of Telematics.** John Benjamins Publishing company, Amsterdam/Philadelphia 1984. Lars Qvortrup et al. (eds.): **Social Experiments with Information Technology and the Challenges of Innovation.** Reidel Publishing Company, Dordrecht/Boston/Lancaster/Tokyo 1987.

Peter H.M. Vervest (1955) studied law and management sciences at the universities of Utrecht and Delft. Doctor's degree in technical sciences (cum laude) from the Technical University Delft. He has been working with Philips International BV Eindhoven since 1979 and is currently group manager Interactive Media Systems/Advanced Consumer Products at Philips Electronics in the United Kingdom. In addition he is associate professor of communications management at the Graduate School of Management of the Erasmus University Rotterdam. He has lectured throughout Europe and has published widely on the subject of electronic mail and message handling systems. His books include **Electronic Mail and Message Handling** (both English and Japanese) and **Innovation in Electronic Mail.** He is co-founder and director of the European Electronic Mail Association.